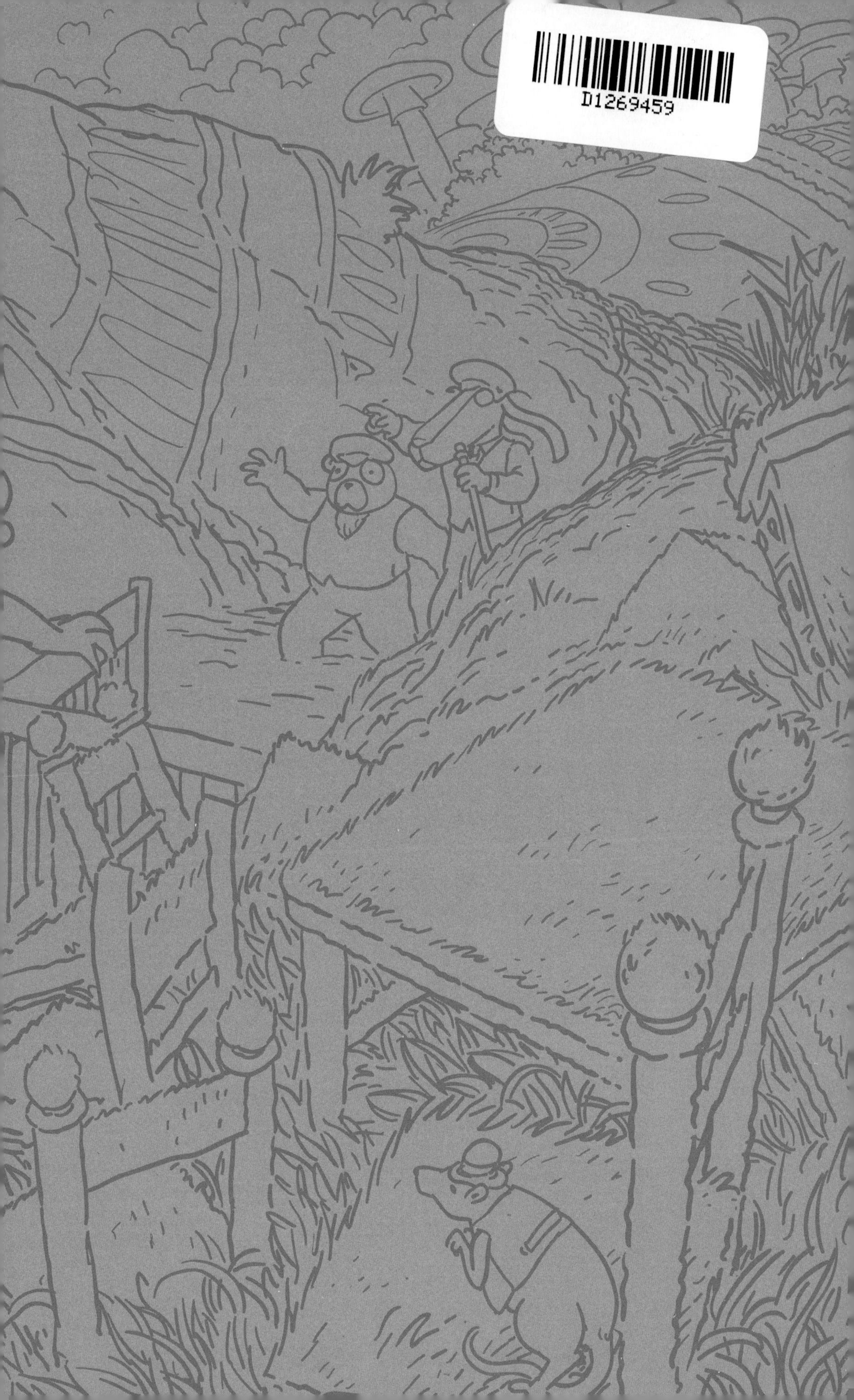

KINGDOM OF THE WICKED

story
Ian Edginton

art
D'Israeli

lettering
Woodrow Phoenix

Dark Horse Books™

To Shirley Ann Davis, for setting me on the path.
To my Gran', my number one fan.
To Jane, for having the patience of a saint.
And to Matt, whose vision, friendship, and good humour know no bounds.

—Ian Edginton

For Alison, for putting up with me the first time round.
For Lynn, for keeping me going during the re-mastering.
And most of all...
For Ian, for not giving up during the twelve years
it took to make this edition happen.

—D'Israeli

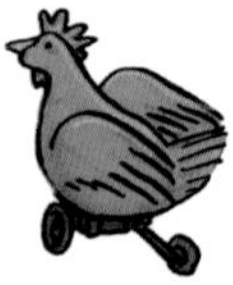

publisher **Mike Richardson**

art director **Lia Ribacchi** *assistant editor* **Katie Moody**

designer **Amy Arendts** *editor* **Dave Land**

KINGDOM OF THE WICKED™

Originally published by Caliber Comics

Dark Horse Books
a division of Dark Horse Comics, Inc.
10956 SE Main Street
Milwaukie, OR 97222

www.darkhorse.com

To find a comic shop in your area
call the Comic Shop Locator Service toll-free at (888) 266-4226

First edition: December 2004
ISBN: 1-59307-187-6

1 3 5 7 9 10 8 6 4 2
Printed in China

prologue
Little Monsters

As I walked upon the stair,
I met a man who wasn't there.
He wasn't there again today.
Oh, how I wish he'd go away.

—Hugh Mearns

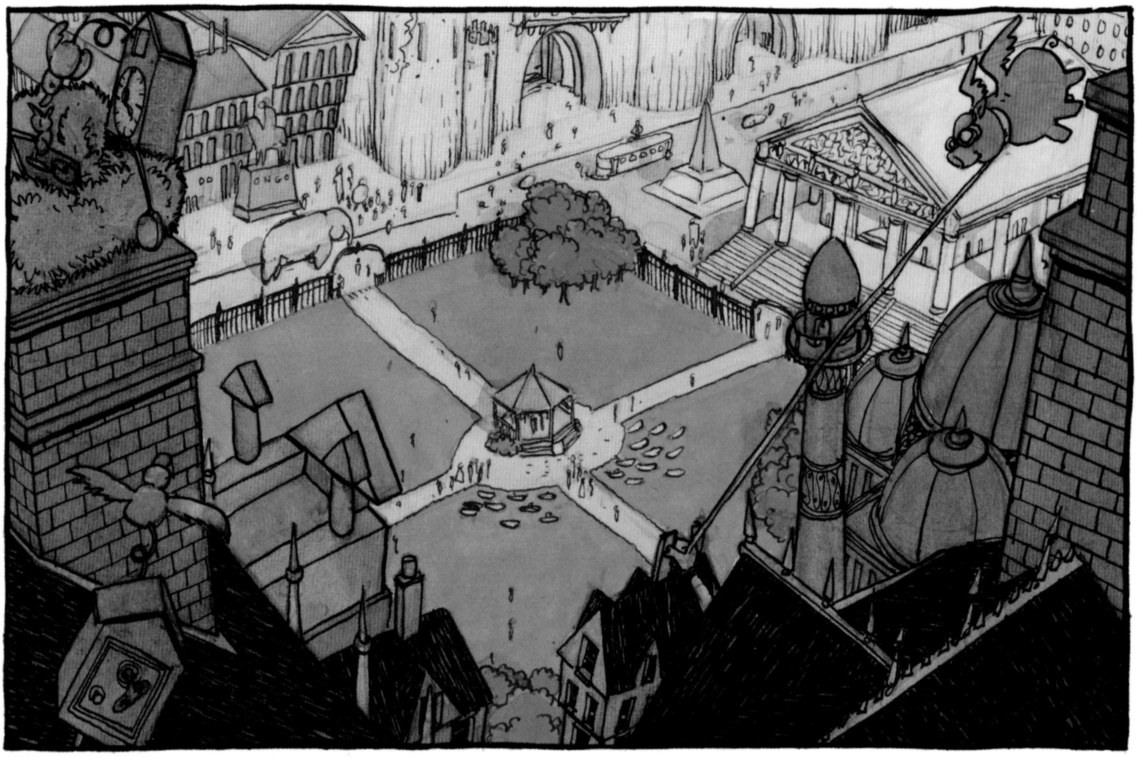

Between the Here-and-Now and the Hereafter...
Between the pen and the page...
There is Castrovalva, city of the twelve shires, where wonders are as free as air and impossibilities fall like spring rain.

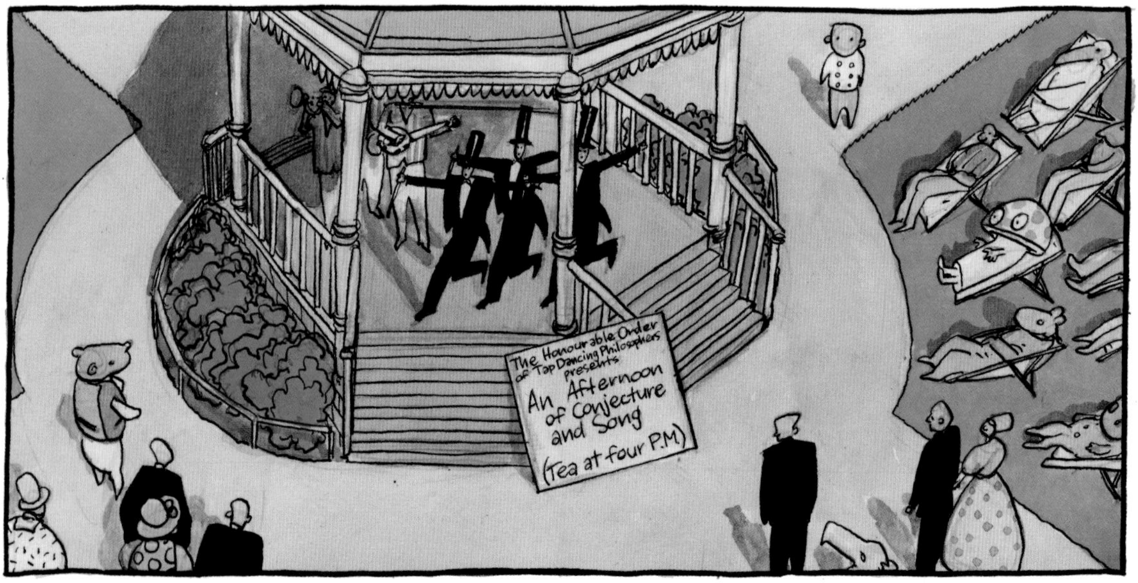
The Honourable Order of Tap Dancing Philosophers presents
An Afternoon of Conjecture and Song
(Tea at four P.M.)

On Sunday afternoons The Honourable Order of Tap-Dancing Philosophers would hoof in heated debate as to the nature of their world.

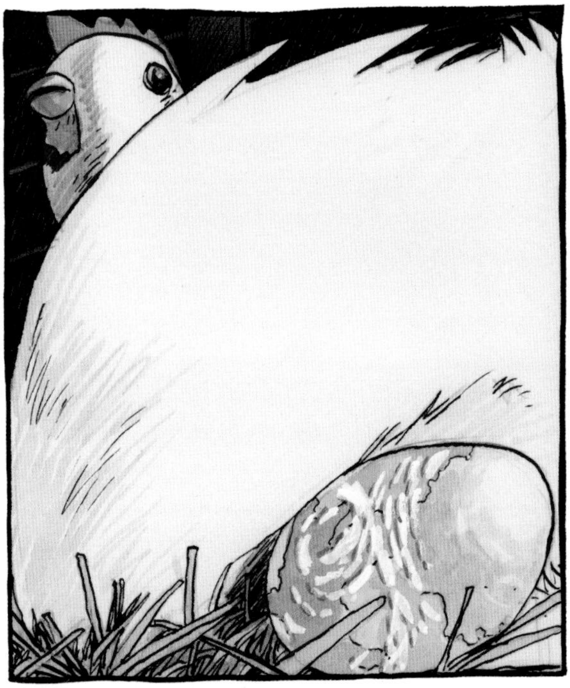

Opinion deviated wildly. One school of thought proposed it was laid by a marvellous celestial chicken.

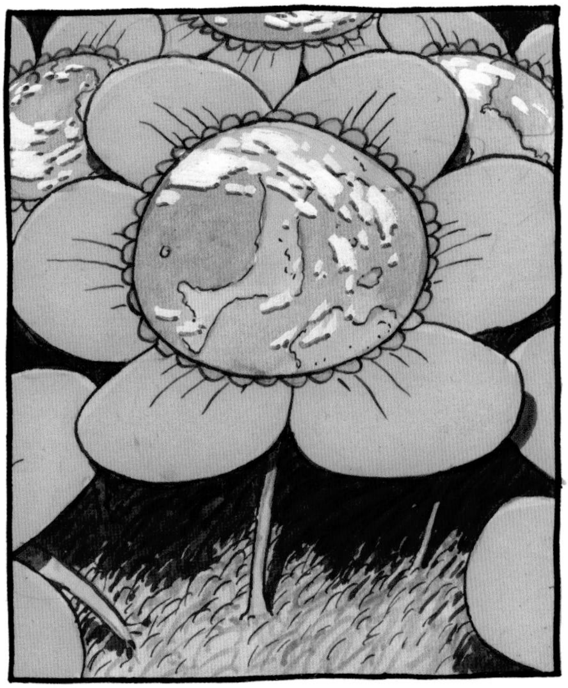

Another, that it grew from seeds in a humus of belly-button fluff and furballs.

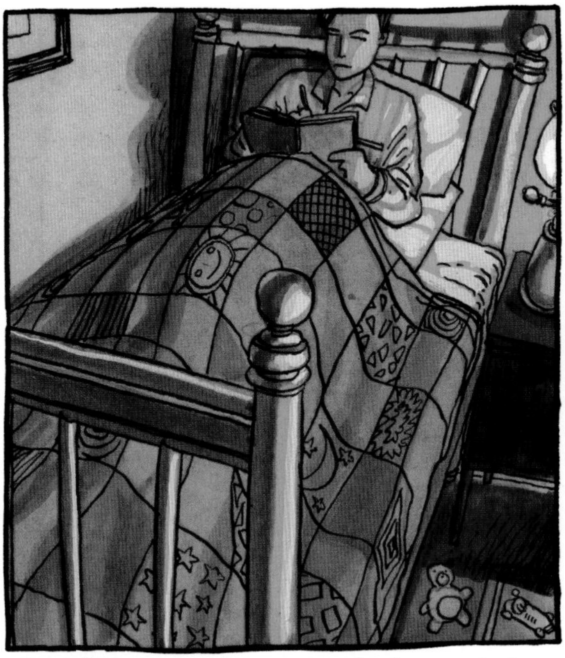

A radical third contended it solely existed in the mind of a small child who'd simply thought them into being.

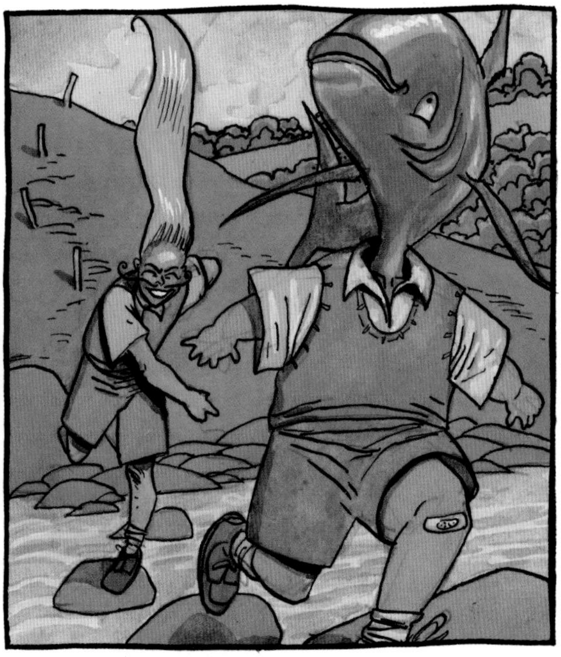

But to Wavy Davy Dali and Tiny Tom Fish Head this meant little.
So long as the sun shone and it snowed at Christmas they were happy.

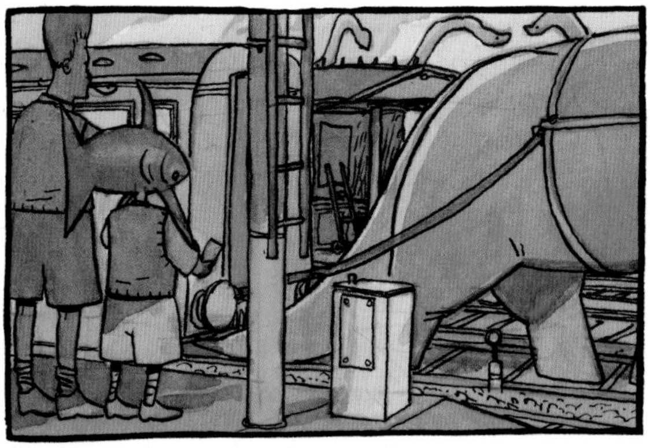

During those endless, balmy summer days there was always something to do.
They could go Dinosaur spotting...

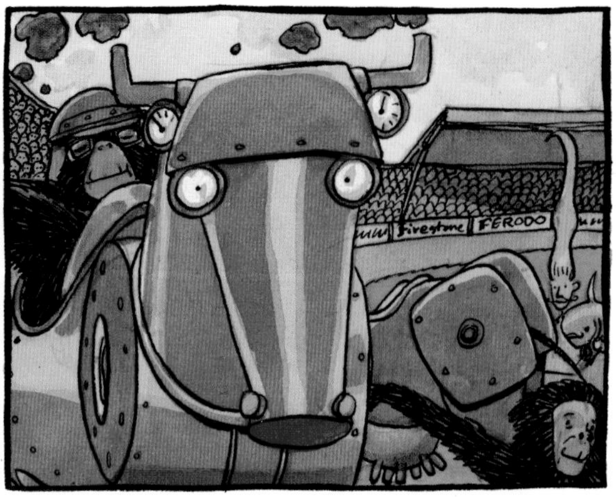
Firestone
FERODO

Watch the chimps race their clock-work cows.

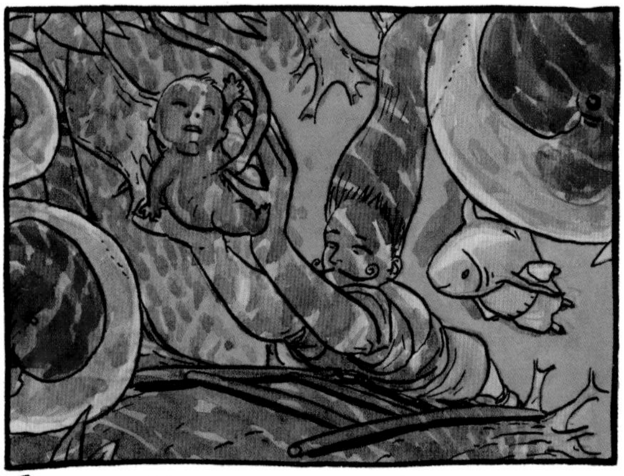

Or sometimes earn pocket money by helping harvest babies from the family trees.

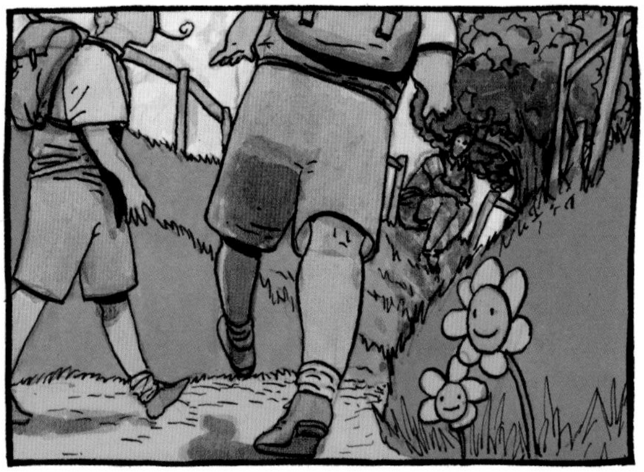

Best of all they would pack up their penknives, balls of string, sandwiches and bottles of pop and go exploring.

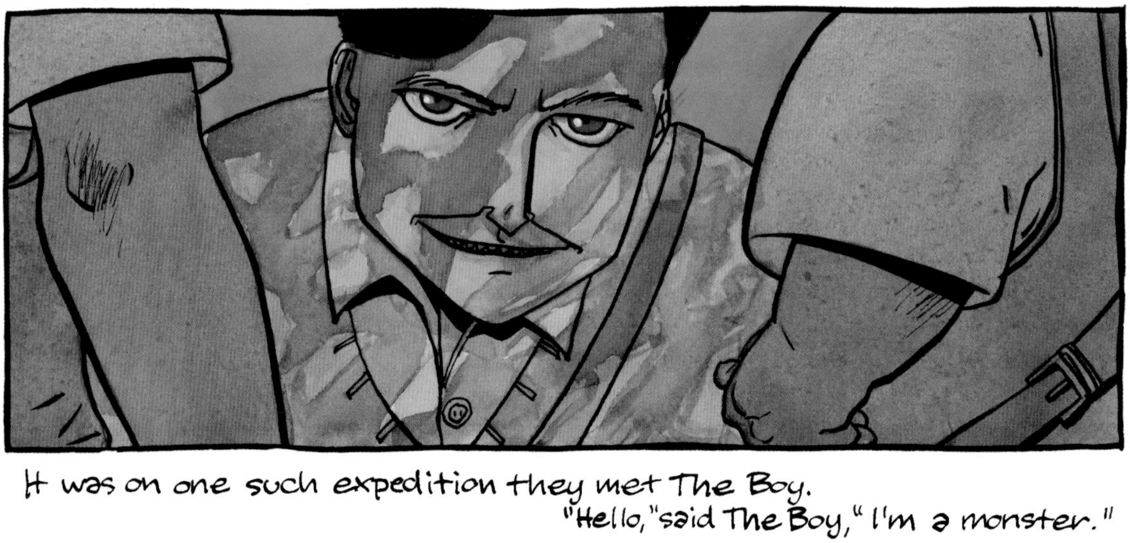

It was on one such expedition they met The Boy.
"Hello," said The Boy, "I'm a monster."

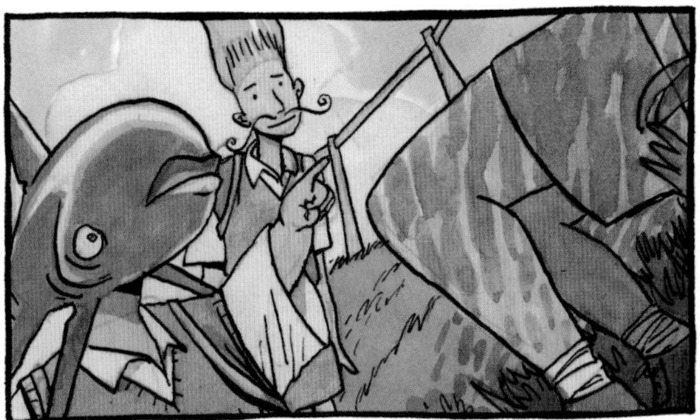

Tiny Tom wasn't convinced. "You can't be," he exclaimed. "Monsters are ugly and vile and live in The Land Under The Bed! You're just a boy."

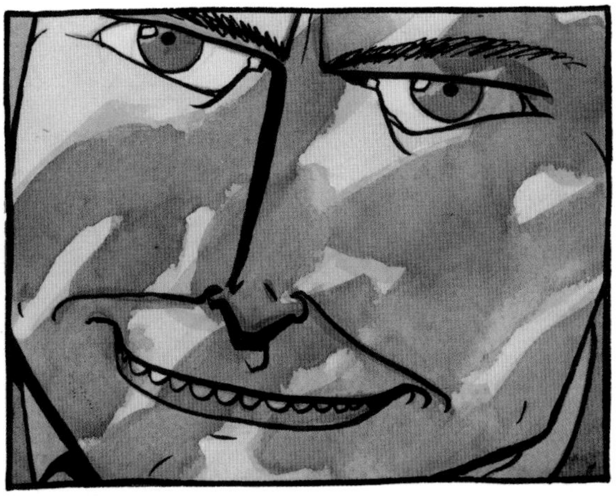

"Ah yes," he grinned, "but you see I'm ugly and vile on the inside."

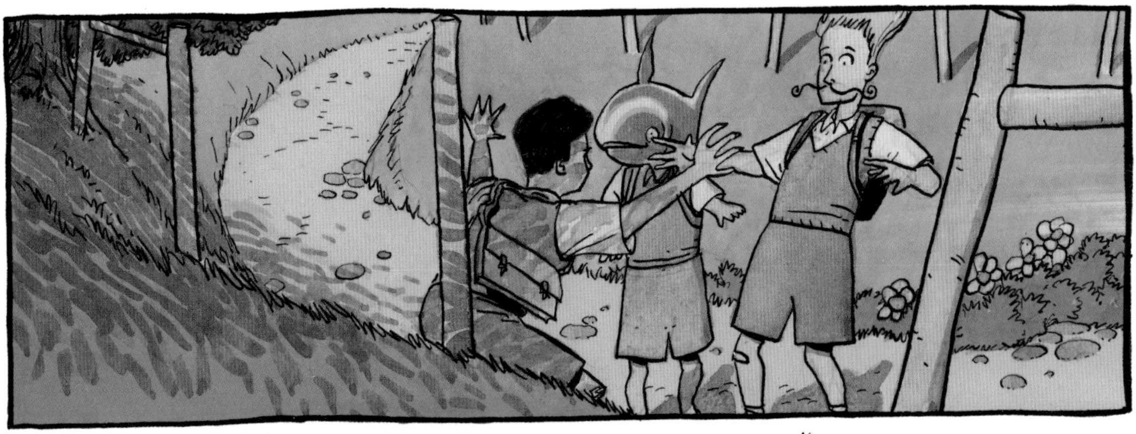

"What's it like," enquired Davy, "being a monster?"

"Oh it's great fun" he replied, "if you're clever and quick you can do whatever you like! No-one can stop you!"

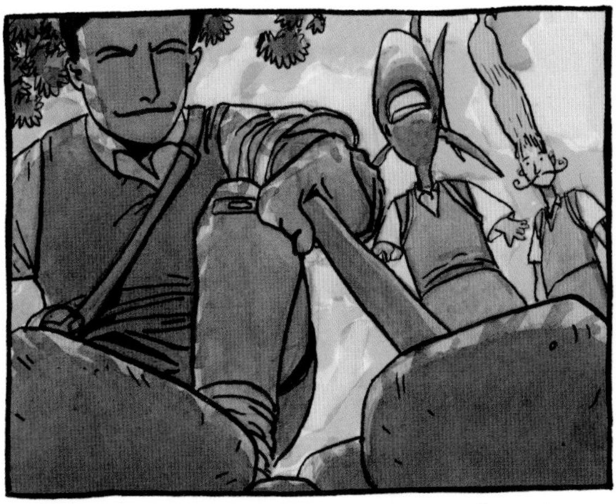

"Aren't monsters supposed to be bad?" asked Tiny Tom.

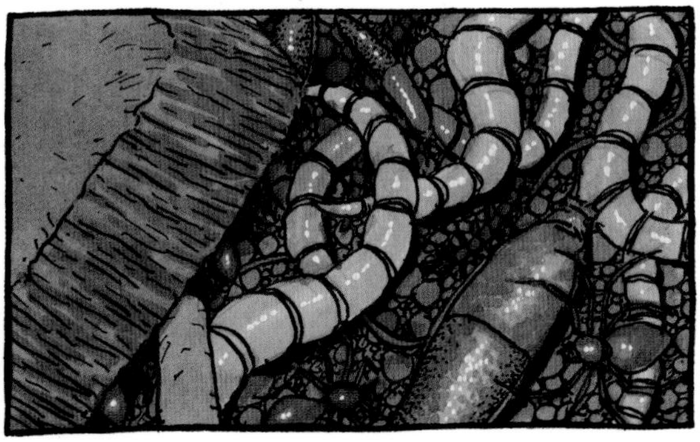

"There have to be monsters!" enthused The Boy, "people expect them. They're the other side of the coin, night after day, the dark face of a stone against the earth."

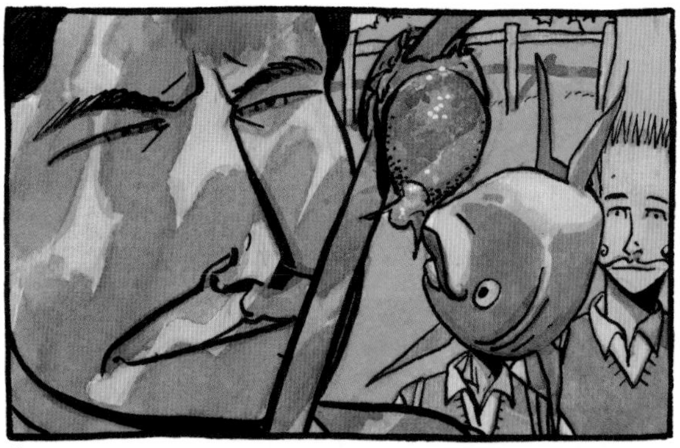

"It's like a see-saw," he trilled, "You need people on both ends to make it work. Only it's such a laugh being a monster, if everyone knew they'd all want to be one!"

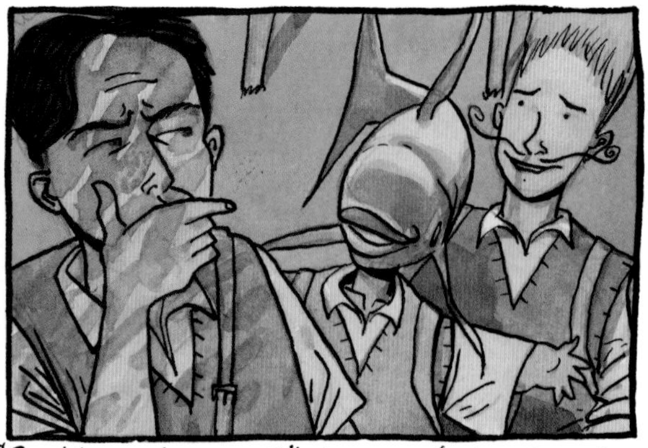

"Could we be one?" chorused the friends. "Well ..." mused The Boy, "perhaps, but it's a very responsible job, you must do everything I say."

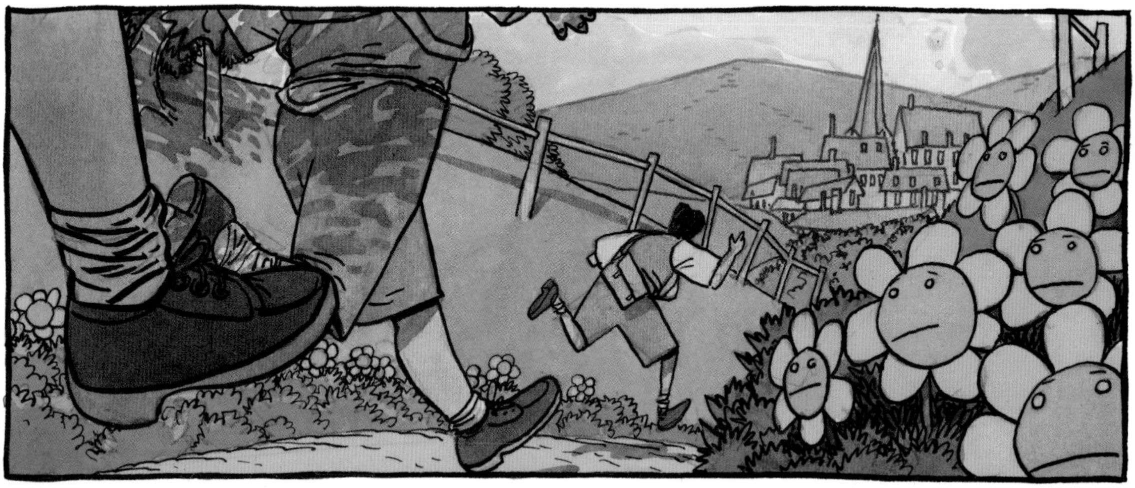

"We will!" replied the eager pair and with that they raced off to start their work.

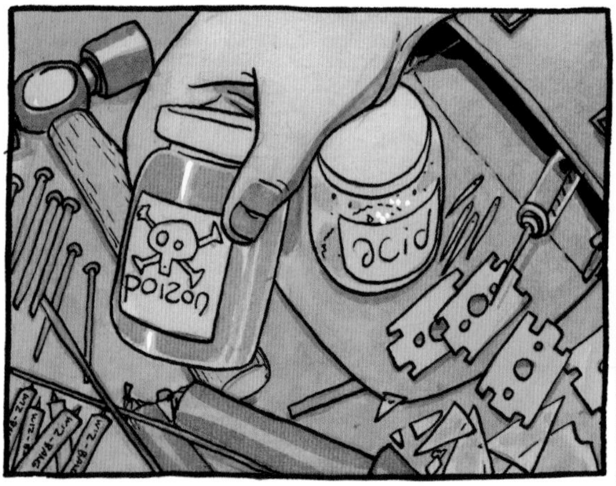
poizon
acid

When they came to a village The Boy gave them each some things from his satchel.

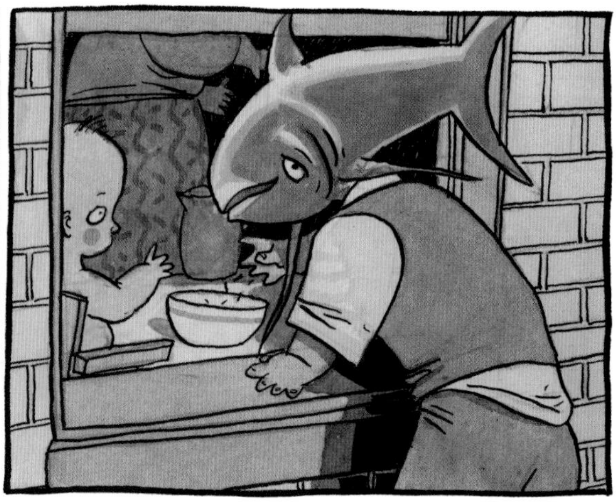

There were needles for a baby's porridge...

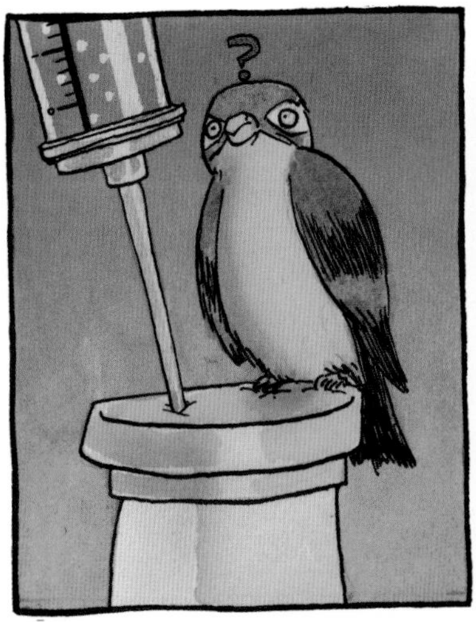

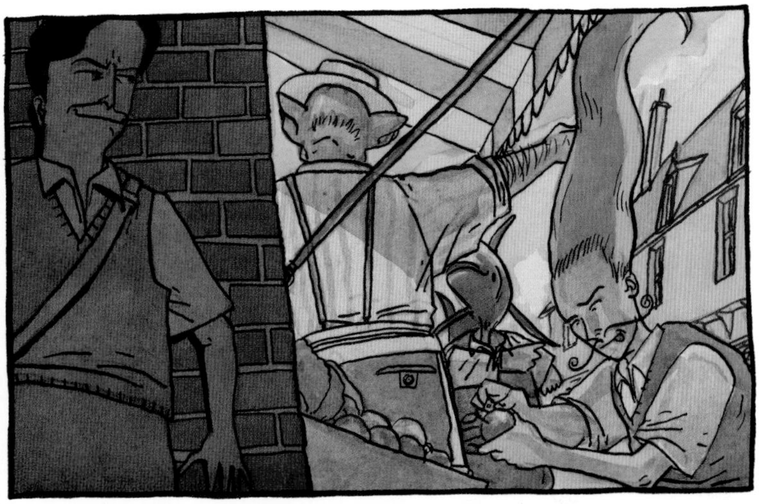

Acid for the morning milk... ... and razor blades for the greengrocers wares.

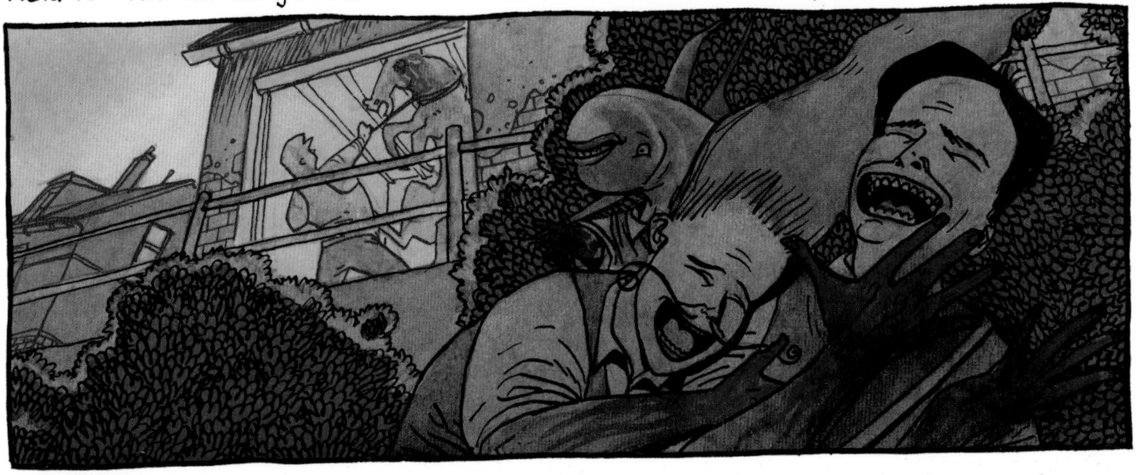

They had such fun. They blinded horses, boiled puppies and turned cats into fiery streaks.

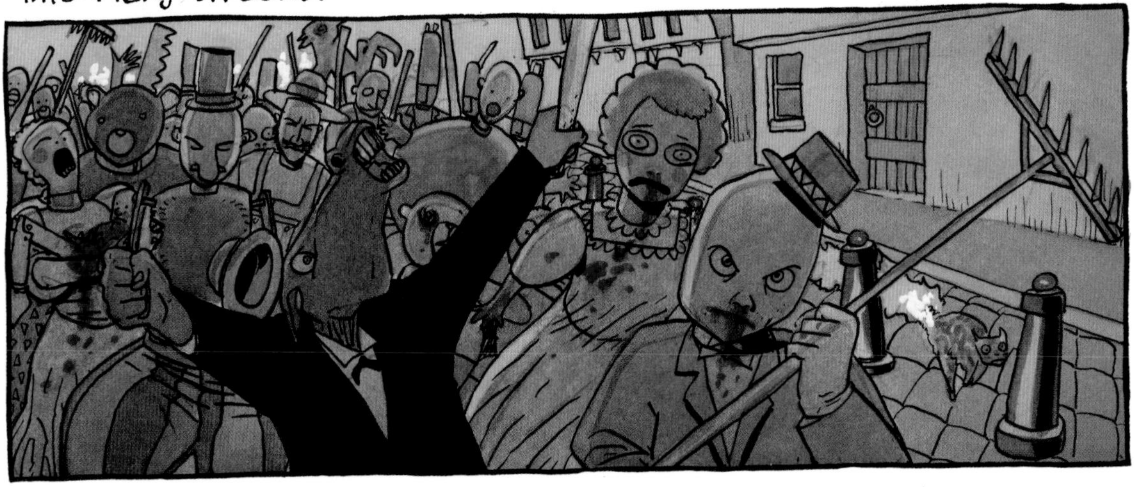

The air was filled with screams and screeches, yells and yowls. There was never such a din before in all the world.

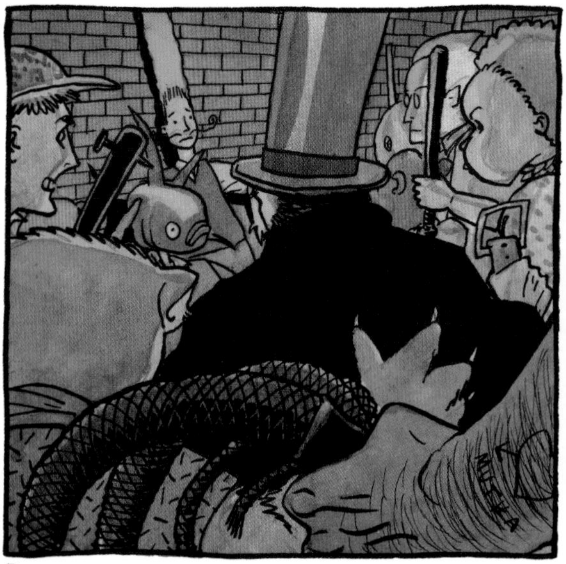

But an angry band knotted and grew.
They found the boys and put them on the spot.
When they saw what they'd done, being a monster didn't seem fun anymore. The Boy was nowhere to be found.

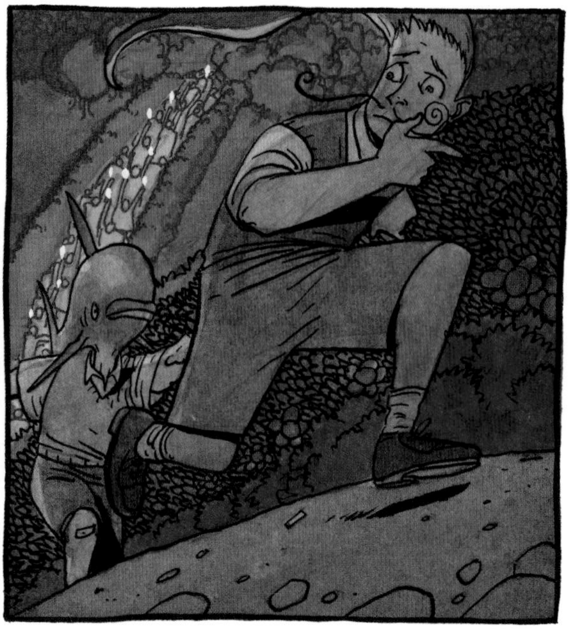

When they tried explaining no-one believed them, calling them monsters and liars.
The frightened friends ran away as fast as they could.

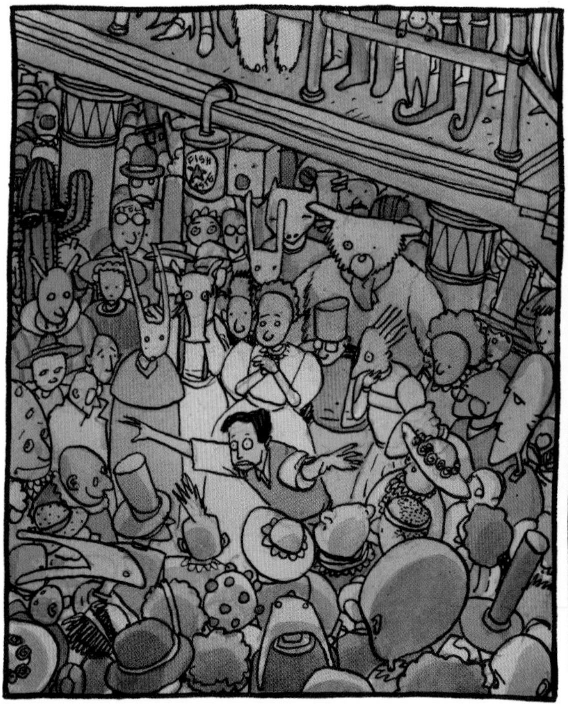
FISH

They couldn't go home as somehow even there everyone knew what they'd done.

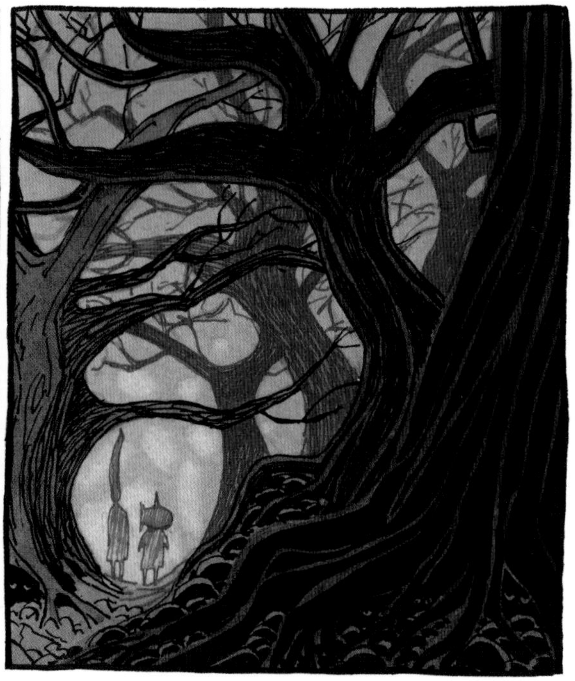

Hungry and scared, they hid in the deep woods around The Land Under The Bed where no-one would dare look for them.

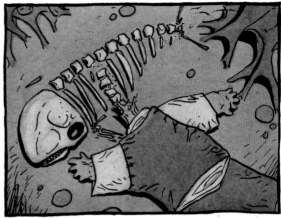

Wavy Davy felt so hungry his stomach hurt. So Tiny Tom Fish Head plucked up his courage and went looking for food for his friend.

But the things in the deep woods found him and he made a dinner for them all.

Wavy Davy Dali, starving and alone sat calling for his friend... and calling.

He called so long he pined away to nothing.

"I told you I was a monster" said The Boy.

D'End!

Chapter
One

❖❖❖

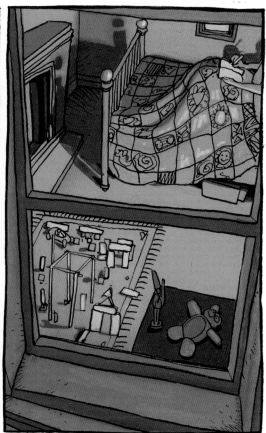

Once upon a time

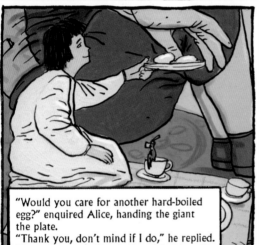

"Would you care for another hard-boiled egg?" enquired Alice, handing the giant the plate.
"Thank you, don't mind if I do," he replied. Then the egg, shell and all vanished into his huge mouth, like a whisper in a cave.

"I hope you don't mind me asking," said Alice, "but is it hard work becoming a giant?"
"Oh no. Not at all," he smiled, showing teeth the size of saucers. "I just sort of grow'd and grow'd and here I was."

"I don't grow up, I grow down," chipped in the ant smartly before taking another nibble from his sugar cube.
"You do not," snapped Alice.
"Don't fib so!"

"Madam," he snorted in the only way that ants can, "ants never fib."
"For your information, when I was your age I was the size of an elephant! Now I'm as small as you see me."

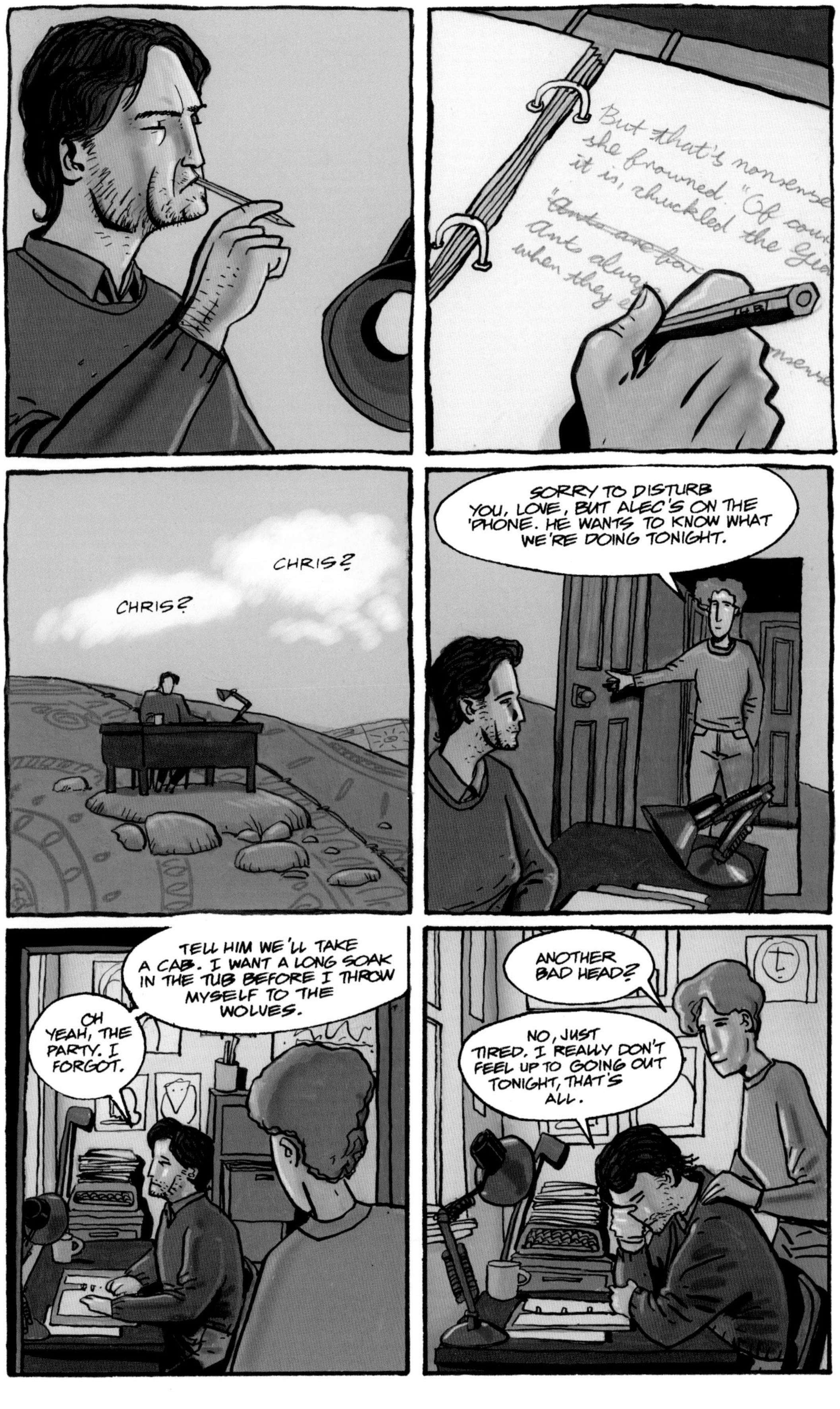
But that's nonsense
CHRIS?
CHRIS?
SORRY TO DISTURB YOU, LOVE, BUT ALEC'S ON THE 'PHONE. HE WANTS TO KNOW WHAT WE'RE DOING TONIGHT.
OH YEAH, THE PARTY. I FORGOT.
TELL HIM WE'LL TAKE A CAB. I WANT A LONG SOAK IN THE TUB BEFORE I THROW MYSELF TO THE WOLVES.
ANOTHER BAD HEAD?
NO, JUST TIRED. I REALLY DON'T FEEL UP TO GOING OUT TONIGHT, THAT'S ALL.

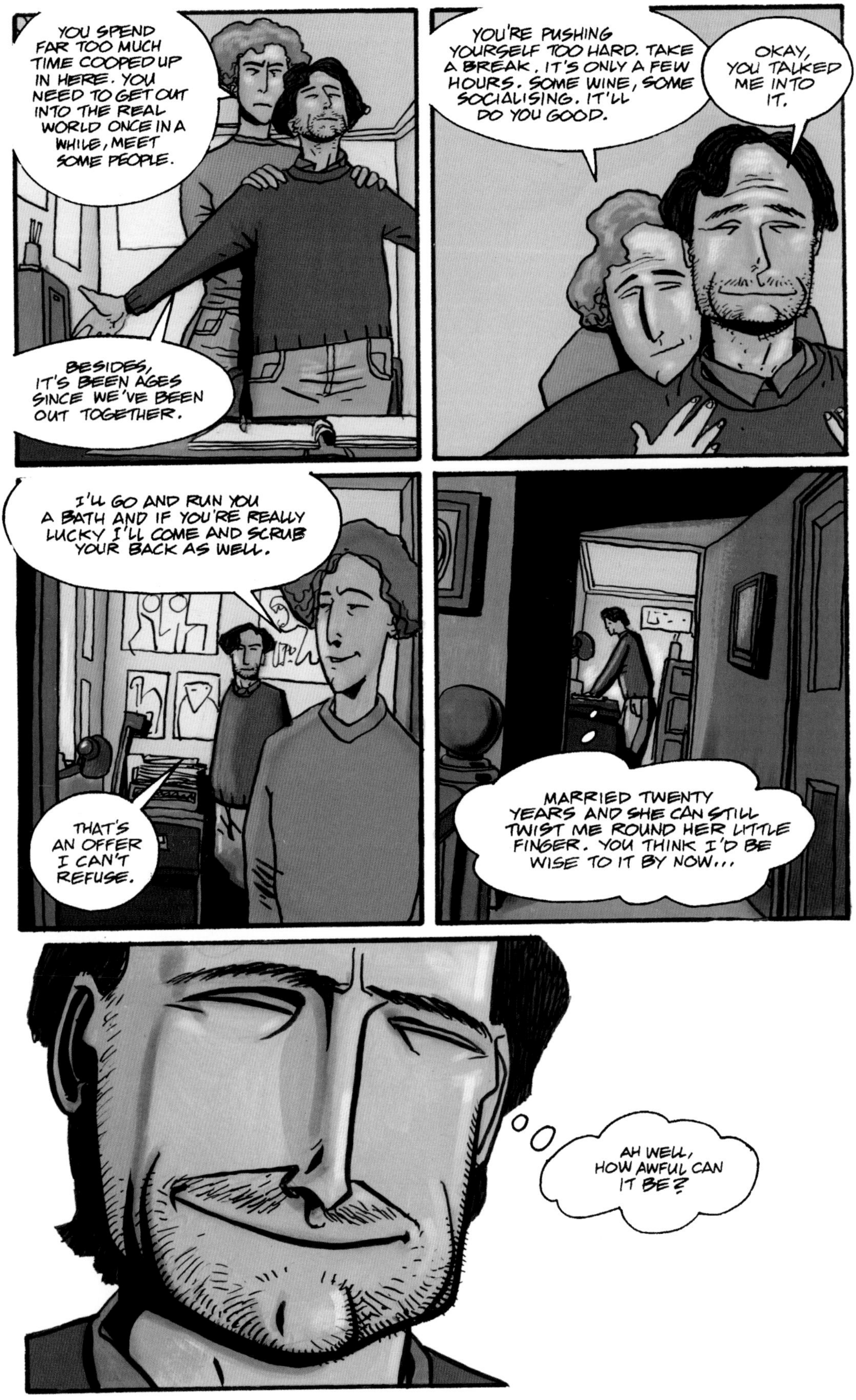
YOU SPEND FAR TOO MUCH TIME COOPED UP IN HERE. YOU NEED TO GET OUT INTO THE REAL WORLD ONCE IN A WHILE, MEET SOME PEOPLE.
BESIDES, IT'S BEEN AGES SINCE WE'VE BEEN OUT TOGETHER.
YOU'RE PUSHING YOURSELF TOO HARD. TAKE A BREAK. IT'S ONLY A FEW HOURS. SOME WINE, SOME SOCIALISING. IT'LL DO YOU GOOD.
OKAY, YOU TALKED ME INTO IT.
I'LL GO AND RUN YOU A BATH AND IF YOU'RE REALLY LUCKY I'LL COME AND SCRUB YOUR BACK AS WELL.
THAT'S AN OFFER I CAN'T REFUSE.
MARRIED TWENTY YEARS AND SHE CAN STILL TWIST ME ROUND HER LITTLE FINGER. YOU THINK I'D BE WISE TO IT BY NOW...
AH WELL, HOW AWFUL CAN IT BE?

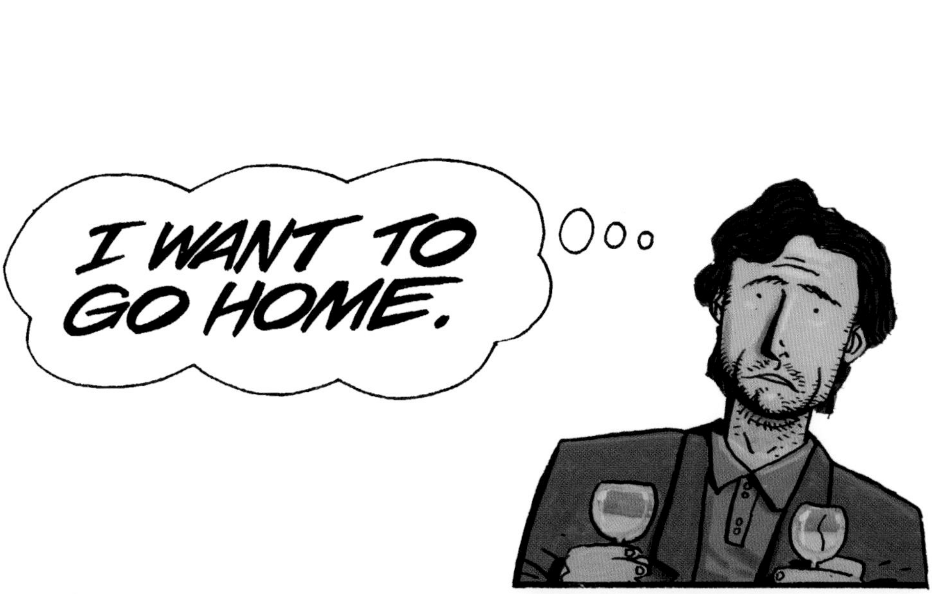
I WANT TO GO HOME.

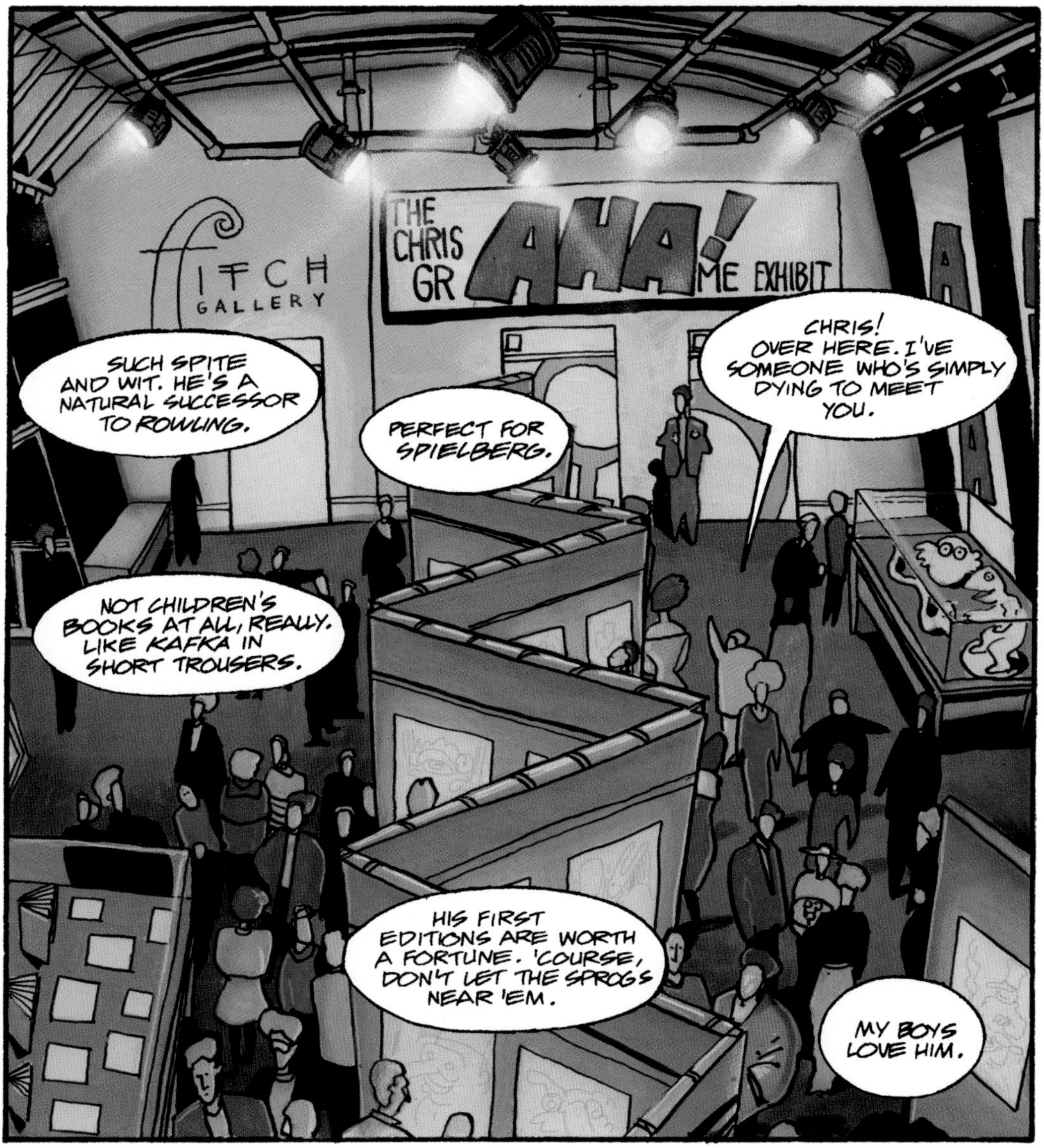
SUCH SPITE AND WIT. HE'S A NATURAL SUCCESSOR TO ROWLING.
PERFECT FOR SPIELBERG.
CHRIS! OVER HERE. I'VE SOMEONE WHO'S SIMPLY DYING TO MEET YOU.
NOT CHILDREN'S BOOKS AT ALL, REALLY. LIKE KAFKA IN SHORT TROUSERS.
HIS FIRST EDITIONS ARE WORTH A FORTUNE. 'COURSE, DON'T LET THE SPROGS NEAR 'EM.
MY BOYS LOVE HIM.

TODD OLIVER, I'D LIKE YOU TO MEET THE STAR OF TONIGHT'S LITTLE SOIREE, CHRIS GRAHAME.

IT'S A PLEASURE.

SORRY, I SEEM TO HAVE MY HANDS FULL.

HERE.

THANKS.

ALEC TELLS ME YOU'RE WORKING ON A FOLLOW-UP TO LEWIS CARROLL'S 'ALICE' NOVELS?

THAT'S RIGHT. IT'S CALLED 'ALICE BEYOND THE PAIL': SHE SORT OF FALLS BACK INTO WONDERLAND THROUGH A HOLE IN A BUCKET.

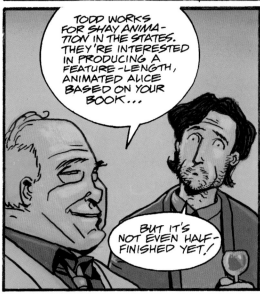

TODD WORKS FOR SHAY ANIMATION IN THE STATES. THEY'RE INTERESTED IN PRODUCING A FEATURE-LENGTH, ANIMATED ALICE BASED ON YOUR BOOK...

BUT IT'S NOT EVEN HALF-FINISHED YET!

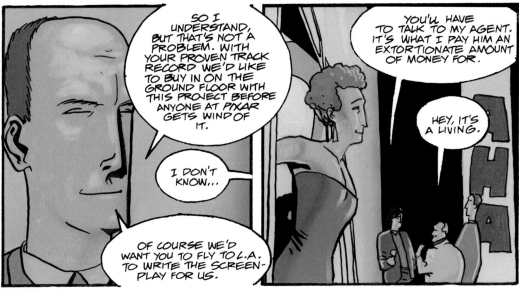

SO I UNDERSTAND, BUT THAT'S NOT A PROBLEM. WITH YOUR PROVEN TRACK RECORD WE'D LIKE TO BUY IN ON THE GROUND FLOOR WITH THIS PROJECT BEFORE ANYONE AT PIXAR GETS WIND OF IT.

I DON'T KNOW...

OF COURSE WE'D WANT YOU TO FLY TO L.A. TO WRITE THE SCREENPLAY FOR US.

YOU'LL HAVE TO TALK TO MY AGENT. IT'S WHAT I PAY HIM AN EXTORTIONATE AMOUNT OF MONEY FOR.

HEY, IT'S A LIVING.

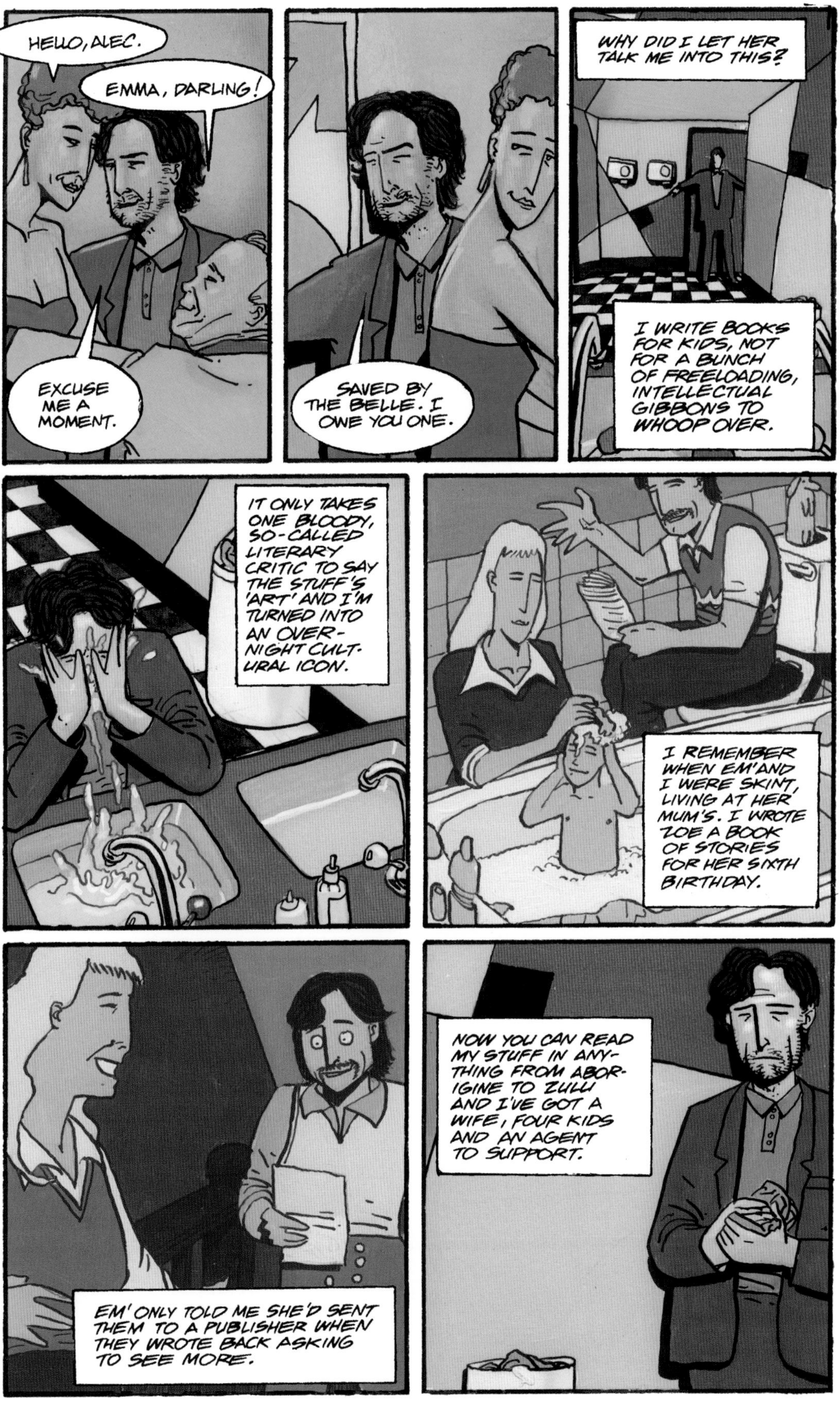
HELLO, ALEC.
EMMA, DARLING!
EXCUSE ME A MOMENT.
SAVED BY THE BELLE. I OWE YOU ONE.
WHY DID I LET HER TALK ME INTO THIS?
I WRITE BOOKS FOR KIDS, NOT FOR A BUNCH OF FREELOADING, INTELLECTUAL GIBBONS TO WHOOP OVER.
IT ONLY TAKES ONE BLOODY, SO-CALLED LITERARY CRITIC TO SAY THE STUFF'S 'ART' AND I'M TURNED INTO AN OVER-NIGHT CULT-URAL ICON.
I REMEMBER WHEN EM' AND I WERE SKINT, LIVING AT HER MUM'S. I WROTE ZOE A BOOK OF STORIES FOR HER SIXTH BIRTHDAY.
EM' ONLY TOLD ME SHE'D SENT THEM TO A PUBLISHER WHEN THEY WROTE BACK ASKING TO SEE MORE.
NOW YOU CAN READ MY STUFF IN ANY-THING FROM ABOR-IGINE TO ZULU AND I'VE GOT A WIFE, FOUR KIDS AND AN AGENT TO SUPPORT.

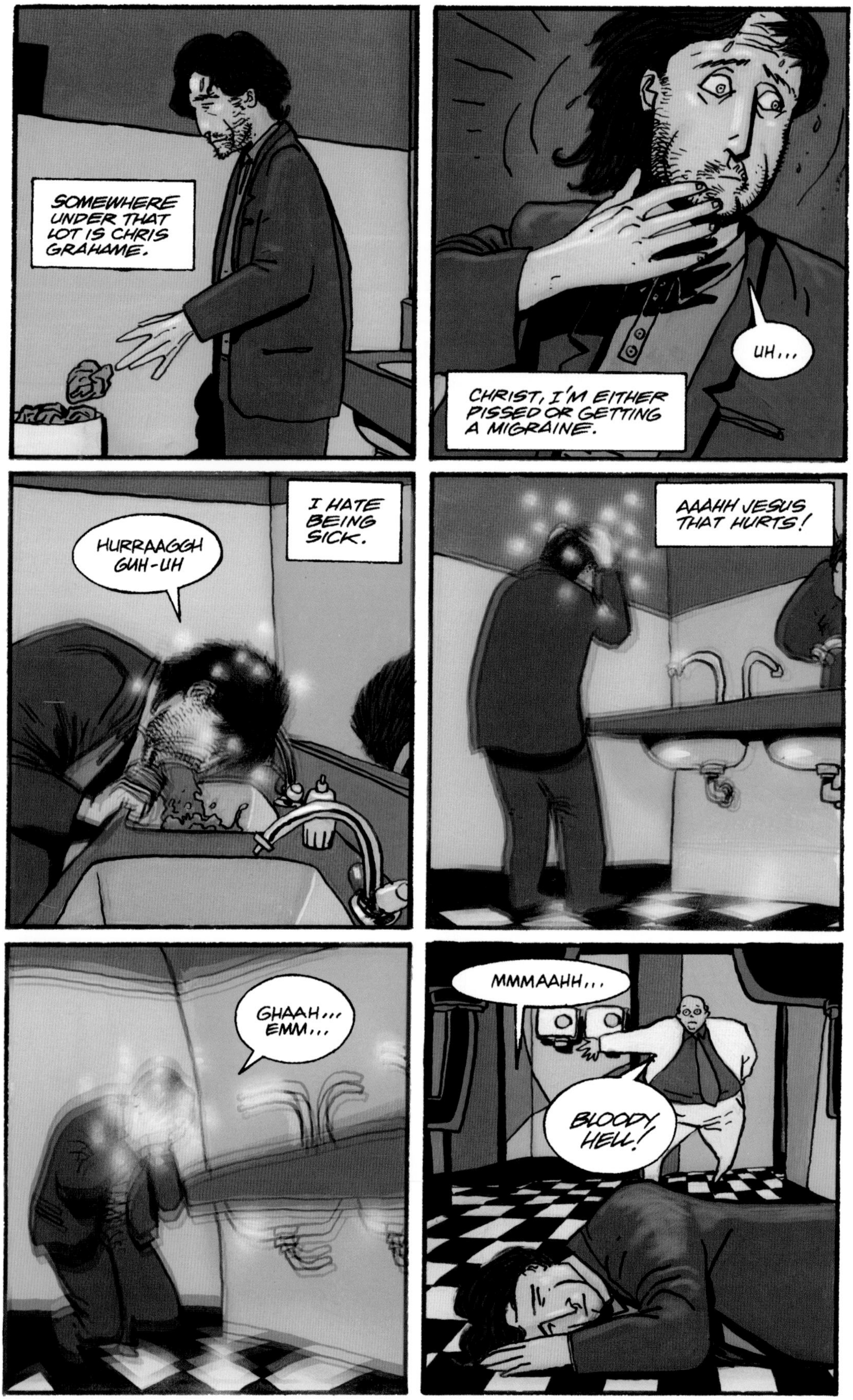
SOMEWHERE UNDER THAT LOT IS CHRIS GRAHAME.
CHRIST, I'M EITHER PISSED OR GETTING A MIGRAINE.
UH...
I HATE BEING SICK.
HURRAAGGH GUH-UH
AAAHH JESUS THAT HURTS!
GHAAH... EMM...
MMMAAHH...
BLOODY HELL!

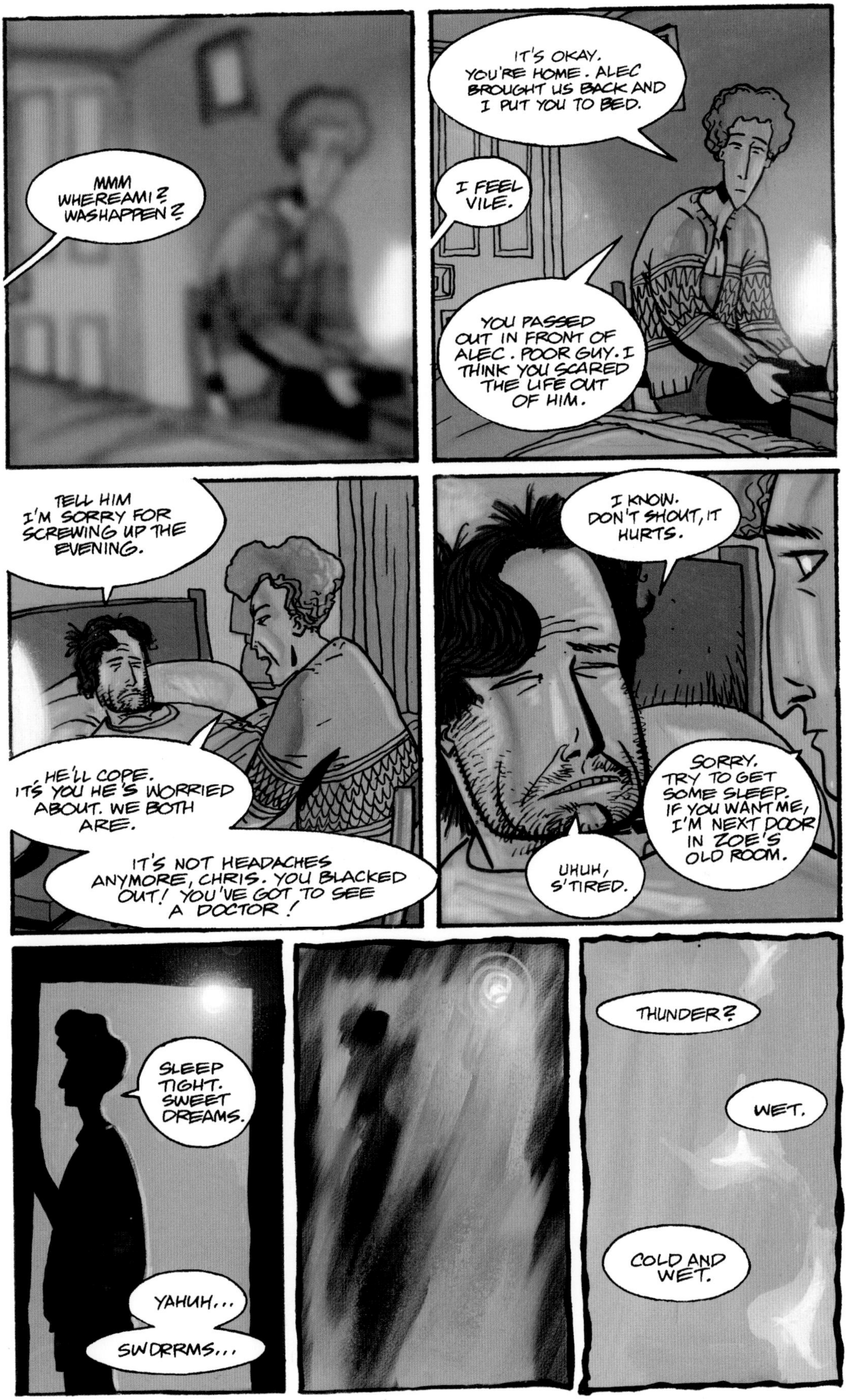
MMM WHEREAMI? WASHAPPEN?
IT'S OKAY. YOU'RE HOME. ALEC BROUGHT US BACK AND I PUT YOU TO BED.
I FEEL VILE.
YOU PASSED OUT IN FRONT OF ALEC. POOR GUY. I THINK YOU SCARED THE LIFE OUT OF HIM.
TELL HIM I'M SORRY FOR SCREWING UP THE EVENING.
HE'LL COPE. IT'S YOU HE'S WORRIED ABOUT. WE BOTH ARE.
IT'S NOT HEADACHES ANYMORE, CHRIS. YOU BLACKED OUT! YOU'VE GOT TO SEE A DOCTOR!
I KNOW. DON'T SHOUT, IT HURTS.
SORRY. TRY TO GET SOME SLEEP. IF YOU WANT ME, I'M NEXT DOOR IN ZOE'S OLD ROOM.
UHUH, S'TIRED.
SLEEP TIGHT. SWEET DREAMS.
YAHUH...
SWDRRMS...
THUNDER?
WET.
COLD AND WET.

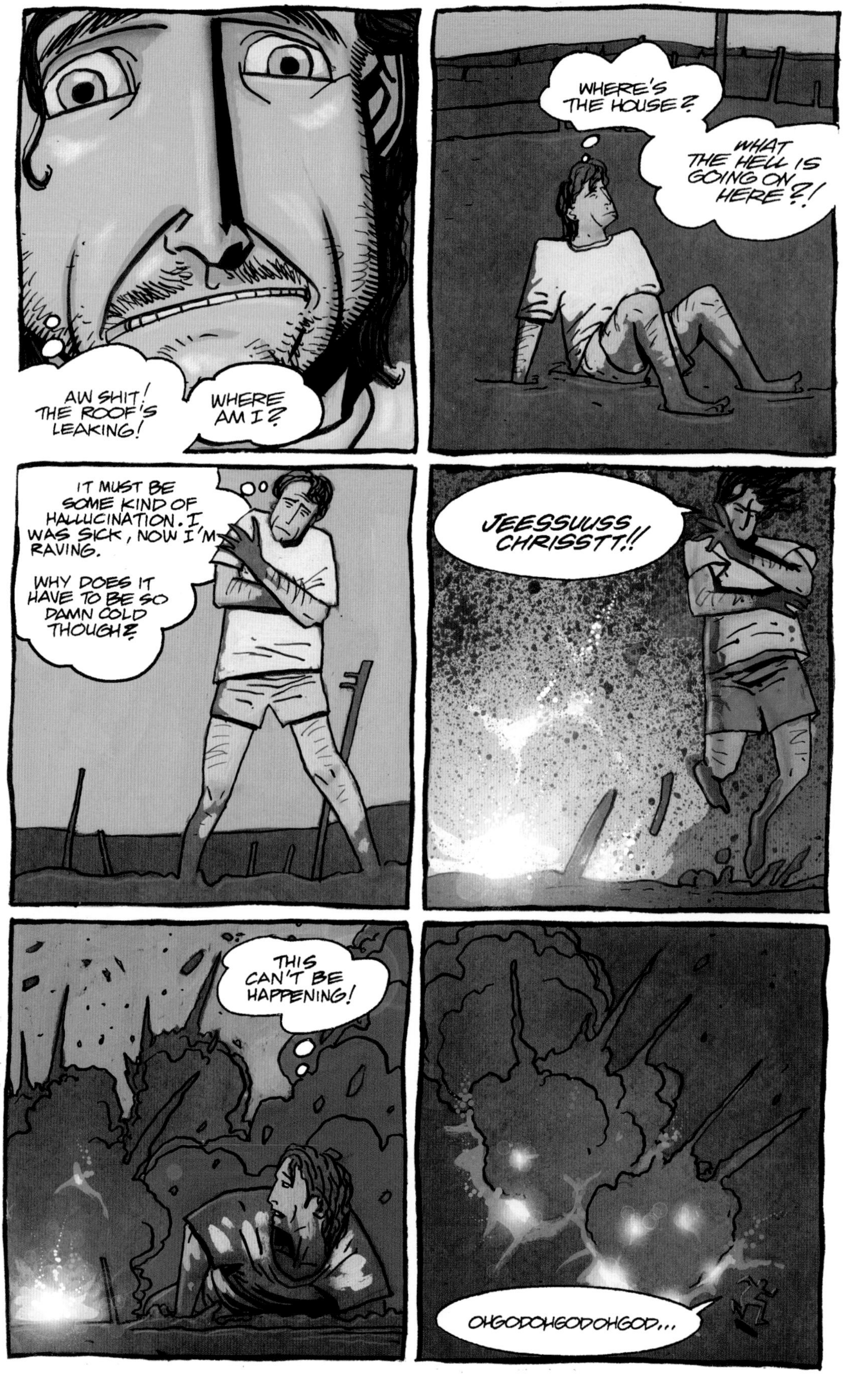
AW SHIT! THE ROOF'S LEAKING!
WHERE AM I?
WHERE'S THE HOUSE?
WHAT THE HELL IS GOING ON HERE?!
IT MUST BE SOME KIND OF HALLUCINATION. I WAS SICK, NOW I'M RAVING.
WHY DOES IT HAVE TO BE SO DAMN COLD THOUGH?
JEESSUUSS CHRISSTT!!
THIS CAN'T BE HAPPENING!
OHGODOHGODOHGOD...

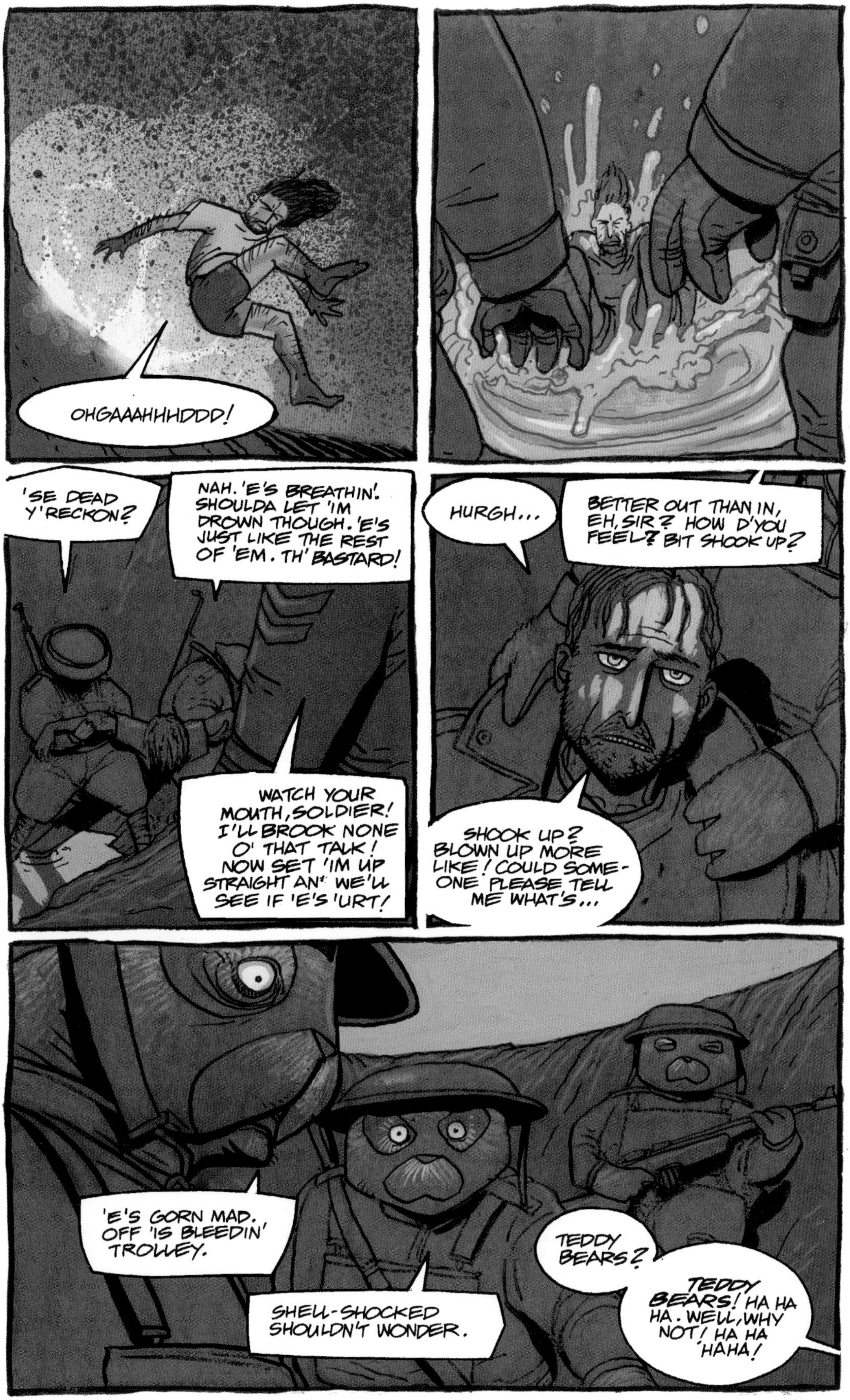
OHGAAAHHHDDD!
'SE DEAD Y'RECKON?
NAH. 'E'S BREATHIN'. SHOULDA LET 'IM DROWN THOUGH. 'E'S JUST LIKE THE REST OF 'EM. TH' BASTARD!
WATCH YOUR MOUTH, SOLDIER! I'LL BROOK NONE O' THAT TALK! NOW SET 'IM UP STRAIGHT AN' WE'LL SEE IF 'E'S 'URT!
HURGH...
BETTER OUT THAN IN, EH, SIR? HOW D'YOU FEEL? BIT SHOOK UP?
SHOOK UP? BLOWN UP MORE LIKE! COULD SOME-ONE PLEASE TELL ME WHAT'S...
'E'S GORN MAD. OFF 'IS BLEEDIN' TROLLEY.
SHELL-SHOCKED SHOULDN'T WONDER.
TEDDY BEARS?
TEDDY BEARS! HA HA HA. WELL, WHY NOT! HA HA HAHA!

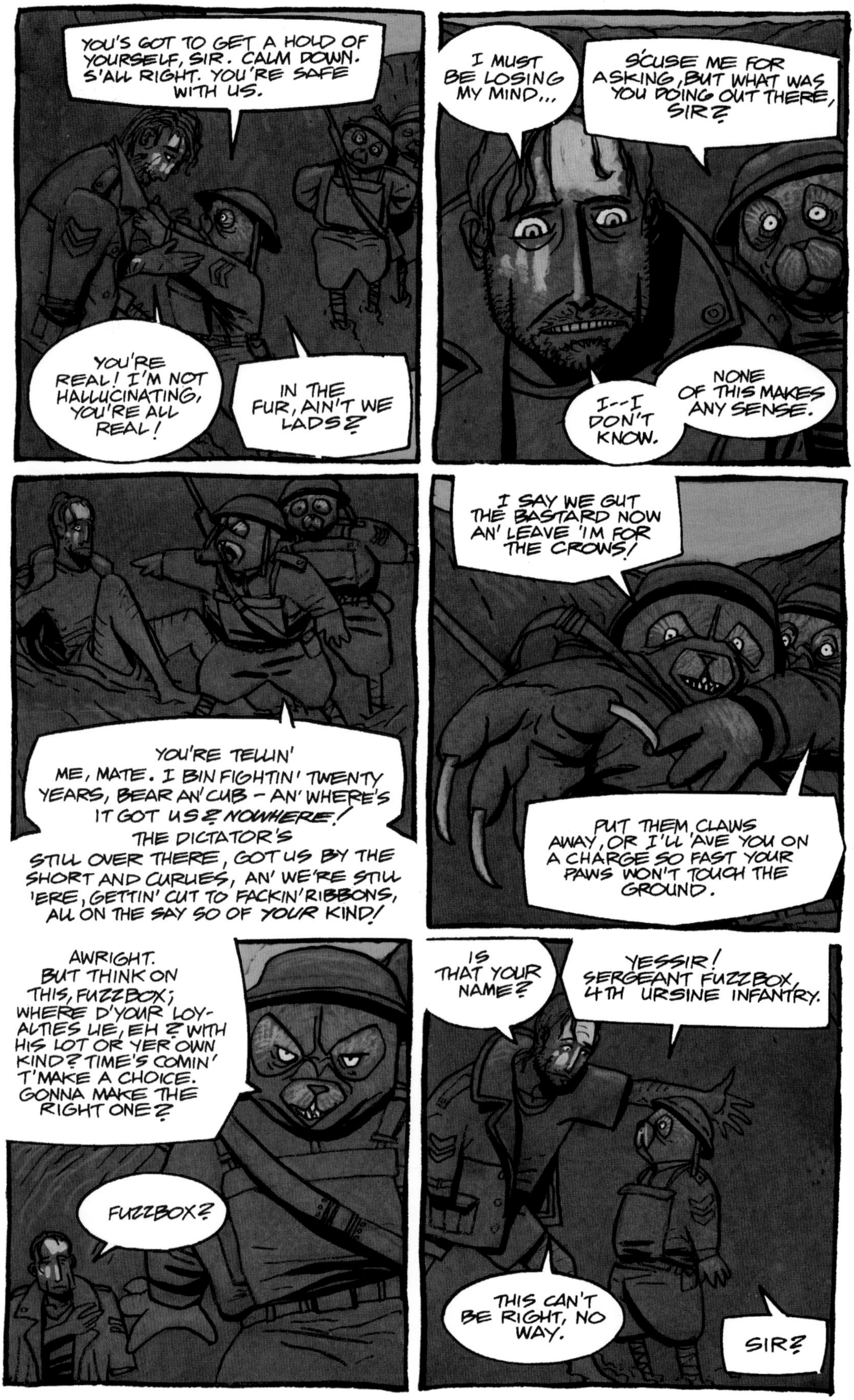
YOU'S GOT TO GET A HOLD OF YOURSELF, SIR. CALM DOWN. S'ALL RIGHT. YOU'RE SAFE WITH US.
YOU'RE REAL! I'M NOT HALLUCINATING, YOU'RE ALL REAL!
IN THE FUR, AIN'T WE LADS?
I MUST BE LOSING MY MIND...
S'CUSE ME FOR ASKING, BUT WHAT WAS YOU DOING OUT THERE, SIR?
I--I DON'T KNOW.
NONE OF THIS MAKES ANY SENSE.
YOU'RE TELLIN' ME, MATE. I BIN FIGHTIN' TWENTY YEARS, BEAR AN' CUB - AN' WHERE'S IT GOT US? NOWHERE! THE DICTATOR'S STILL OVER THERE, GOT US BY THE SHORT AND CURLIES, AN' WE'RE STILL 'ERE, GETTIN' CUT TO FACKIN' RIBBONS, ALL ON THE SAY SO OF YOUR KIND!
I SAY WE GUT THE BASTARD NOW AN' LEAVE 'IM FOR THE CROWS!
PUT THEM CLAWS AWAY, OR I'LL 'AVE YOU ON A CHARGE SO FAST YOUR PAWS WON'T TOUCH THE GROUND.
AWRIGHT. BUT THINK ON THIS, FUZZBOX; WHERE D'YOUR LOY-ALTIES LIE, EH? WITH HIS LOT OR YER OWN KIND? TIME'S COMIN' T'MAKE A CHOICE. GONNA MAKE THE RIGHT ONE?
FUZZBOX?
IS THAT YOUR NAME?
YESSIR! SERGEANT FUZZBOX, 4TH URSINE INFANTRY.
THIS CAN'T BE RIGHT, NO WAY.
SIR?

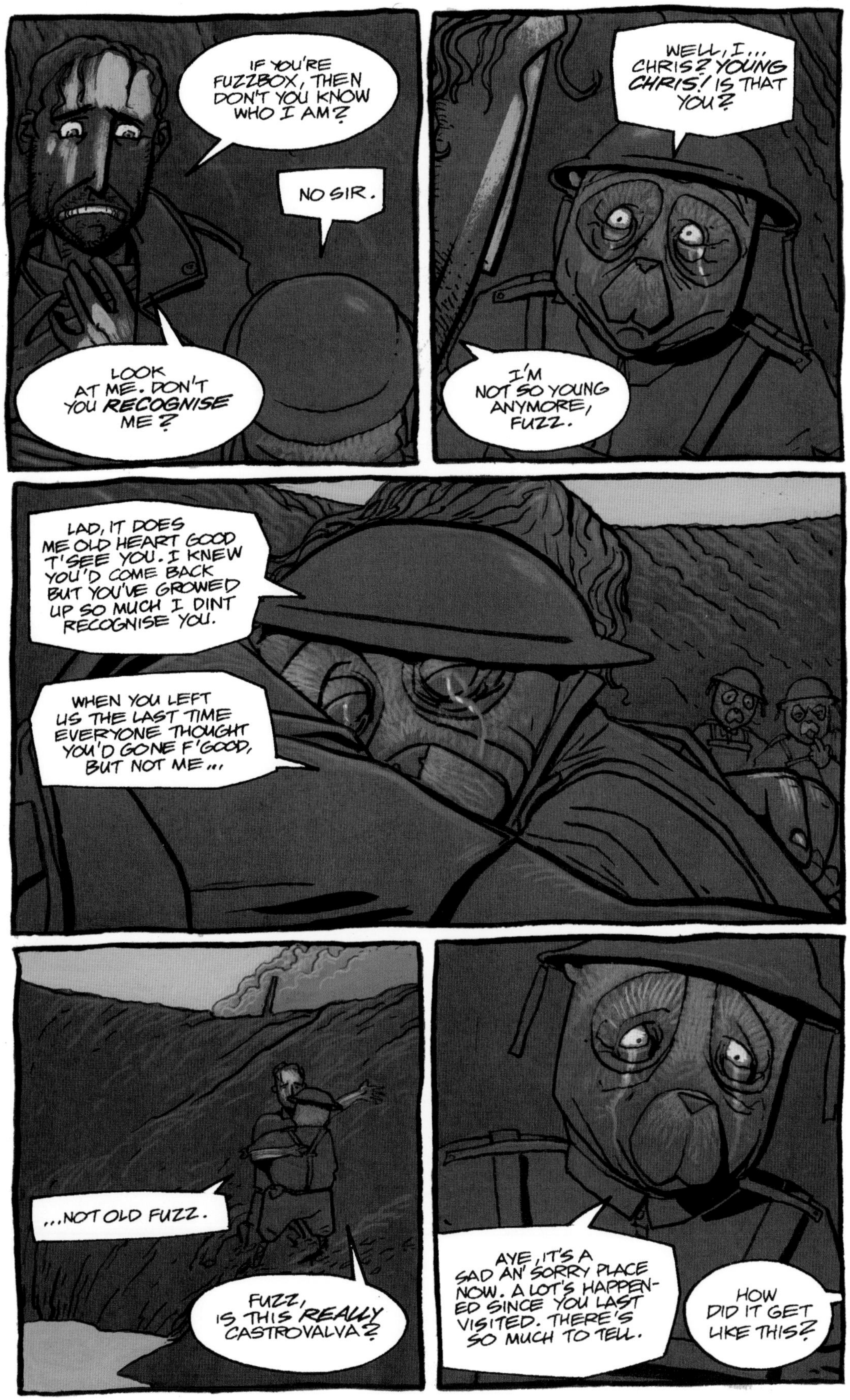
IF YOU'RE FUZZBOX, THEN DON'T YOU KNOW WHO I AM?
NO SIR.
LOOK AT ME. DON'T YOU RECOGNISE ME?
WELL, I... CHRIS? YOUNG CHRIS! IS THAT YOU?
I'M NOT SO YOUNG ANYMORE, FUZZ.
LAD, IT DOES ME OLD HEART GOOD T'SEE YOU. I KNEW YOU'D COME BACK BUT YOU'VE GROWED UP SO MUCH I DINT RECOGNISE YOU.
WHEN YOU LEFT US THE LAST TIME EVERYONE THOUGHT YOU'D GONE F'GOOD, BUT NOT ME...
...NOT OLD FUZZ.
FUZZ, IS THIS REALLY CASTROVALVA?
AYE, IT'S A SAD AN' SORRY PLACE NOW. A LOT'S HAPPEN-ED SINCE YOU LAST VISITED. THERE'S SO MUCH TO TELL.
HOW DID IT GET LIKE THIS?

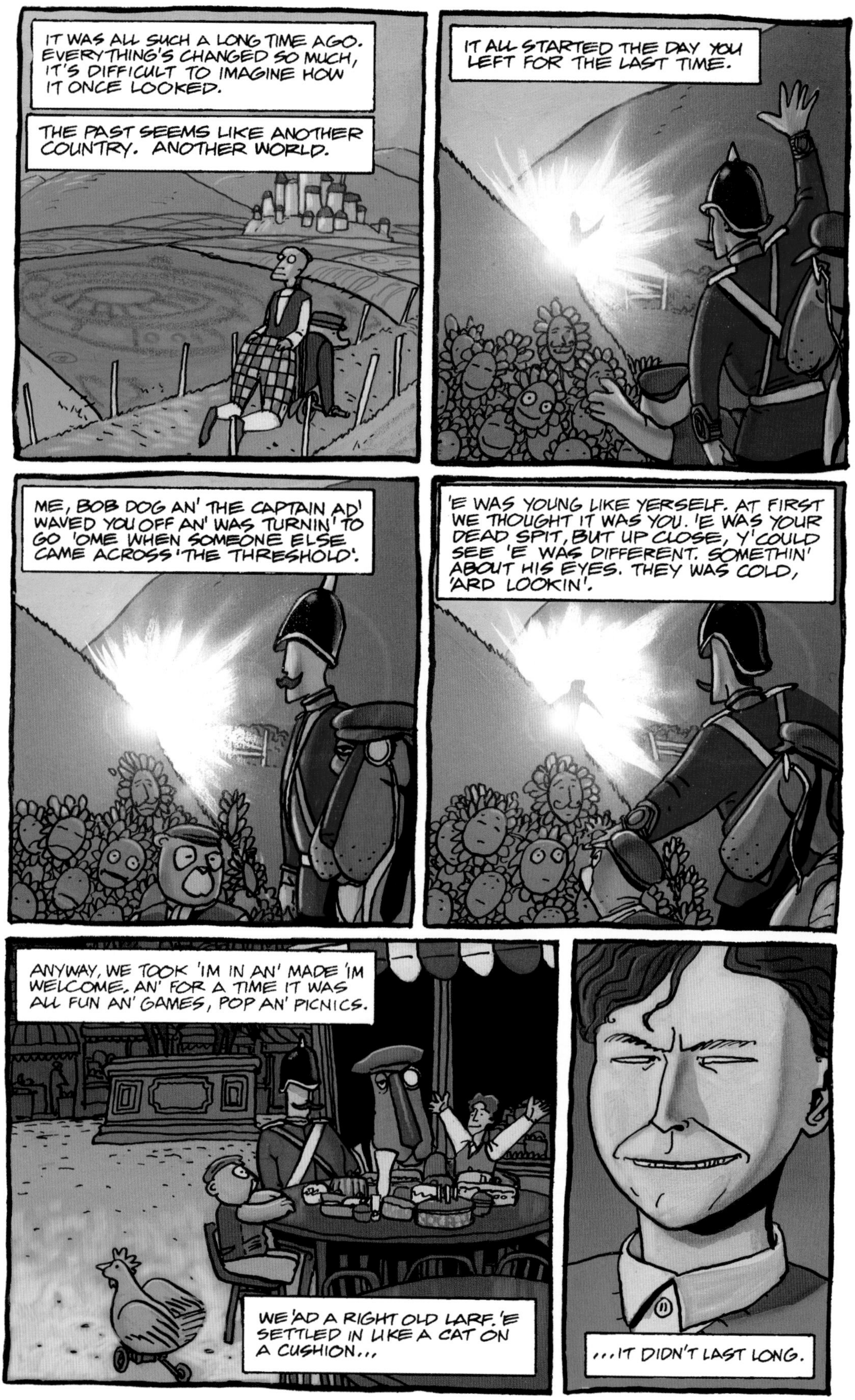
IT WAS ALL SUCH A LONG TIME AGO. EVERYTHING'S CHANGED SO MUCH, IT'S DIFFICULT TO IMAGINE HOW IT ONCE LOOKED.
THE PAST SEEMS LIKE ANOTHER COUNTRY. ANOTHER WORLD.
IT ALL STARTED THE DAY YOU LEFT FOR THE LAST TIME.
ME, BOB DOG AN' THE CAPTAIN 'AD WAVED YOU OFF AN' WAS TURNIN' TO GO 'OME WHEN SOMEONE ELSE CAME ACROSS 'THE THRESHOLD'.
'E WAS YOUNG LIKE YERSELF. AT FIRST WE THOUGHT IT WAS YOU. 'E WAS YOUR DEAD SPIT, BUT UP CLOSE, Y'COULD SEE 'E WAS DIFFERENT. SOMETHIN' ABOUT HIS EYES. THEY WAS COLD, 'ARD LOOKIN'.
ANYWAY, WE TOOK 'IM IN AN' MADE 'IM WELCOME. AN' FOR A TIME IT WAS ALL FUN AN' GAMES, POP AN' PICNICS.
WE 'AD A RIGHT OLD LARF. 'E SETTLED IN LIKE A CAT ON A CUSHION...
...IT DIDN'T LAST LONG.

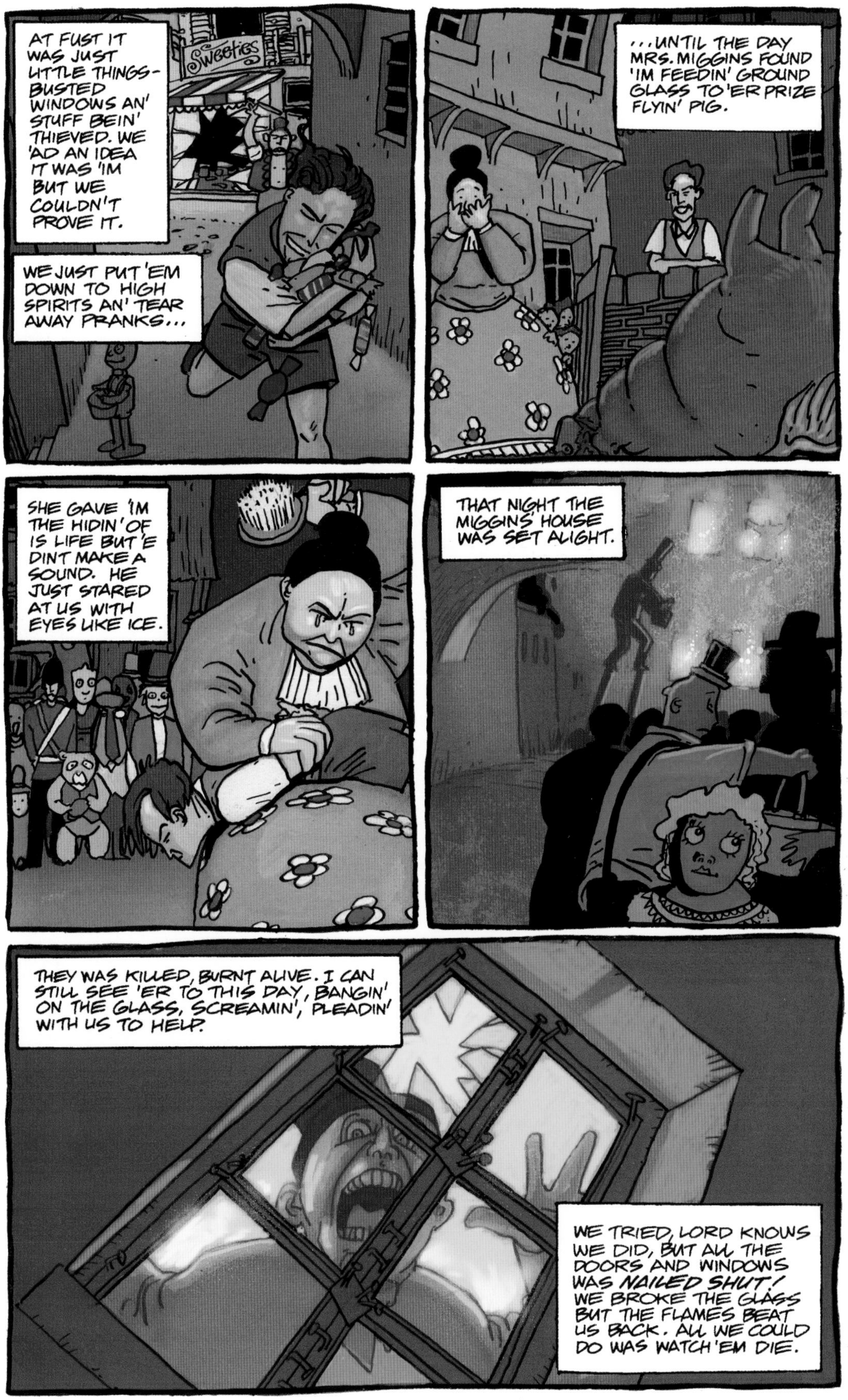
AT FUST IT WAS JUST LITTLE THINGS- BUSTED WINDOWS AN' STUFF BEIN' THIEVED. WE 'AD AN IDEA IT WAS 'IM BUT WE COULDN'T PROVE IT.
Sweeties
WE JUST PUT 'EM DOWN TO HIGH SPIRITS AN' TEAR AWAY PRANKS...
...UNTIL THE DAY MRS. MIGGINS FOUND 'IM FEEDIN' GROUND GLASS TO 'ER PRIZE FLYIN' PIG.
SHE GAVE 'IM THE HIDIN' OF 'IS LIFE BUT 'E DINT MAKE A SOUND. HE JUST STARED AT US WITH EYES LIKE ICE.
THAT NIGHT THE MIGGINS' HOUSE WAS SET ALIGHT.
THEY WAS KILLED, BURNT ALIVE. I CAN STILL SEE 'ER TO THIS DAY, BANGIN' ON THE GLASS, SCREAMIN', PLEADIN' WITH US TO HELP.
WE TRIED, LORD KNOWS WE DID, BUT ALL THE DOORS AND WINDOWS WAS NAILED SHUT! WE BROKE THE GLASS BUT THE FLAMES BEAT US BACK. ALL WE COULD DO WAS WATCH 'EM DIE.

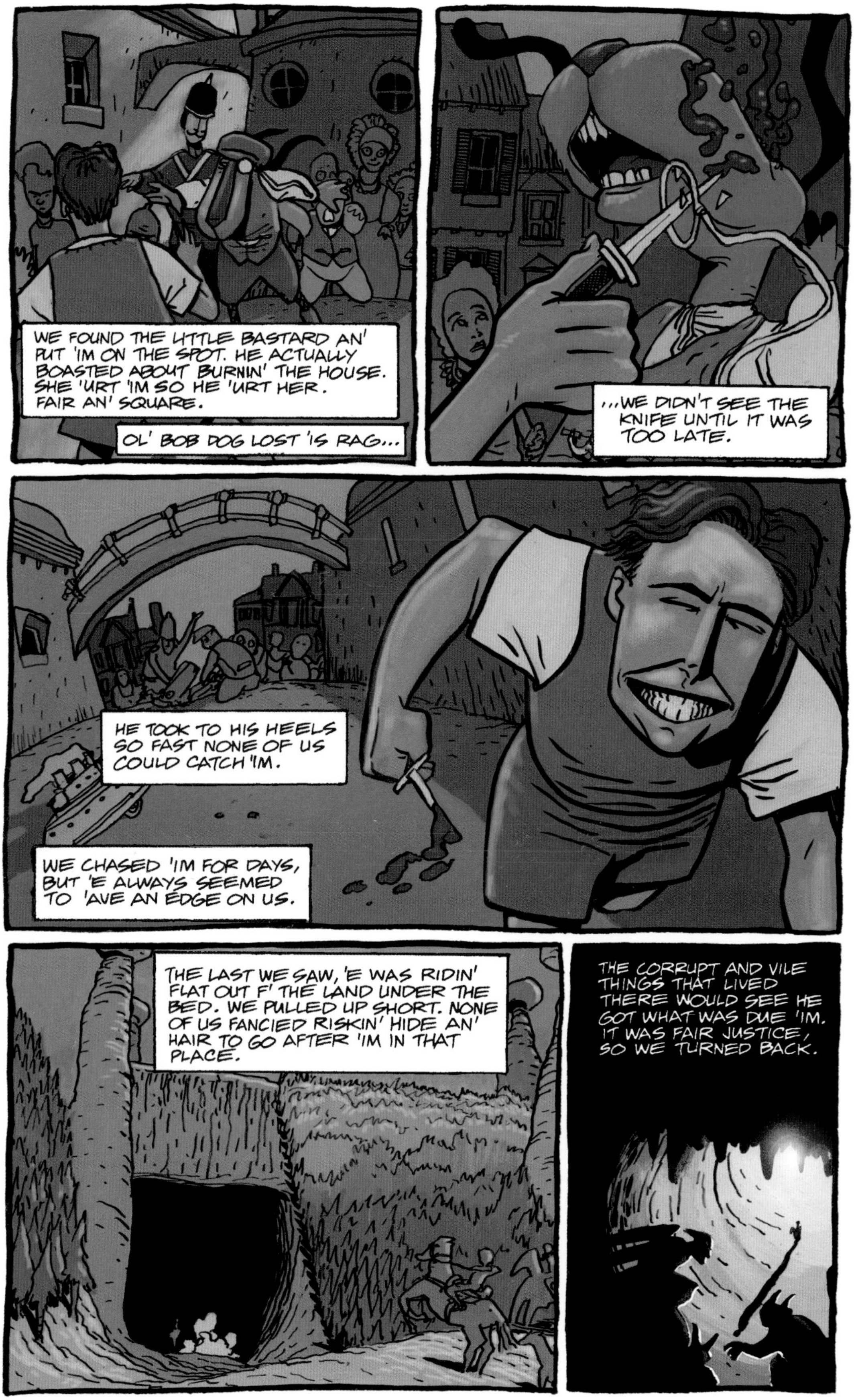
WE FOUND THE LITTLE BASTARD AN' PUT 'IM ON THE SPOT. HE ACTUALLY BOASTED ABOUT BURNIN' THE HOUSE. SHE 'URT 'IM SO HE 'URT HER. FAIR AN' SQUARE.
OL' BOB DOG LOST 'IS RAG...
...WE DIDN'T SEE THE KNIFE UNTIL IT WAS TOO LATE.
HE TOOK TO HIS HEELS SO FAST NONE OF US COULD CATCH 'IM.
WE CHASED 'IM FOR DAYS, BUT 'E ALWAYS SEEMED TO 'AVE AN EDGE ON US.
THE LAST WE SAW, 'E WAS RIDIN' FLAT OUT F' THE LAND UNDER THE BED. WE PULLED UP SHORT. NONE OF US FANCIED RISKIN' HIDE AN' HAIR TO GO AFTER 'IM IN THAT PLACE.
THE CORRUPT AND VILE THINGS THAT LIVED THERE WOULD SEE HE GOT WHAT WAS DUE 'IM. IT WAS FAIR JUSTICE, SO WE TURNED BACK.

IN TIME, 'E BECAME JUST A BAD MEMORY; A STORY TO FRIGHTEN NAUGHTY CUBS.

I GOT MARRIED TO LIL' AN' OPENED ME OWN BAKERY. Y'SHOULD'VE TASTED MY HONEY TARTS. GOLDEN AS SUNLIGHT AN' SWEET AS ANGELS' KISSES.

A FEW YEARS ON, LIL' HAD TWO CUBS. GREW UP T'BE STRAPPING LADS, BIGGER 'N ME. I CALLED THE ELDEST CHRIS, IN Y'HONOUR!

I MISSED YOU, LAD. I LOVED YOU LIKE ONE OF ME OWN BUT I KNEW YOU'D BE BACK SOMEDAY, AN' COME SWEEPIN' IN LIKE A SUMMER BREEZE..

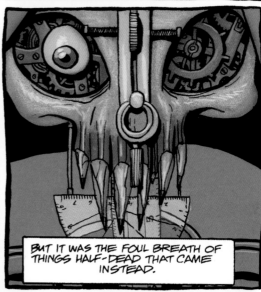

BUT IT WAS THE FOUL BREATH OF THINGS HALF-DEAD THAT CAME INSTEAD.

OUT FROM UNDER THE BED THEY CAME. RIDIN' AN' FLYIN' ON ENGINES OF DEATH, CUTTIN' ACROSS THE LAND LIKE LIGHTNING.

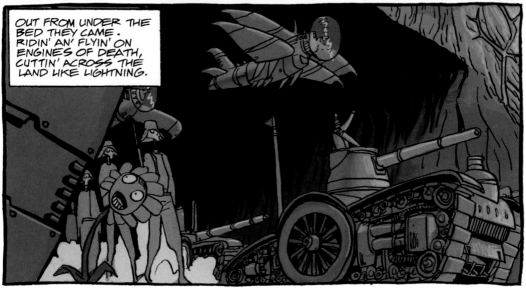

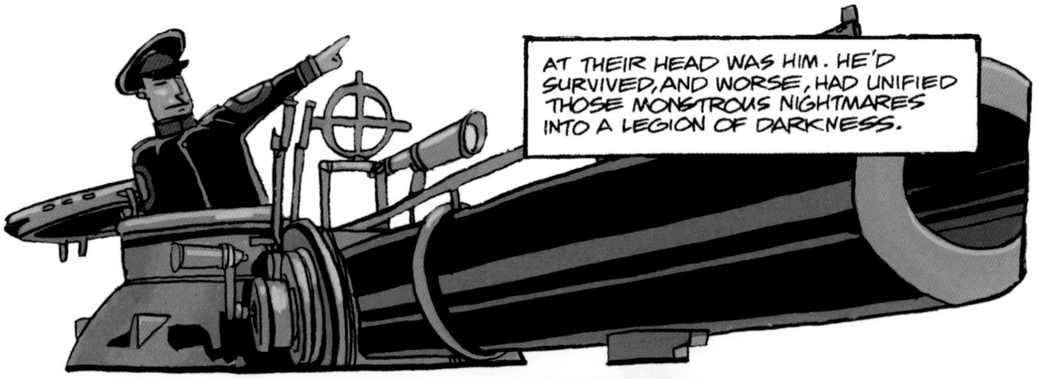
AT THEIR HEAD WAS HIM. HE'D SURVIVED, AND WORSE, HAD UNIFIED THOSE MONSTROUS NIGHTMARES INTO A LEGION OF DARKNESS.

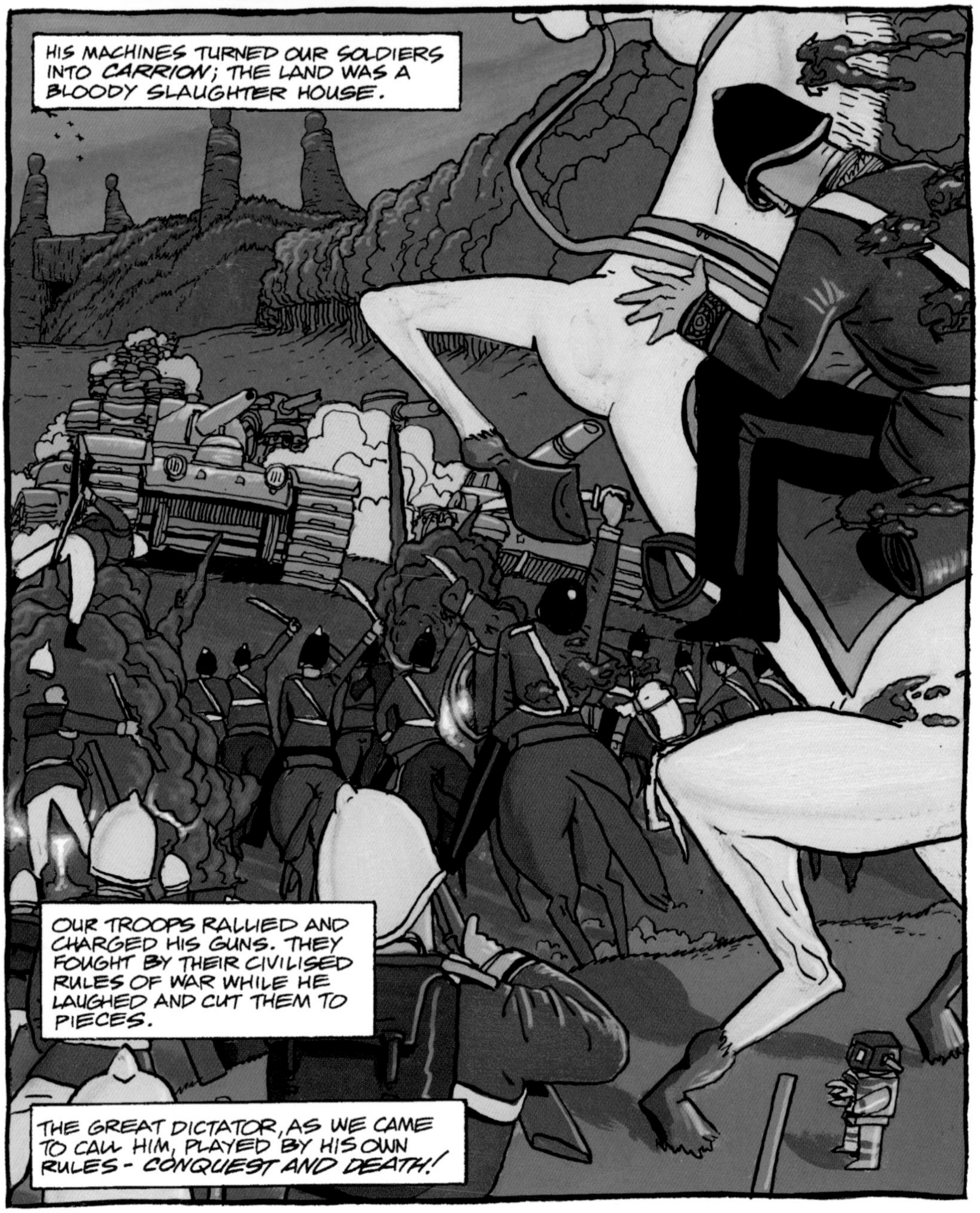
HIS MACHINES TURNED OUR SOLDIERS INTO *CARRION*; THE LAND WAS A BLOODY SLAUGHTER HOUSE.
OUR TROOPS RALLIED AND CHARGED HIS GUNS. THEY FOUGHT BY THEIR CIVILISED RULES OF WAR WHILE HE LAUGHED AND CUT THEM TO PIECES.
THE GREAT DICTATOR, AS WE CAME TO CALL HIM, PLAYED BY HIS OWN RULES - *CONQUEST AND DEATH!*

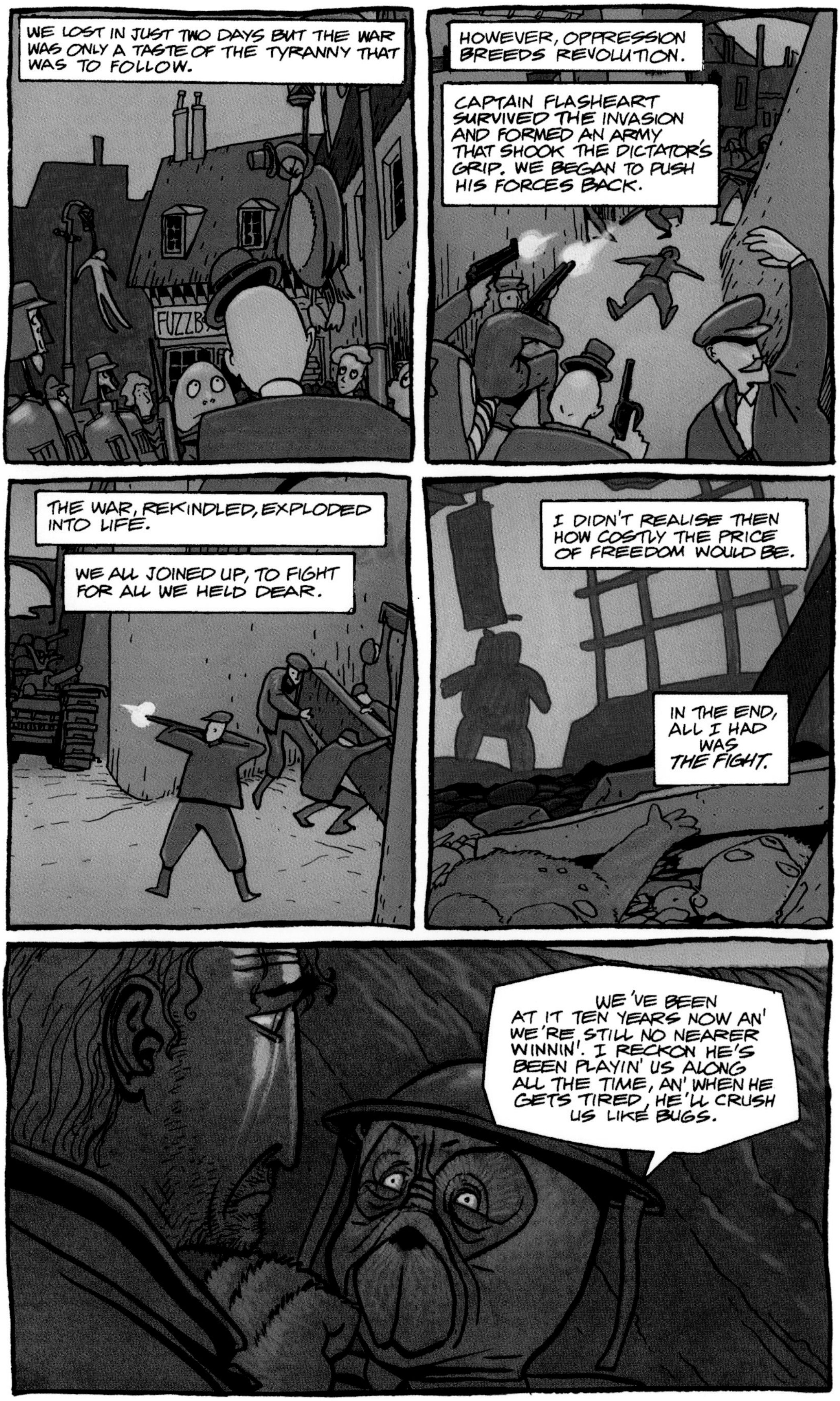
WE LOST IN JUST TWO DAYS BUT THE WAR WAS ONLY A TASTE OF THE TYRANNY THAT WAS TO FOLLOW.
HOWEVER, OPPRESSION BREEDS REVOLUTION.
CAPTAIN FLASHEART SURVIVED THE INVASION AND FORMED AN ARMY THAT SHOOK THE DICTATOR'S GRIP. WE BEGAN TO PUSH HIS FORCES BACK.
THE WAR, REKINDLED, EXPLODED INTO LIFE.
WE ALL JOINED UP, TO FIGHT FOR ALL WE HELD DEAR.
I DIDN'T REALISE THEN HOW COSTLY THE PRICE OF FREEDOM WOULD BE.
IN THE END, ALL I HAD WAS *THE FIGHT.*
WE'VE BEEN AT IT TEN YEARS NOW AN' WE'RE STILL NO NEARER WINNIN'. I RECKON HE'S BEEN PLAYIN' US ALONG ALL THE TIME, AN' WHEN HE GETS TIRED, HE'LL CRUSH US LIKE BUGS.

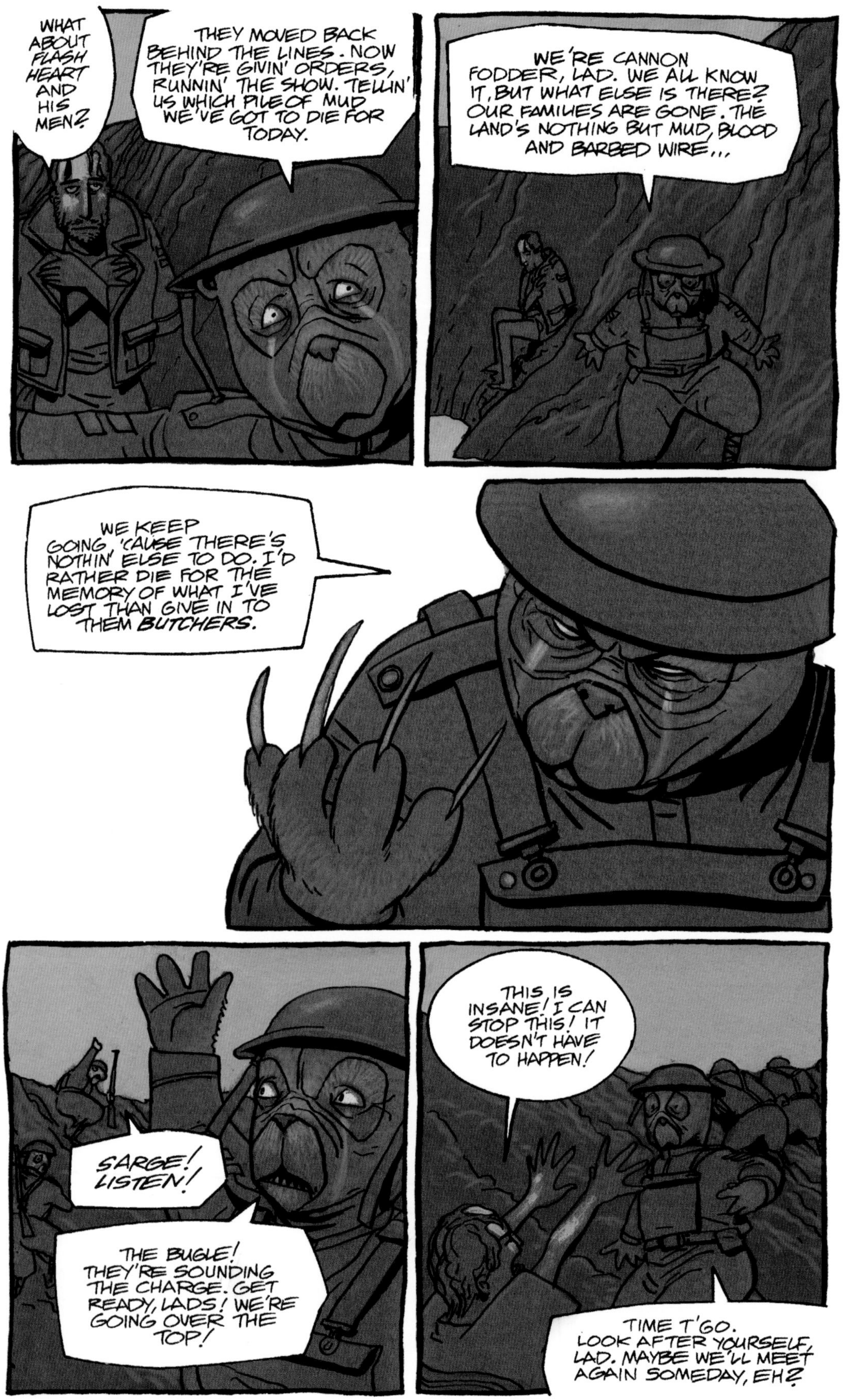
WHAT ABOUT FLASH HEART AND HIS MEN?
THEY MOVED BACK BEHIND THE LINES. NOW THEY'RE GIVIN' ORDERS, RUNNIN' THE SHOW. TELLIN' US WHICH PILE OF MUD WE'VE GOT TO DIE FOR TODAY.
WE'RE CANNON FODDER, LAD. WE ALL KNOW IT, BUT WHAT ELSE IS THERE? OUR FAMILIES ARE GONE. THE LAND'S NOTHING BUT MUD, BLOOD AND BARBED WIRE...
WE KEEP GOING 'CAUSE THERE'S NOTHIN' ELSE TO DO. I'D RATHER DIE FOR THE MEMORY OF WHAT I'VE LOST THAN GIVE IN TO THEM BUTCHERS.
SARGE! LISTEN!
THE BUGLE! THEY'RE SOUNDING THE CHARGE. GET READY, LADS! WE'RE GOING OVER THE TOP!
THIS IS INSANE! I CAN STOP THIS! IT DOESN'T HAVE TO HAPPEN!
TIME T'GO. LOOK AFTER YOURSELF, LAD. MAYBE WE'LL MEET AGAIN SOMEDAY, EH?

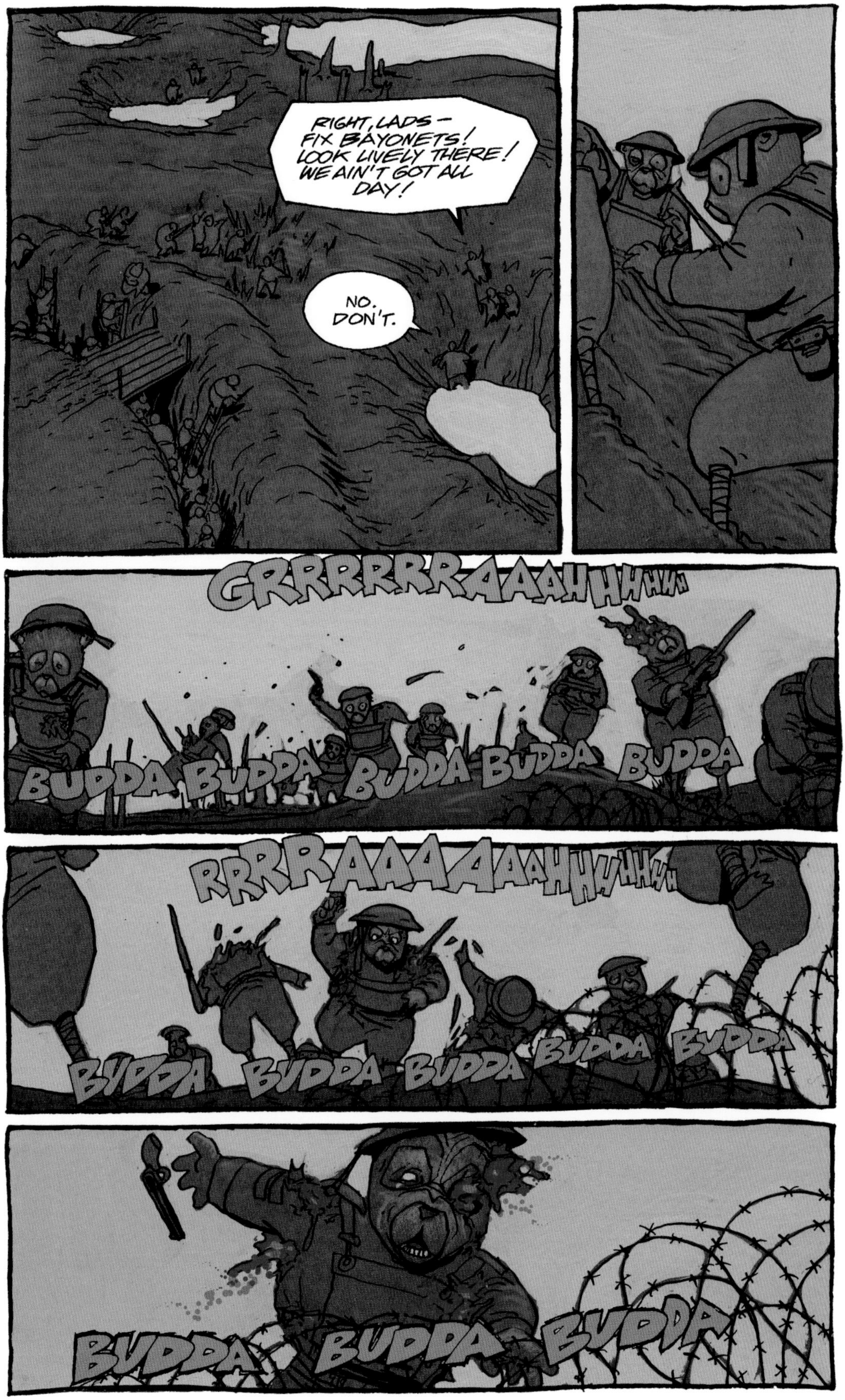
RIGHT, LADS — FIX BAYONETS! LOOK LIVELY THERE! WE AIN'T GOT ALL DAY!
NO. DON'T.
GRRRRRRAAAHHHHHH
BUDDA BUDDA BUDDA BUDDA BUDDA
RRRRAAAAAAAHHHHHHH
BUDDA BUDDA BUDDA BUDDA BUDDA
BUDDA BUDDA BUDDA

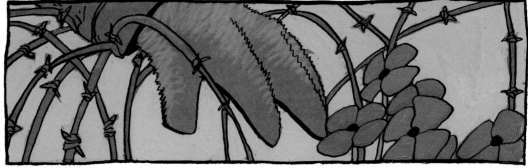

NOOOOO!!

NO! NO! DON'T GOOO! I CAN SAVE YOU!

CHRIS! FOR GOD'S SAKE, WHAT'S *WRONG*?

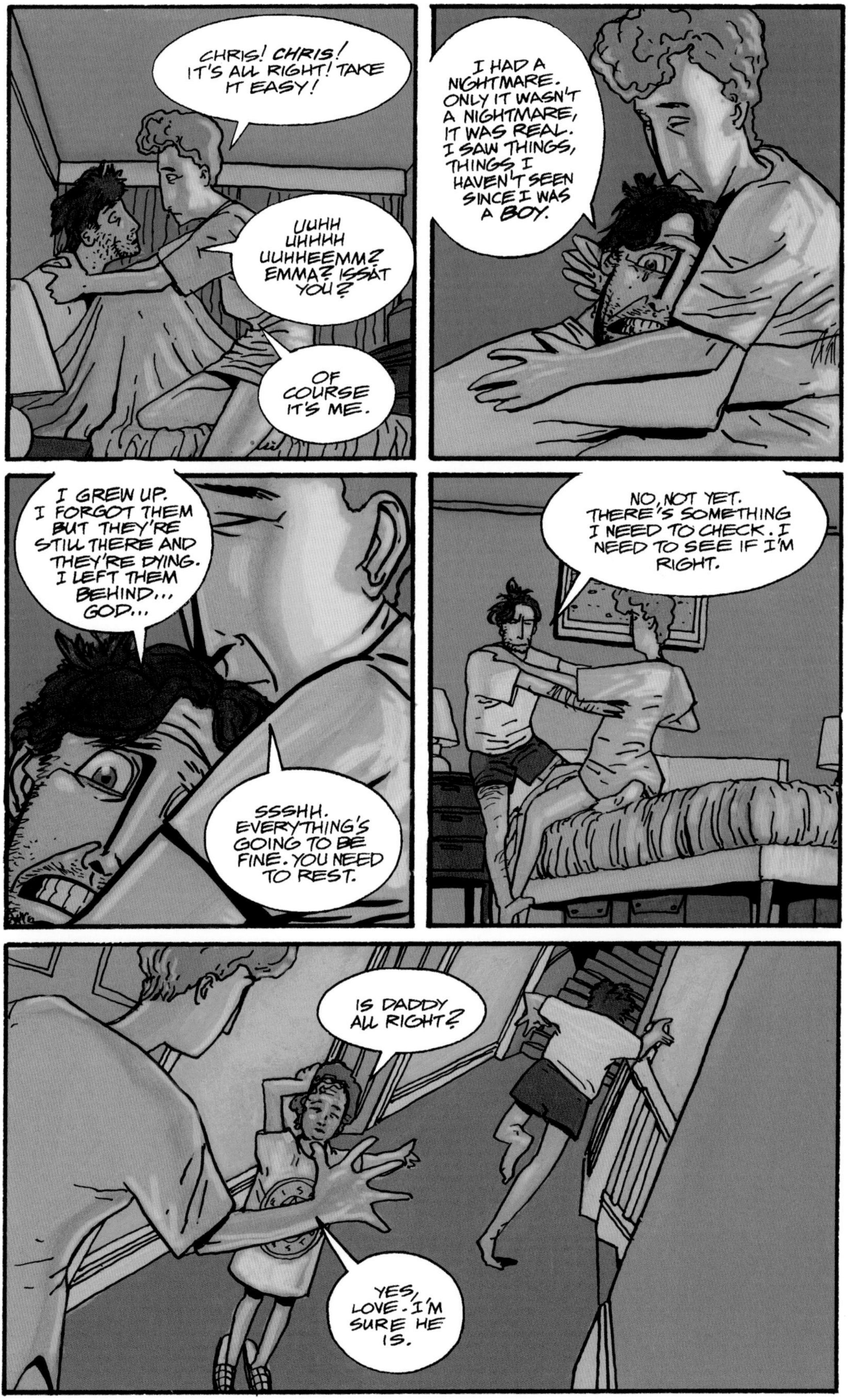
CHRIS! CHRIS! IT'S ALL RIGHT! TAKE IT EASY!
UUHH UHHHH UUHHEEMM? EMMA? ISSÁT YOU?
OF COURSE IT'S ME.
I HAD A NIGHTMARE. ONLY IT WASN'T A NIGHTMARE, IT WAS REAL. I SAW THINGS, THINGS I HAVEN'T SEEN SINCE I WAS A BOY.
I GREW UP. I FORGOT THEM BUT THEY'RE STILL THERE AND THEY'RE DYING. I LEFT THEM BEHIND... GOD...
SSSHH. EVERYTHING'S GOING TO BE FINE. YOU NEED TO REST.
NO, NOT YET. THERE'S SOMETHING I NEED TO CHECK. I NEED TO SEE IF I'M RIGHT.
IS DADDY ALL RIGHT?
YES, LOVE. I'M SURE HE IS.

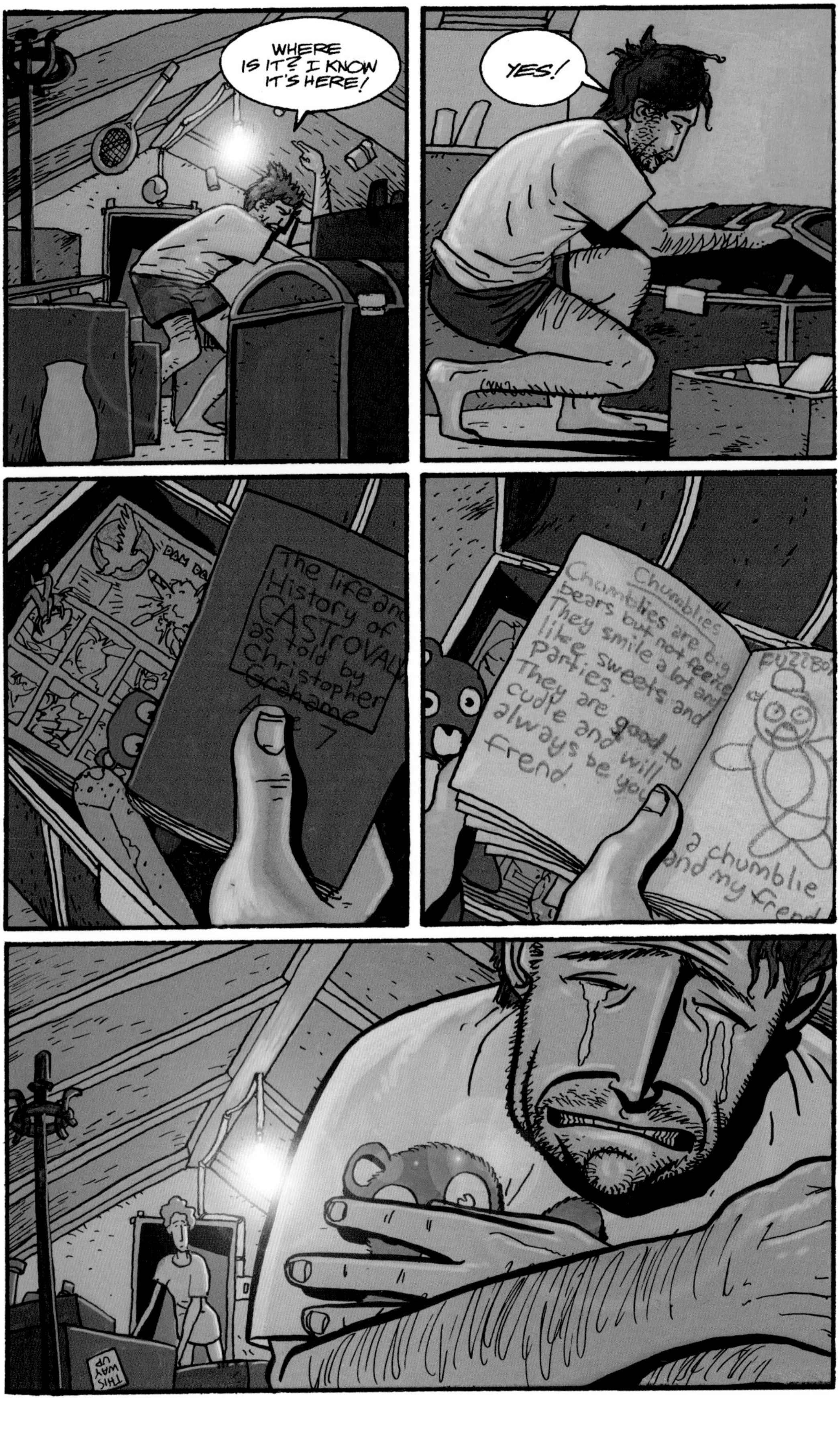
WHERE IS IT? I KNOW IT'S HERE!
YES!
The life and
History of
CASTROVAL
as told by
Christopher
Grahame
Chumblies
Chumblies are big bears but not feerce
They smile a lot and like sweets and parties.
They are good to cudle and will always be you
frend.
a chumblie
and my frend
THIS WAY UP

Chapter Two

◆◆◆

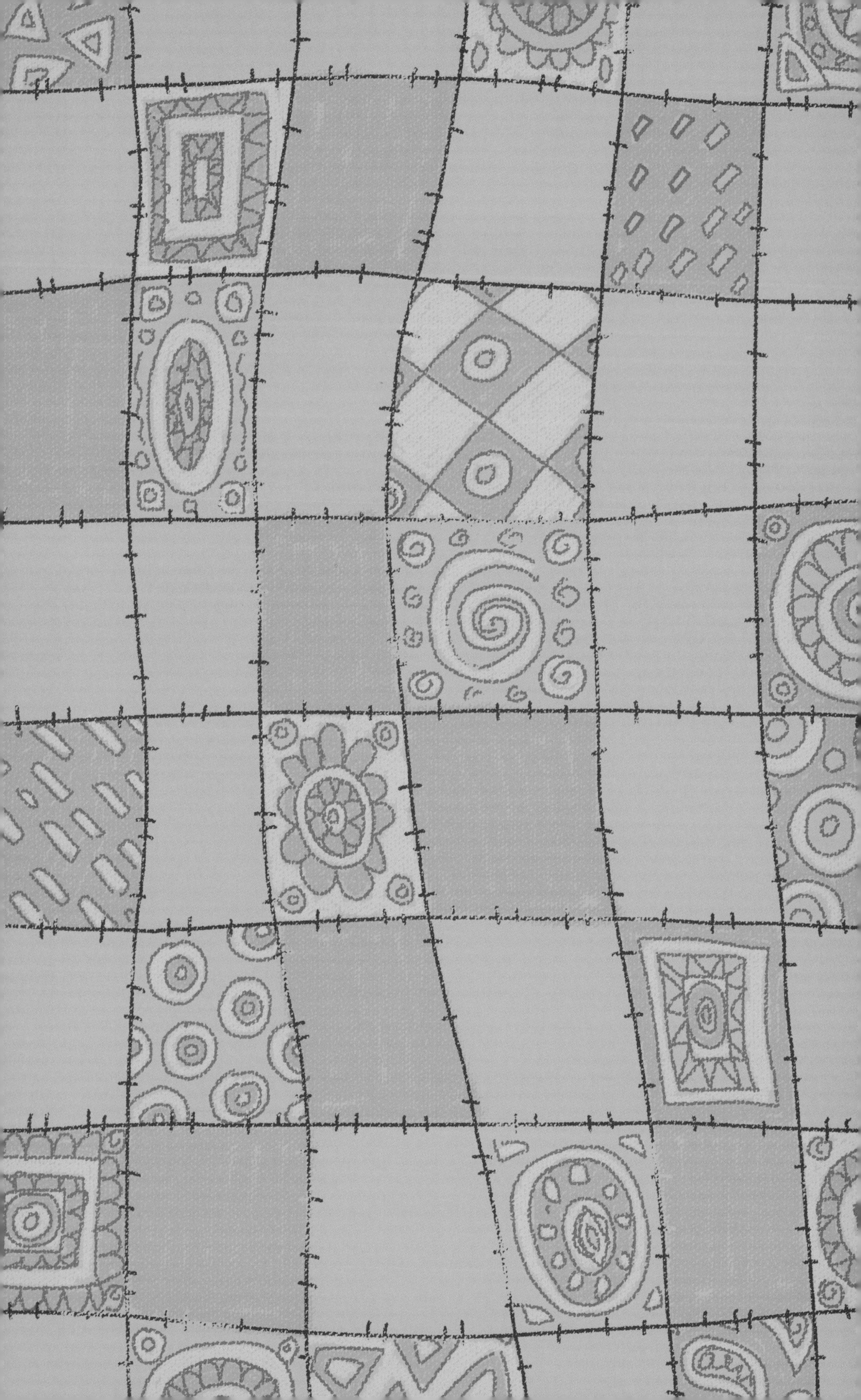

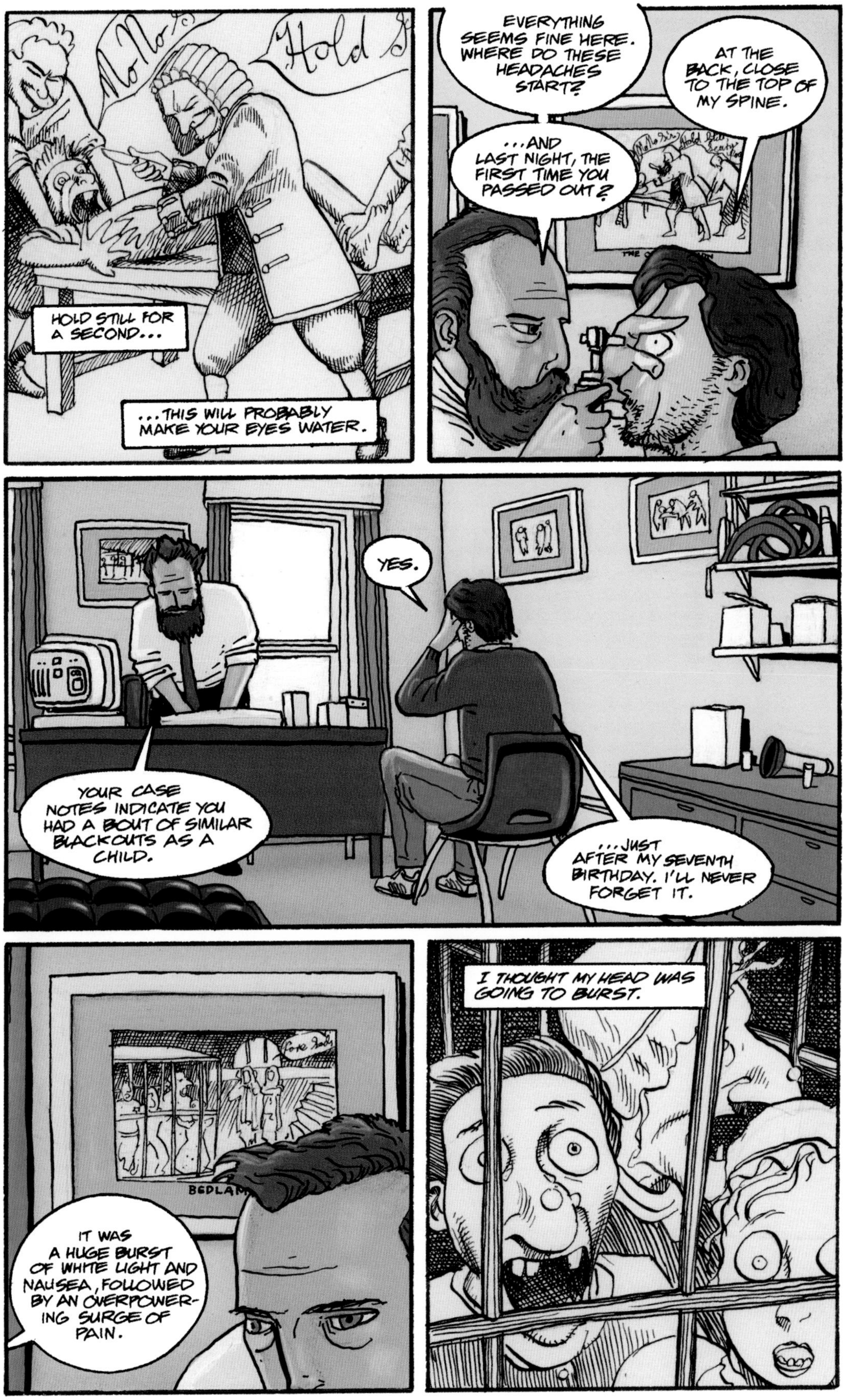
HOLD STILL FOR A SECOND...
...THIS WILL PROBABLY MAKE YOUR EYES WATER.
EVERYTHING SEEMS FINE HERE. WHERE DO THESE HEADACHES START?
AT THE BACK, CLOSE TO THE TOP OF MY SPINE.
...AND LAST NIGHT, THE FIRST TIME YOU PASSED OUT?
YES.
YOUR CASE NOTES INDICATE YOU HAD A BOUT OF SIMILAR BLACKOUTS AS A CHILD.
...JUST AFTER MY SEVENTH BIRTHDAY. I'LL NEVER FORGET IT.
IT WAS A HUGE BURST OF WHITE LIGHT AND NAUSEA, FOLLOWED BY AN OVERPOWERING SURGE OF PAIN.
I THOUGHT MY HEAD WAS GOING TO BURST.

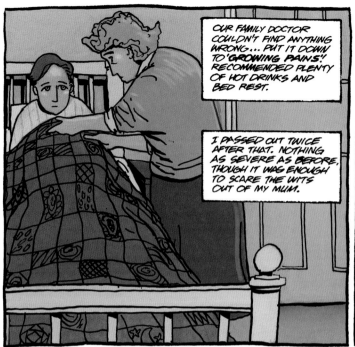

OUR FAMILY DOCTOR COULDN'T FIND ANYTHING WRONG... PUT IT DOWN TO 'GROWING PAINS'! RECOMMENDED PLENTY OF HOT DRINKS AND BED REST.

I PASSED OUT TWICE AFTER THAT. NOTHING AS SEVERE AS BEFORE, THOUGH IT WAS ENOUGH TO SCARE THE WITS OUT OF MY MUM.

BEING AN ONLY CHILD, SHE PAMPERED ME CONSTANTLY, KILLING ME WITH KINDNESS. I WAS A PRISONER IN MY OWN ROOM, EXILED FROM LIFE, DYING OF BOREDOM...

...UNTIL DAD AND THE VILLAGE LIBRARY ARRIVED LIKE THE SEVENTH CAVALRY TO SAVE THE DAY.

HE'D ALWAYS BEEN A DISTANT MAN, REMOTE, KEEPING HIS EMOTIONS IN CHECK. YET THAT DAY I SAW A NEW SIDE TO HIM, A WARMTH I'D NEVER ASSOCIATED WITH MY FATHER.

IT CHANGED BOTH OUR LIVES. HE FIRED A NEW APPETITE IN ME. I READ VORACIOUSLY, A STARVING MAN AT A BANQUET.

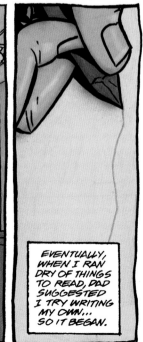

EVENTUALLY, WHEN I RAN DRY OF THINGS TO READ, DAD SUGGESTED I TRY WRITING MY OWN... SO IT BEGAN.

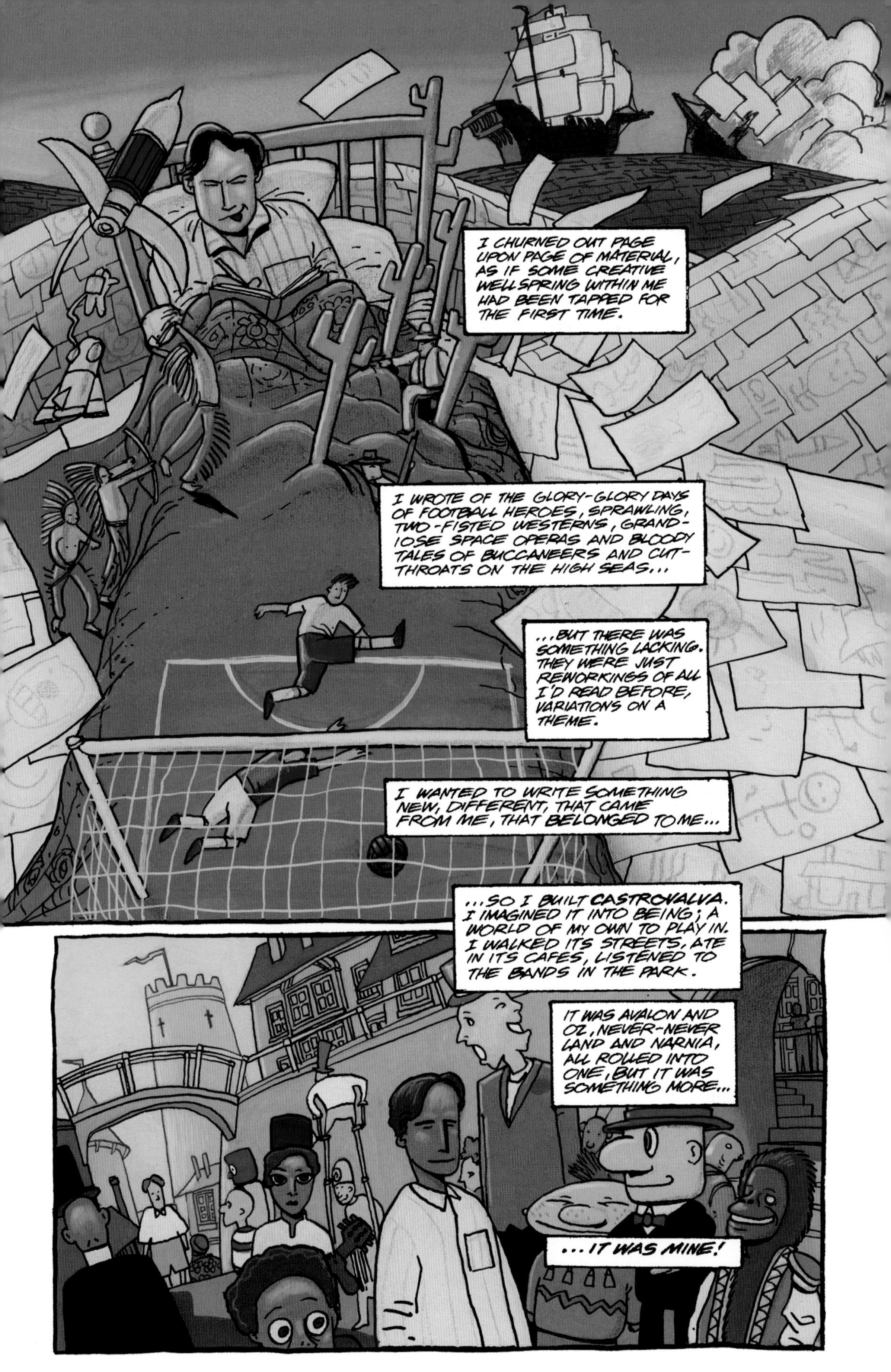
I CHURNED OUT PAGE UPON PAGE OF MATERIAL, AS IF SOME CREATIVE WELLSPRING WITHIN ME HAD BEEN TAPPED FOR THE FIRST TIME.
I WROTE OF THE GLORY-GLORY DAYS OF FOOTBALL HEROES, SPRAWLING, TWO-FISTED WESTERNS, GRANDIOSE SPACE OPERAS AND BLOODY TALES OF BUCCANEERS AND CUT-THROATS ON THE HIGH SEAS...
...BUT THERE WAS SOMETHING LACKING. THEY WERE JUST REWORKINGS OF ALL I'D READ BEFORE, VARIATIONS ON A THEME.
I WANTED TO WRITE SOMETHING NEW, DIFFERENT, THAT CAME FROM ME, THAT BELONGED TO ME...
...SO I BUILT CASTROVALVA. I IMAGINED IT INTO BEING; A WORLD OF MY OWN TO PLAY IN. I WALKED ITS STREETS, ATE IN ITS CAFES, LISTENED TO THE BANDS IN THE PARK.
IT WAS AVALON AND OZ, NEVER-NEVER LAND AND NARNIA, ALL ROLLED INTO ONE, BUT IT WAS SOMETHING MORE...
...IT WAS MINE!

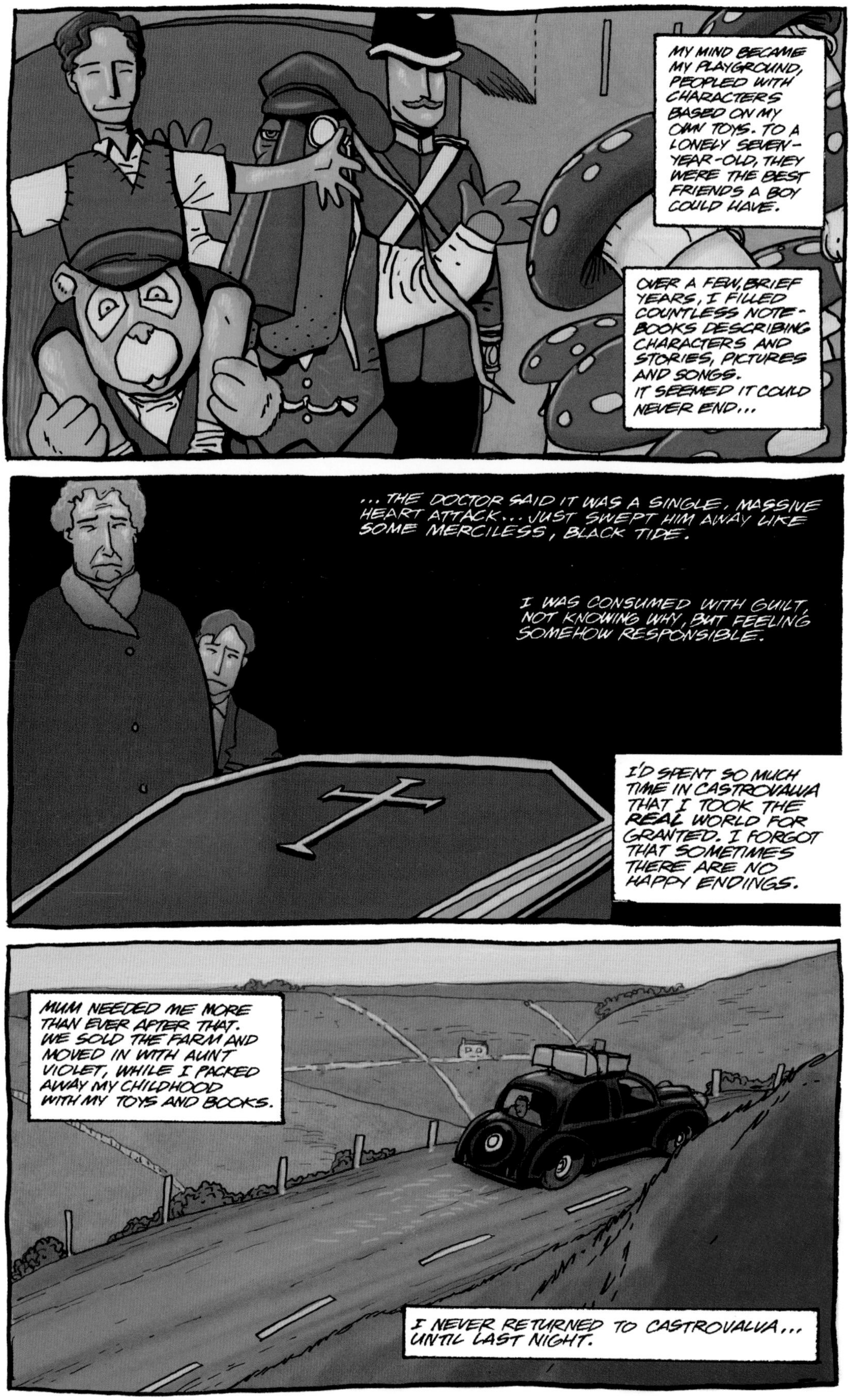
MY MIND BECAME MY PLAYGROUND, PEOPLED WITH CHARACTERS BASED ON MY OWN TOYS. TO A LONELY SEVEN-YEAR-OLD, THEY WERE THE BEST FRIENDS A BOY COULD HAVE.
OVER A FEW, BRIEF YEARS, I FILLED COUNTLESS NOTE-BOOKS DESCRIBING CHARACTERS AND STORIES, PICTURES AND SONGS. IT SEEMED IT COULD NEVER END...
...THE DOCTOR SAID IT WAS A SINGLE, MASSIVE HEART ATTACK... JUST SWEPT HIM AWAY LIKE SOME MERCILESS, BLACK TIDE.
I WAS CONSUMED WITH GUILT, NOT KNOWING WHY, BUT FEELING SOMEHOW RESPONSIBLE.
I'D SPENT SO MUCH TIME IN CASTROVALVA THAT I TOOK THE REAL WORLD FOR GRANTED. I FORGOT THAT SOMETIMES THERE ARE NO HAPPY ENDINGS.
MUM NEEDED ME MORE THAN EVER AFTER THAT. WE SOLD THE FARM AND MOVED IN WITH AUNT VIOLET, WHILE I PACKED AWAY MY CHILDHOOD WITH MY TOYS AND BOOKS.
I NEVER RETURNED TO CASTROVALVA... UNTIL LAST NIGHT.

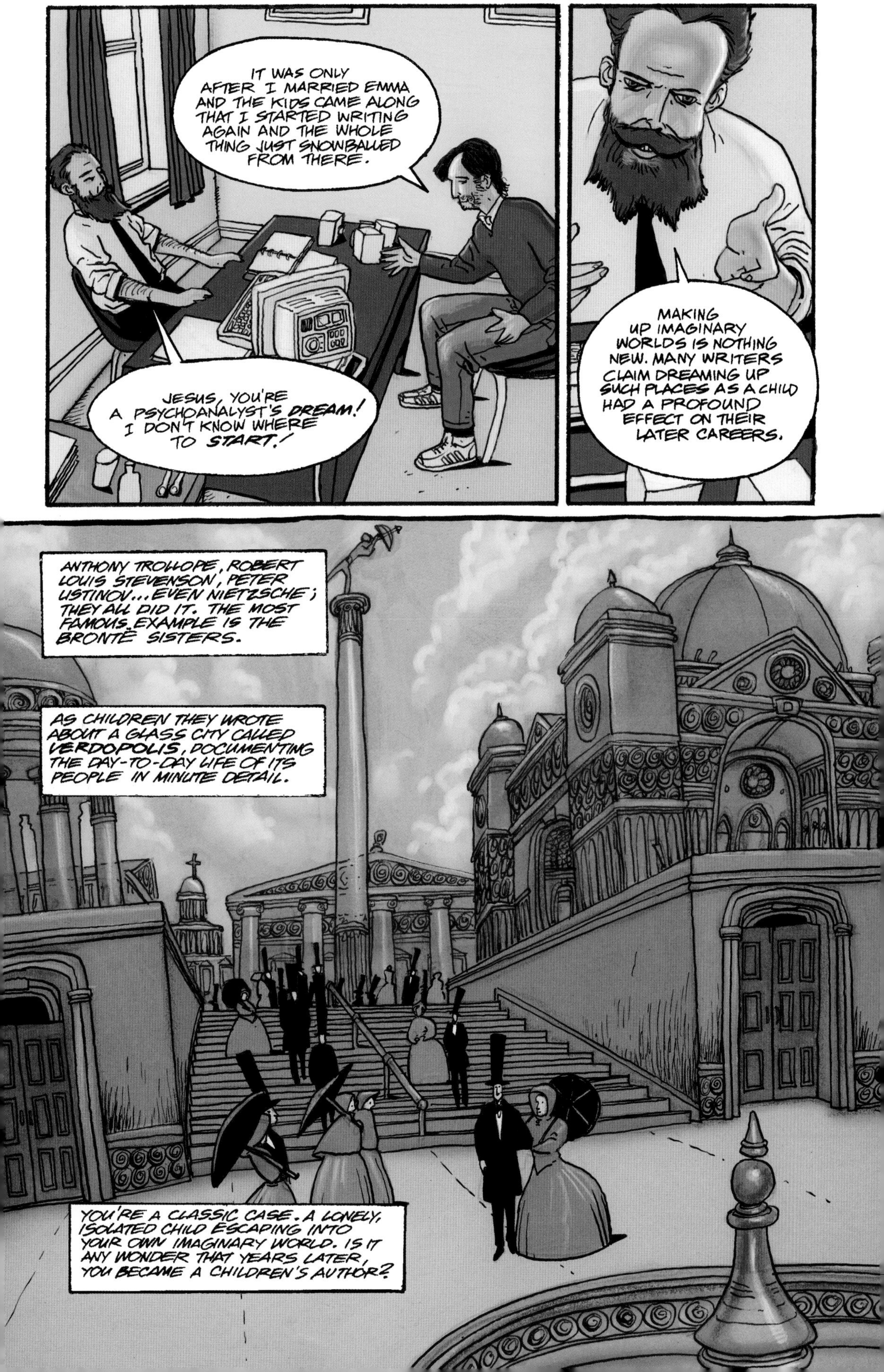
IT WAS ONLY AFTER I MARRIED EMMA AND THE KIDS CAME ALONG THAT I STARTED WRITING AGAIN AND THE WHOLE THING JUST SNOWBALLED FROM THERE.
JESUS, YOU'RE A PSYCHOANALYST'S **DREAM!** I DON'T KNOW WHERE TO **START!**
MAKING UP IMAGINARY WORLDS IS NOTHING NEW. MANY WRITERS CLAIM DREAMING UP SUCH PLACES AS A CHILD HAD A PROFOUND EFFECT ON THEIR LATER CAREERS.
ANTHONY TROLLOPE, ROBERT LOUIS STEVENSON, PETER USTINOV... EVEN NIETZSCHE; THEY ALL DID IT. THE MOST FAMOUS EXAMPLE IS THE BRONTË SISTERS.
AS CHILDREN THEY WROTE ABOUT A GLASS CITY CALLED **VERDOPOLIS**, DOCUMENTING THE DAY-TO-DAY LIFE OF ITS PEOPLE IN MINUTE DETAIL.
YOU'RE A CLASSIC CASE. A LONELY, ISOLATED CHILD ESCAPING INTO YOUR OWN IMAGINARY WORLD. IS IT ANY WONDER THAT YEARS LATER, YOU BECAME A CHILDREN'S AUTHOR?

I THINK THE BLACKOUT COULD BE PSYCHOSOMATIC; A MANIFESTATION OF STRESS, OVERWORK. WHEN THINGS GET TOO MUCH, YOU SIMPLY SHUT DOWN...

I DON'T KNOW...

THE NIGHTMARE YOU HAD WAS A SHATTERED ESCAPIST IDEAL, A REFUGE VIOLATED, MEANING YOU CAN'T AVOID THE PROBLEM, WHATEVER IT IS. YOU HAVE TO FACE IT.

HMM. PERHAPS.

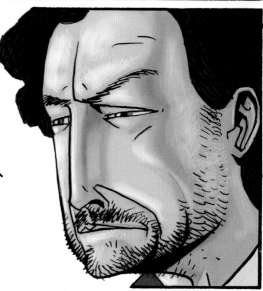

I CAN'T HELP BUT SENSE THERE'S SOME KIND OF UNCOMFORTABLE SYNCHRONICITY BETWEEN THE BLACKOUT AND THE NIGHTMARE.

PERSONALLY I THINK YOU'RE READING TOO MUCH INTO THINGS...

...BUT HEY, I'M A FAMILY DOCTOR, NOT SIGMUND FREUD...

...AND I'M AN OVER-WORKED WRITER WITH AN OVER-ACTIVE IMAGINATION, RIGHT?

I NEVER SAID THAT, BUT I AM BOOKING YOU IN FOR X-RAYS AND A CAT-SCAN AT ST. LUKE'S. I WANT TO BE SURE IT'S NOTHING PHYSICAL.

OH.

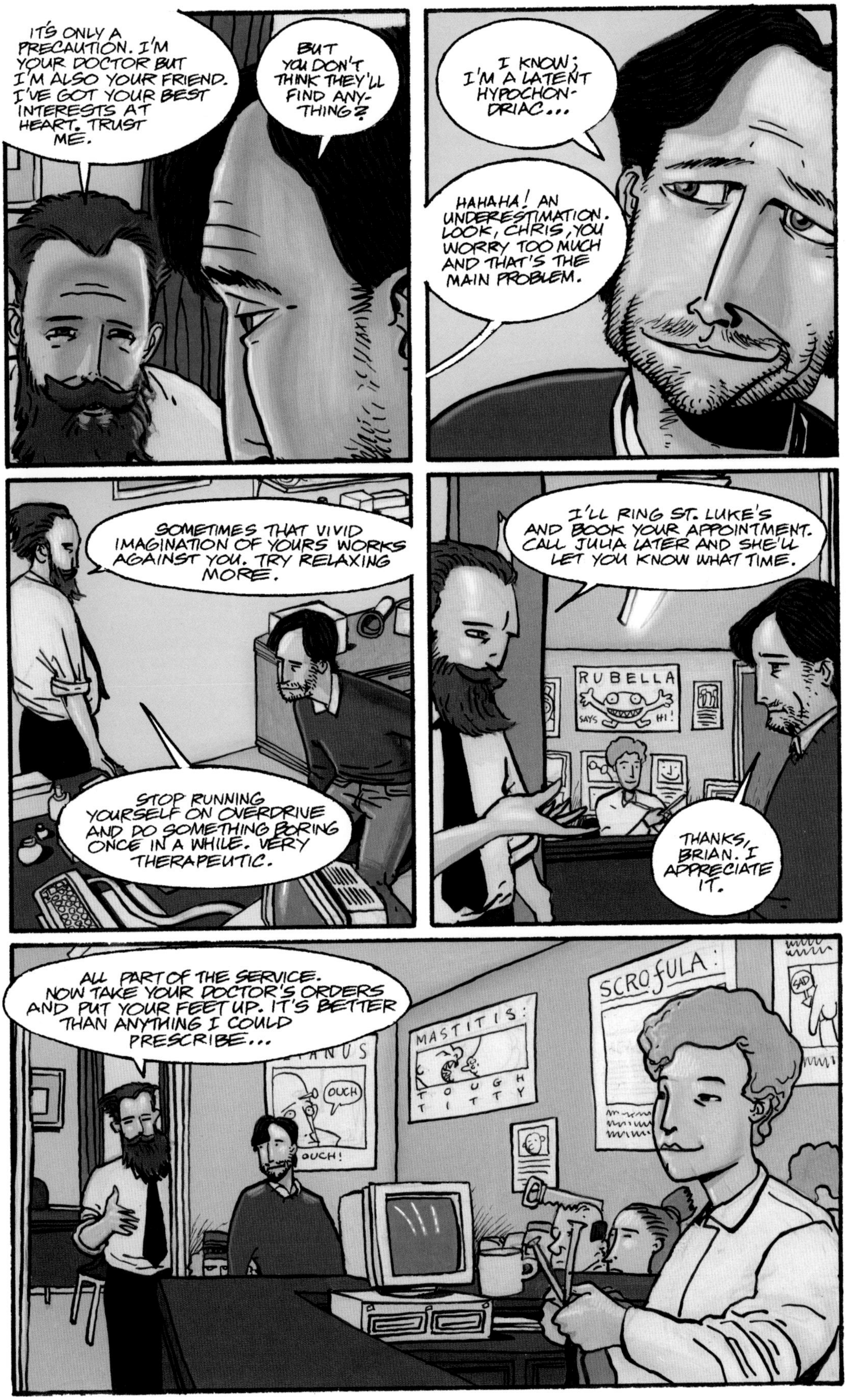
IT'S ONLY A PRECAUTION. I'M YOUR DOCTOR BUT I'M ALSO YOUR FRIEND. I'VE GOT YOUR BEST INTERESTS AT HEART. TRUST ME.
BUT YOU DON'T THINK THEY'LL FIND ANYTHING?
I KNOW; I'M A LATENT HYPOCHONDRIAC...
HAHAHA! AN UNDERESTIMATION. LOOK, CHRIS, YOU WORRY TOO MUCH AND THAT'S THE MAIN PROBLEM.
SOMETIMES THAT VIVID IMAGINATION OF YOURS WORKS AGAINST YOU. TRY RELAXING MORE.
STOP RUNNING YOURSELF ON OVERDRIVE AND DO SOMETHING BORING ONCE IN A WHILE. VERY THERAPEUTIC.
I'LL RING ST. LUKE'S AND BOOK YOUR APPOINTMENT. CALL JULIA LATER AND SHE'LL LET YOU KNOW WHAT TIME.
RUBELLA
SAYS HI!
THANKS, BRIAN. I APPRECIATE IT.
ALL PART OF THE SERVICE. NOW TAKE YOUR DOCTOR'S ORDERS AND PUT YOUR FEET UP. IT'S BETTER THAN ANYTHING I COULD PRESCRIBE...
SCROFULA:
MASTITIS:
TOUGH TITTY
OUCH
OUCH!
SAD

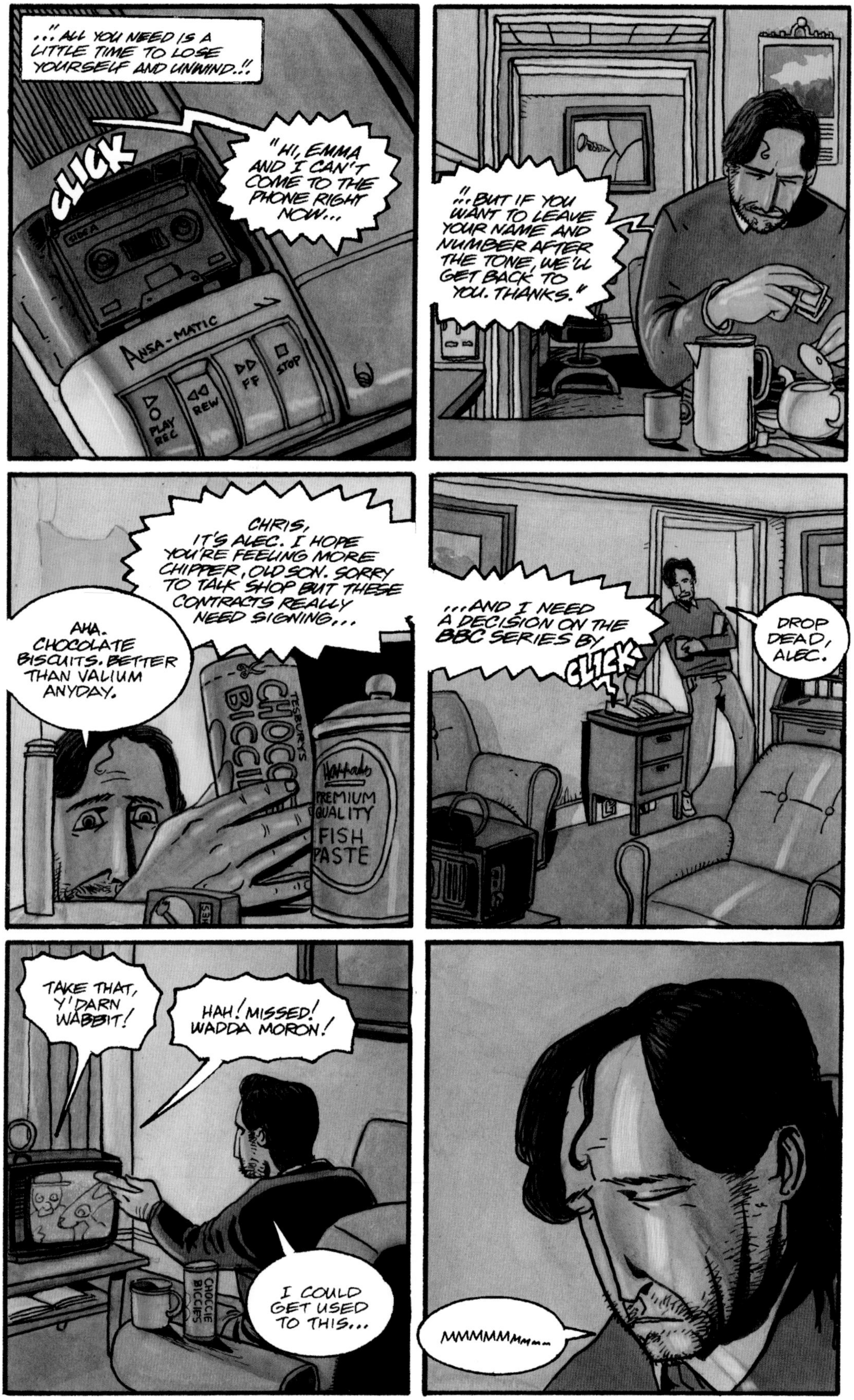
..."ALL YOU NEED IS A LITTLE TIME TO LOSE YOURSELF AND UNWIND..!!
CLICK
"HI, EMMA AND I CAN'T COME TO THE PHONE RIGHT NOW...
ANSA-MATIC
PLAY REC
REW
FF
STOP
...BUT IF YOU WANT TO LEAVE YOUR NAME AND NUMBER AFTER THE TONE, WE'LL GET BACK TO YOU. THANKS."
CHRIS, IT'S ALEC. I HOPE YOU'RE FEELING MORE CHIPPER, OLD SON. SORRY TO TALK SHOP BUT THESE CONTRACTS REALLY NEED SIGNING...
AHA. CHOCOLATE BISCUITS. BETTER THAN VALIUM ANYDAY.
TESBURYS
CHOCCIE BICCIES
PREMIUM QUALITY
FISH PASTE
...AND I NEED A DECISION ON THE BBC SERIES BY
CLICK
DROP DEAD, ALEC.
TAKE THAT, Y'DARN WABBIT!
HAH! MISSED! WADDA MORON!
CHOCCIE BICCIES
I COULD GET USED TO THIS...
MMMMMMmm...

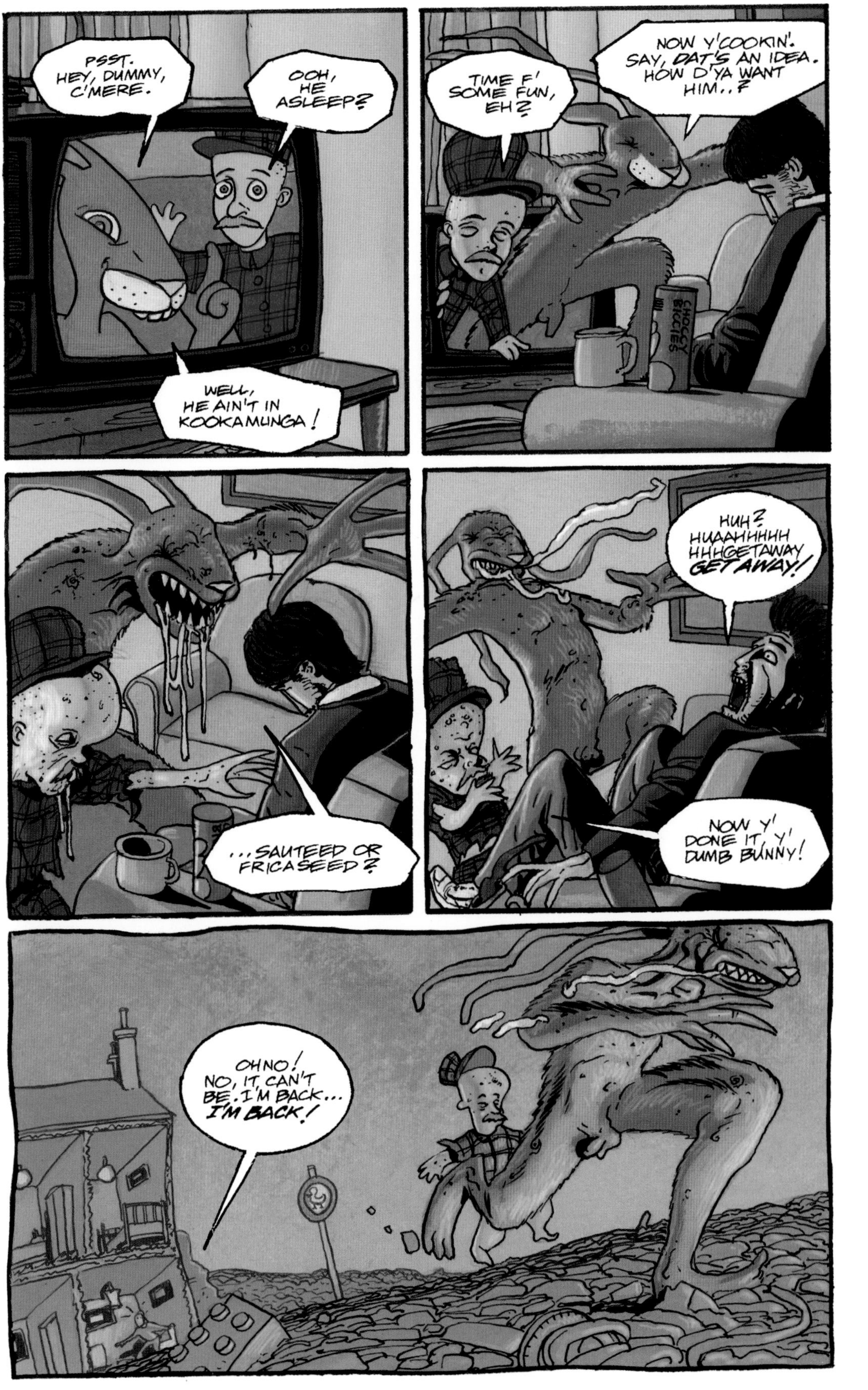
PSST. HEY, DUMMY, C'MERE.
OOH, HE ASLEEP?
WELL, HE AIN'T IN KOOKAMUNGA!
TIME F' SOME FUN, EH?
NOW Y'COOKIN'. SAY, DAT'S AN IDEA. HOW D'YA WANT HIM..?
CHOCCY BICCIES
...SAUTEED OR FRICASEED?
HUH? HUAAHHHHH HHHGETAWAY GETAWAY!
NOW Y' DONE IT, Y' DUMB BUNNY!
OH NO! NO, IT CAN'T BE. I'M BACK... I'M BACK!

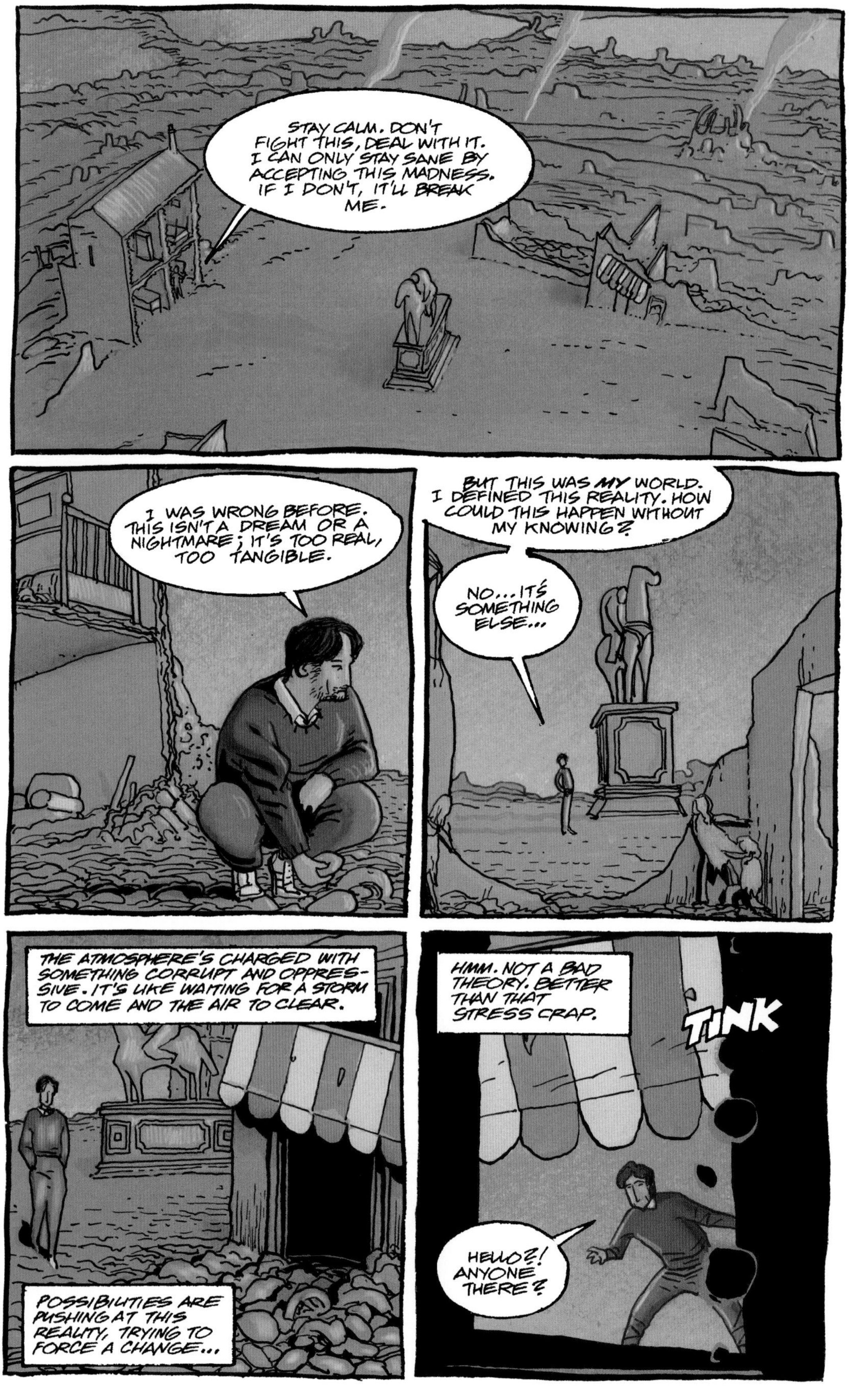
STAY CALM. DON'T FIGHT THIS, DEAL WITH IT. I CAN ONLY STAY SANE BY ACCEPTING THIS MADNESS. IF I DON'T, IT'LL BREAK ME.
I WAS WRONG BEFORE. THIS ISN'T A DREAM OR A NIGHTMARE; IT'S TOO REAL, TOO TANGIBLE.
BUT THIS WAS MY WORLD. I DEFINED THIS REALITY. HOW COULD THIS HAPPEN WITHOUT MY KNOWING?
NO... IT'S SOMETHING ELSE...
THE ATMOSPHERE'S CHARGED WITH SOMETHING CORRUPT AND OPPRES-SIVE. IT'S LIKE WAITING FOR A STORM TO COME AND THE AIR TO CLEAR.
POSSIBILITIES ARE PUSHING AT THIS REALITY, TRYING TO FORCE A CHANGE...
HMM. NOT A BAD THEORY. BETTER THAN THAT STRESS CRAP.
TINK
HELLO?! ANYONE THERE?

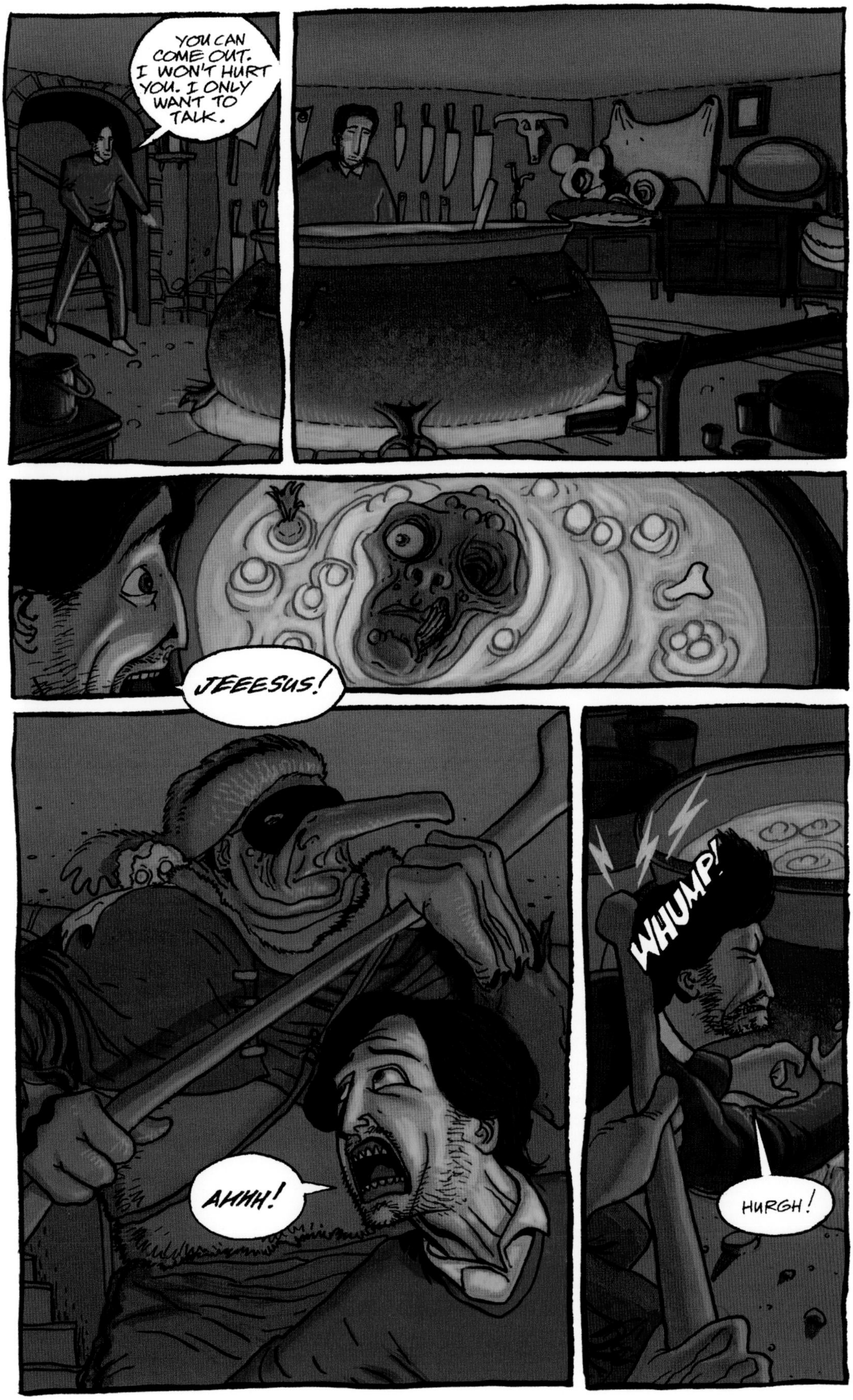
YOU CAN COME OUT. I WON'T HURT YOU. I ONLY WANT TO TALK.
JEEESUS!
AHHH!
WHUMP!
HURGH!

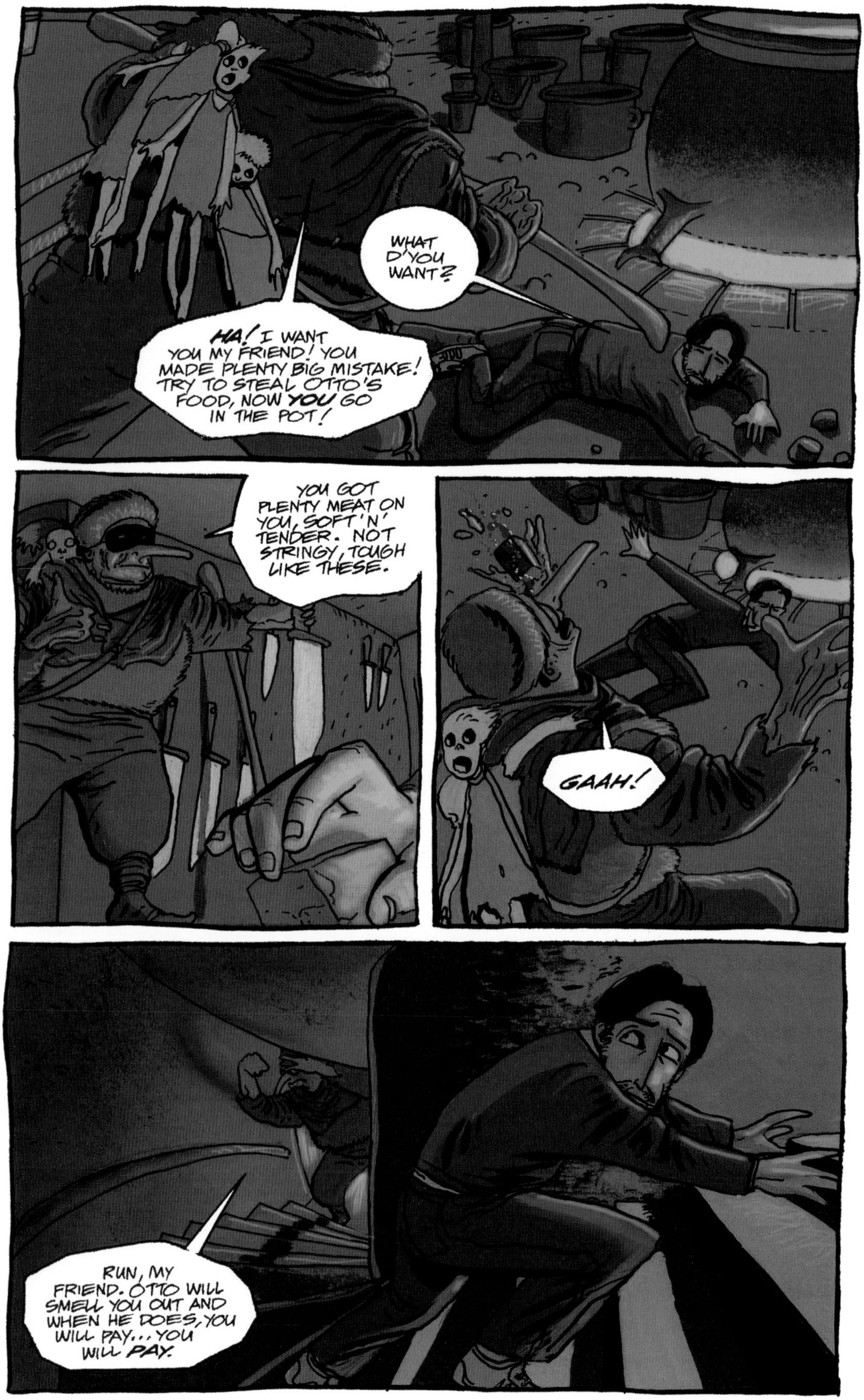
WHAT D'YOU WANT?
HA! I WANT YOU MY FRIEND! YOU MADE PLENTY BIG MISTAKE! TRY TO STEAL OTTO'S FOOD, NOW YOU GO IN THE POT!
YOU GOT PLENTY MEAT ON YOU, SOFT 'N' TENDER. NOT STRINGY, TOUGH LIKE THESE.
GAAH!
RUN, MY FRIEND. OTTO WILL SMELL YOU OUT AND WHEN HE DOES, YOU WILL PAY... YOU WILL PAY.

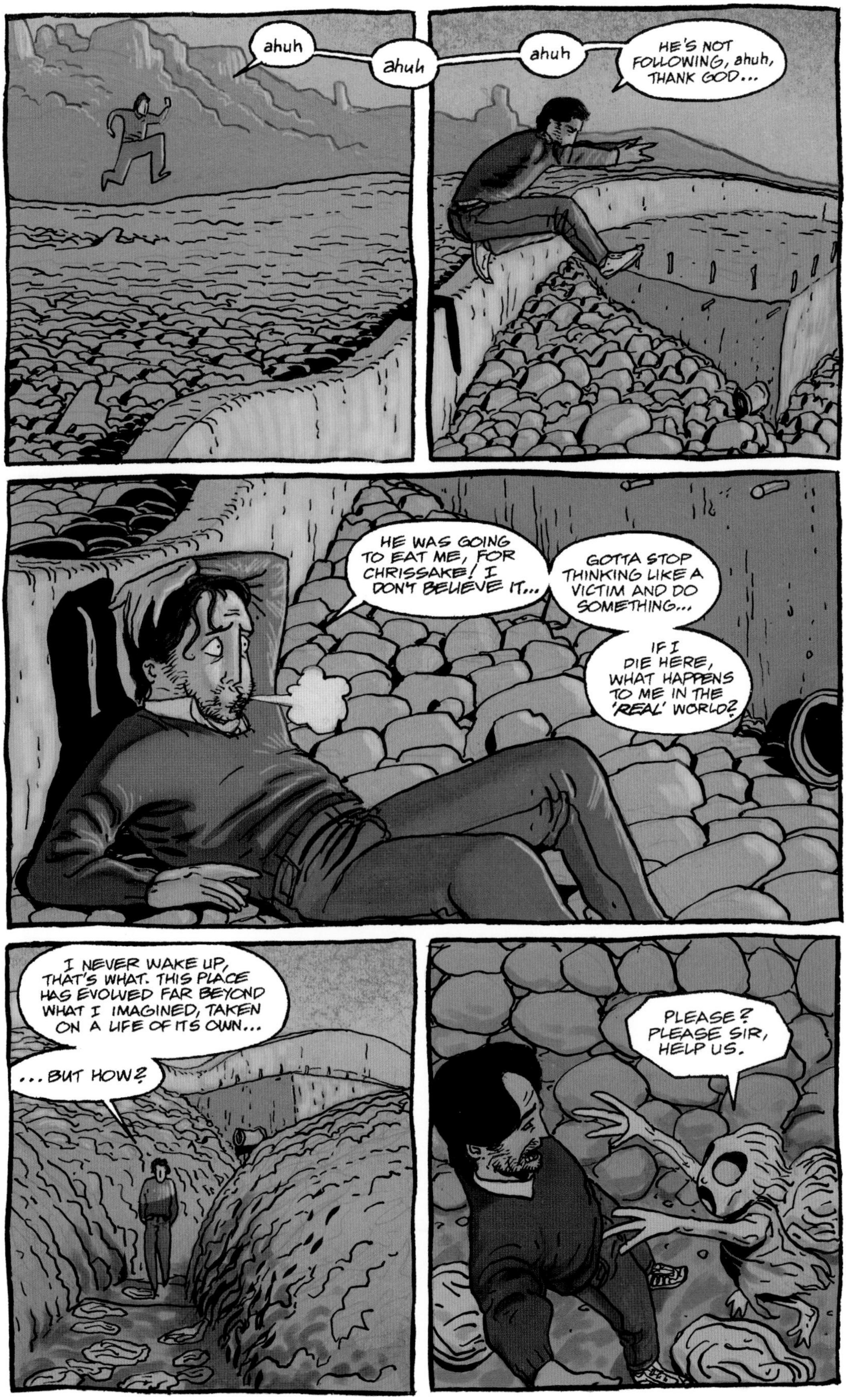
ahuh
ahuh
ahuh
HE'S NOT FOLLOWING, ahuh, THANK GOD...
HE WAS GOING TO EAT ME, FOR CHRISSAKE! I DON'T BELIEVE IT...
GOTTA STOP THINKING LIKE A VICTIM AND DO SOMETHING...
IF I DIE HERE, WHAT HAPPENS TO ME IN THE 'REAL' WORLD?
I NEVER WAKE UP, THAT'S WHAT. THIS PLACE HAS EVOLVED FAR BEYOND WHAT I IMAGINED, TAKEN ON A LIFE OF ITS OWN...
...BUT HOW?
PLEASE? PLEASE SIR, HELP US.

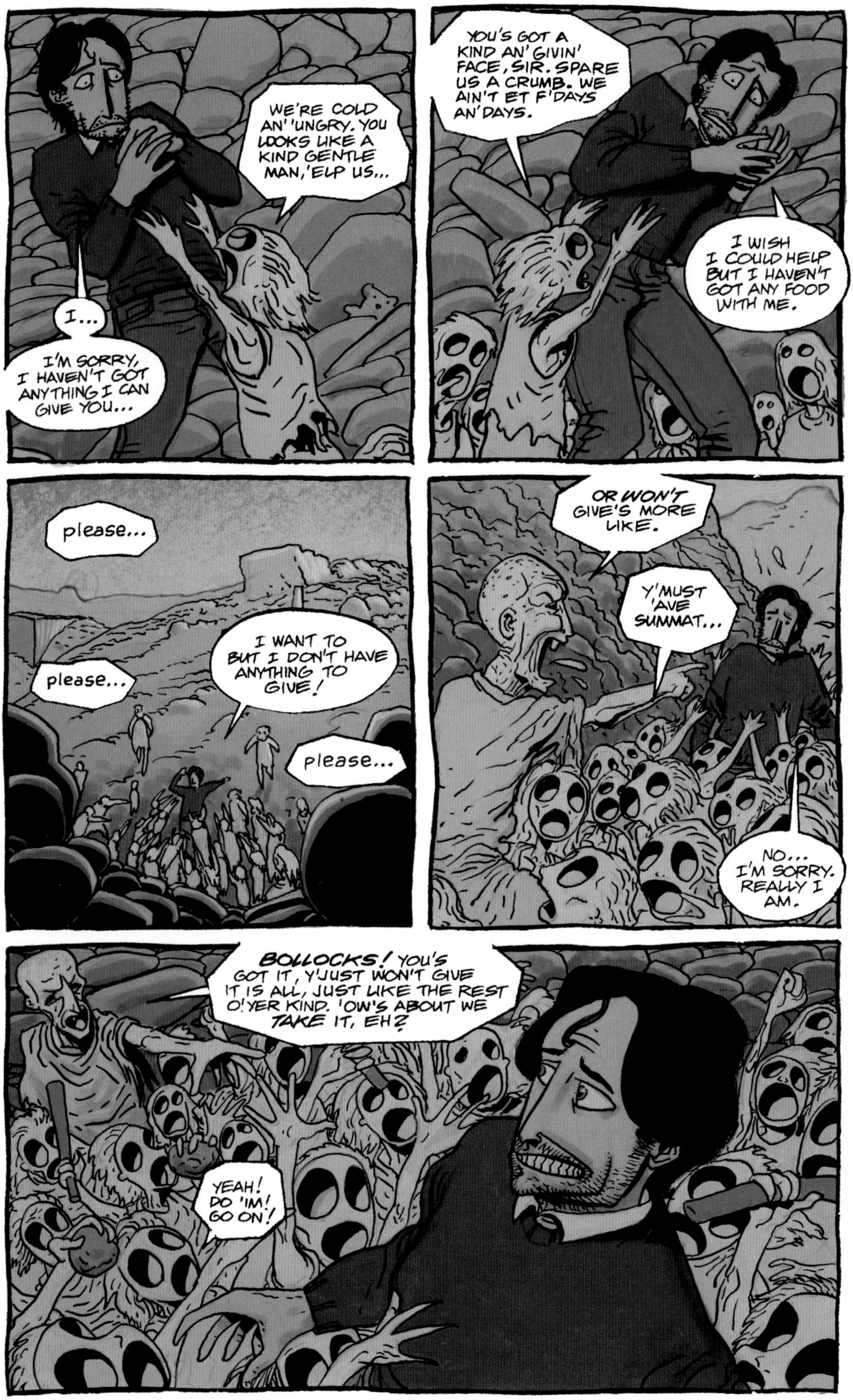

WE'RE COLD AN' 'UNGRY. YOU LOOKS LIKE A KIND GENTLE MAN, 'ELP US...
I...
I'M SORRY, I HAVEN'T GOT ANYTHING I CAN GIVE YOU...
YOU'S GOT A KIND AN' GIVIN' FACE, SIR. SPARE US A CRUMB. WE AIN'T ET F'DAYS AN' DAYS.
I WISH I COULD HELP BUT I HAVEN'T GOT ANY FOOD WITH ME.
please...
please...
I WANT TO BUT I DON'T HAVE ANYTHING TO GIVE!
please...
OR WON'T GIVE'S MORE LIKE.
Y'MUST 'AVE SUMMAT...
NO... I'M SORRY. REALLY I AM.
BOLLOCKS! YOU'S GOT IT, Y'JUST WON'T GIVE IT IS ALL, JUST LIKE THE REST O' YER KIND. 'OW'S ABOUT WE TAKE IT, EH?
YEAH! DO 'IM! GO ON!

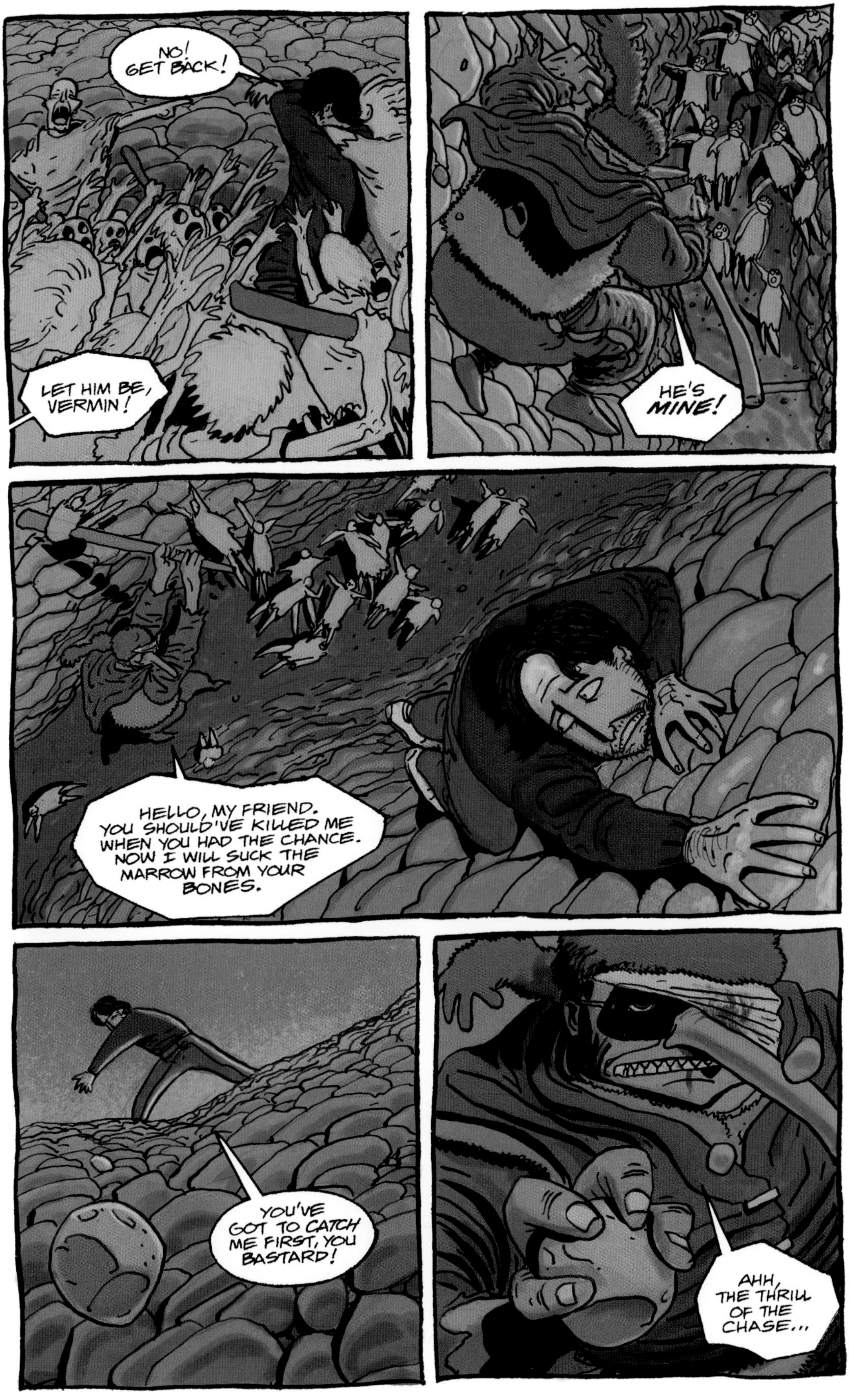
NO! GET BACK!
LET HIM BE, VERMIN!
HE'S MINE!
HELLO, MY FRIEND. YOU SHOULD'VE KILLED ME WHEN YOU HAD THE CHANCE. NOW I WILL SUCK THE MARROW FROM YOUR BONES.
YOU'VE GOT TO CATCH ME FIRST, YOU BASTARD!
AHH, THE THRILL OF THE CHASE...

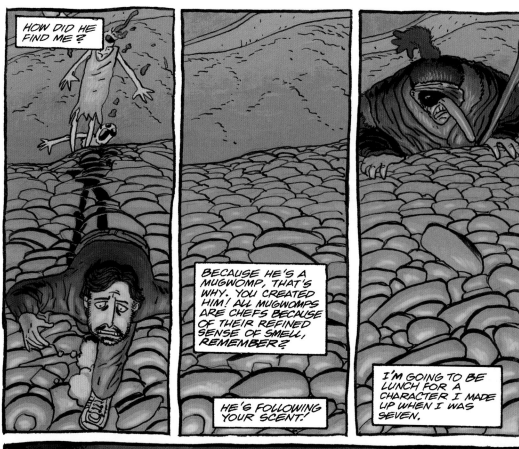

HOW DID HE FIND ME?

BECAUSE HE'S A MUGWOMP, THAT'S WHY. YOU CREATED HIM! ALL MUGWOMPS ARE CHEFS BECAUSE OF THEIR REFINED SENSE OF SMELL, REMEMBER?

HE'S FOLLOWING YOUR SCENT!

I'M GOING TO BE LUNCH FOR A CHARACTER I MADE UP WHEN I WAS SEVEN.

THIS IS INSANE.

YOU CAN'T HIDE FROM ME, MY FRIEND. I CAN SMELL YOUR FEAR.

IT'S DELICIOUS.

SNMYFNUFSNURFF

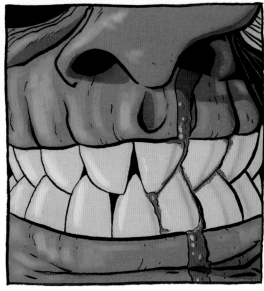

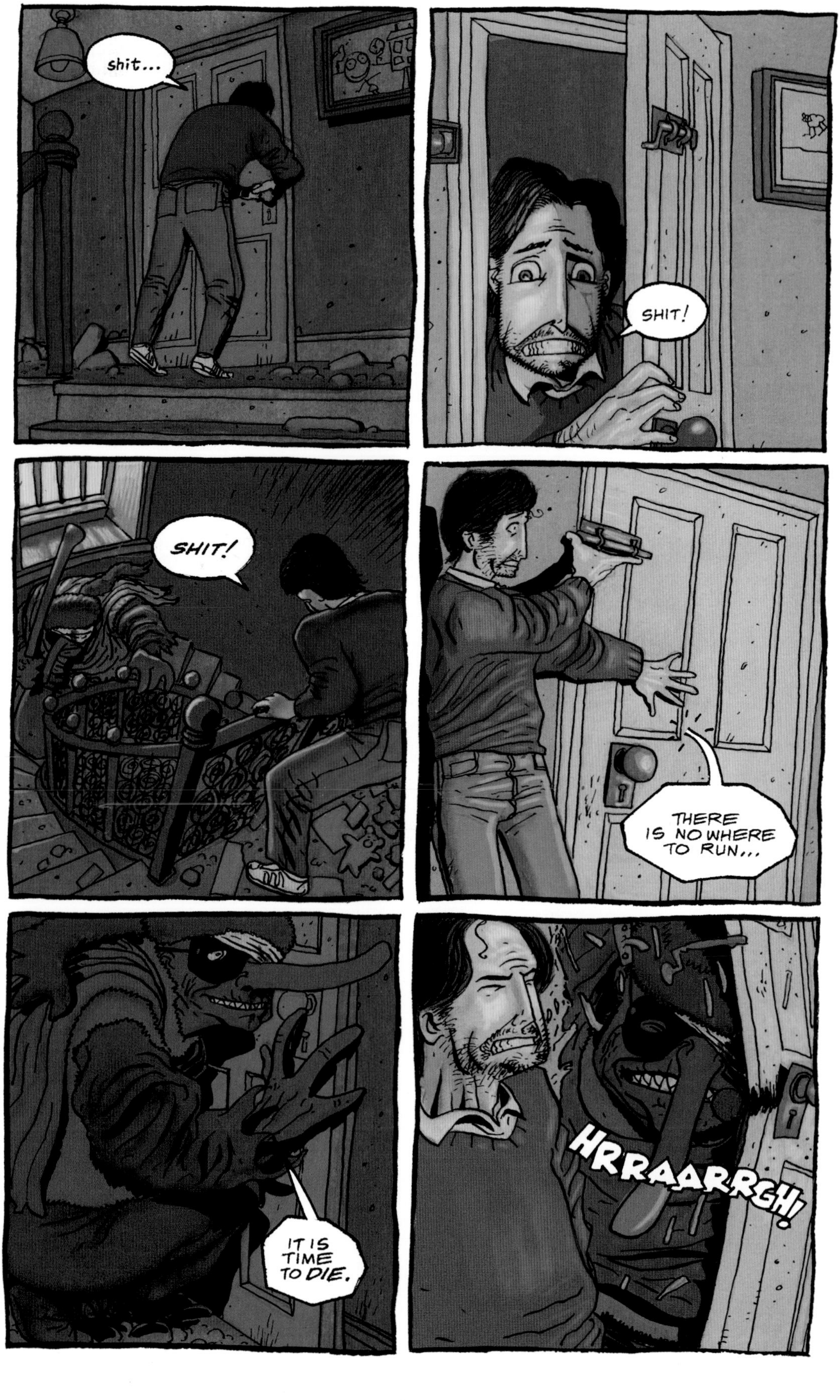
shit...
SHIT!
SHIT!
THERE IS NO WHERE TO RUN...
IT IS TIME TO DIE.
HRRAARRGH!

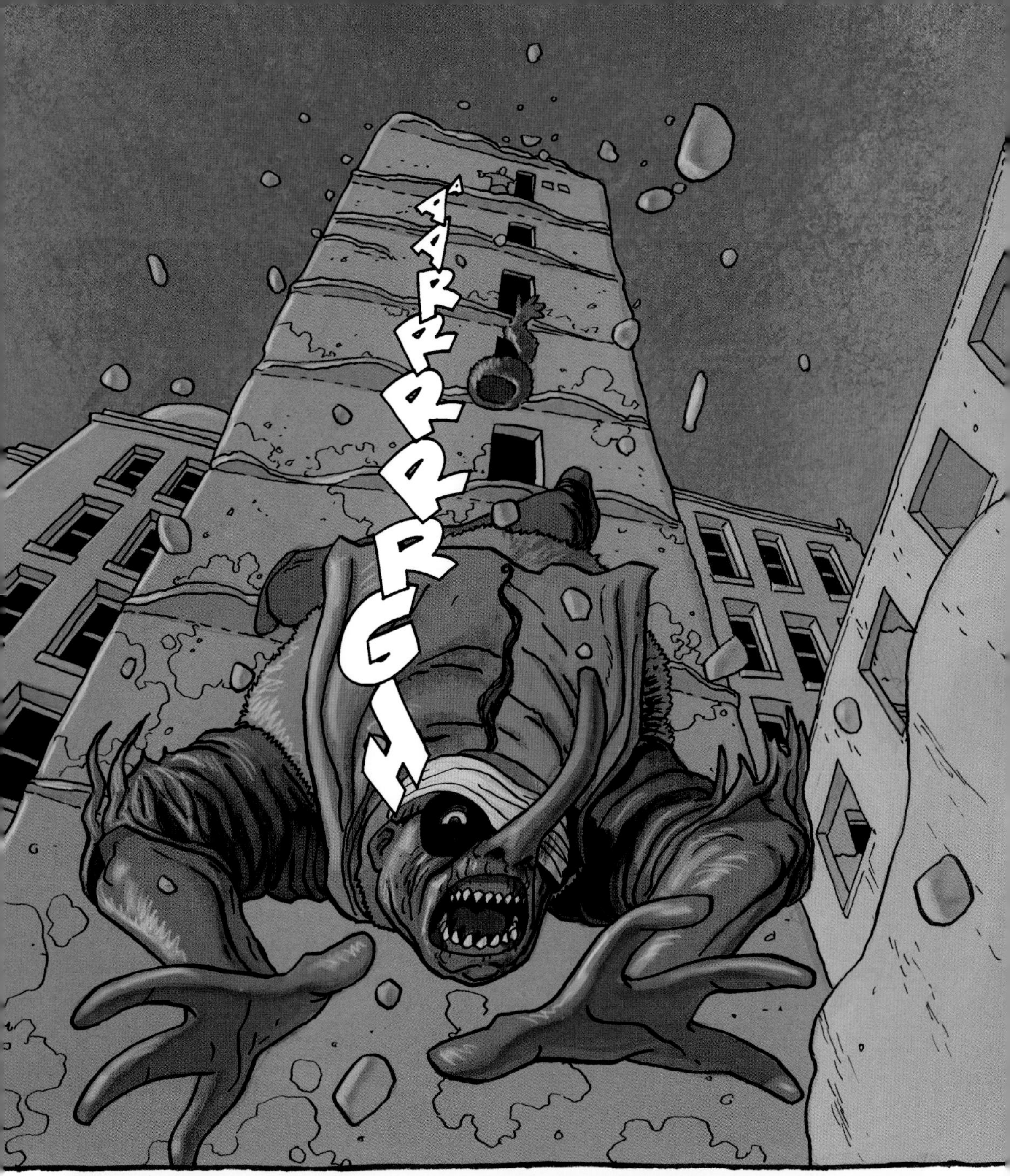
AAARRRRRGH

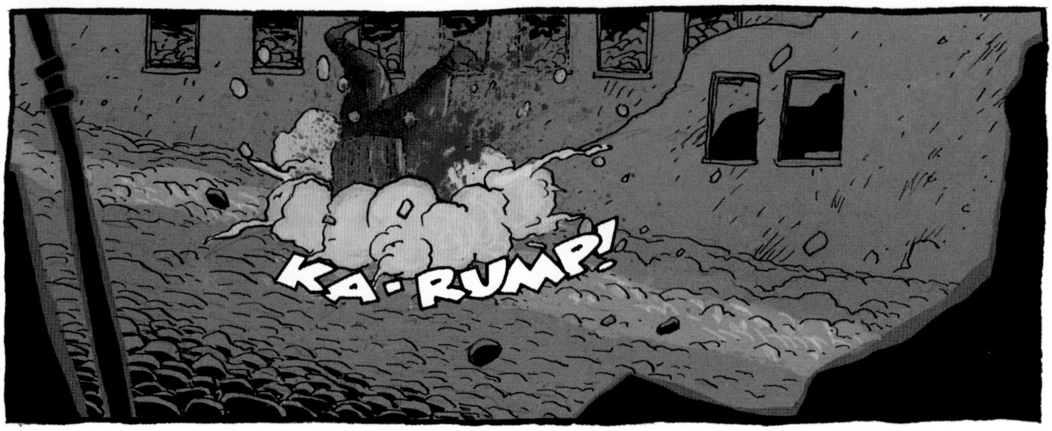
KA-RUMP!

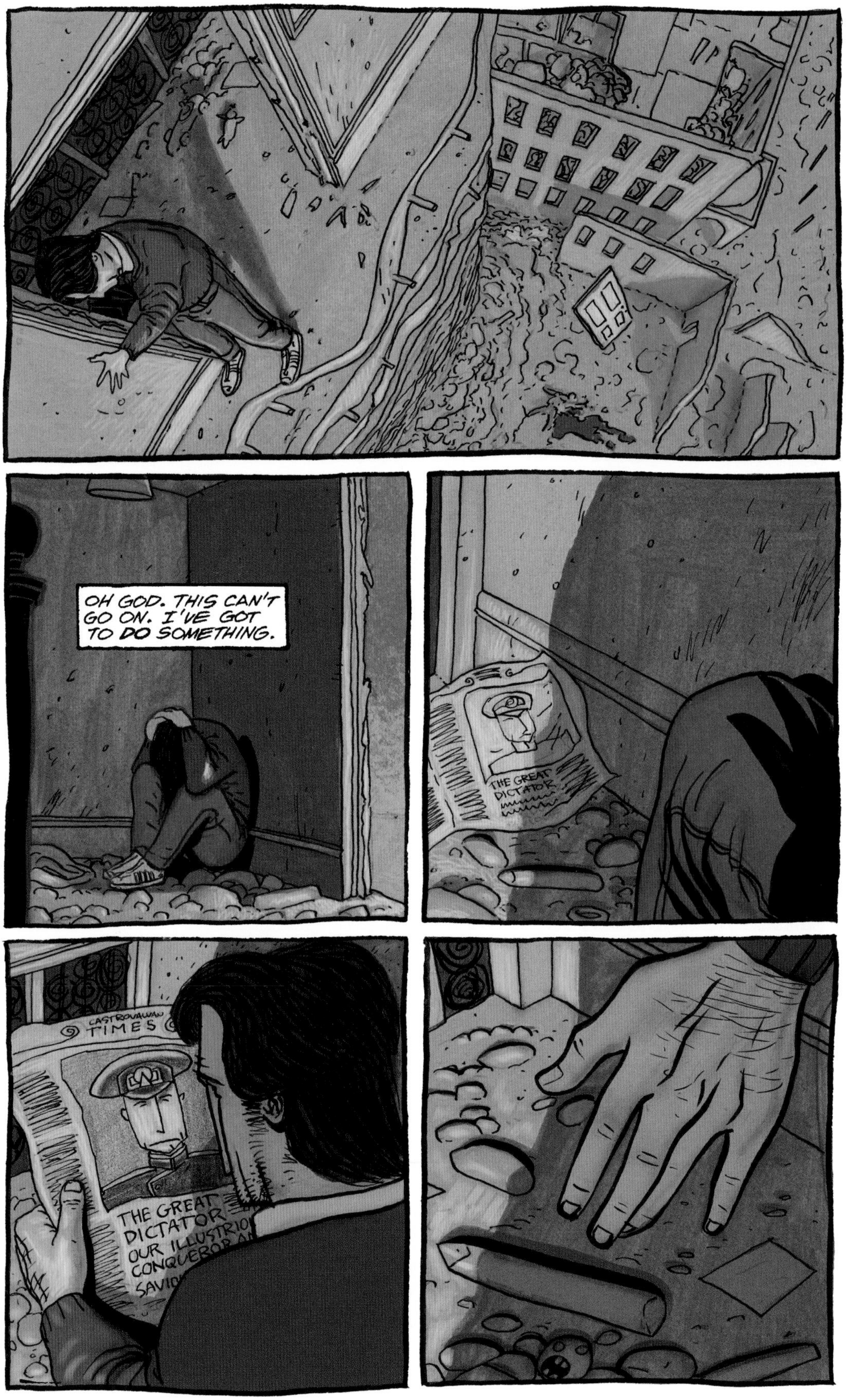
OH GOD. THIS CAN'T GO ON. I'VE GOT TO DO SOMETHING.
THE GREAT DICTATOR
CASTROVALVAN TIMES
THE GREAT DICTATOR

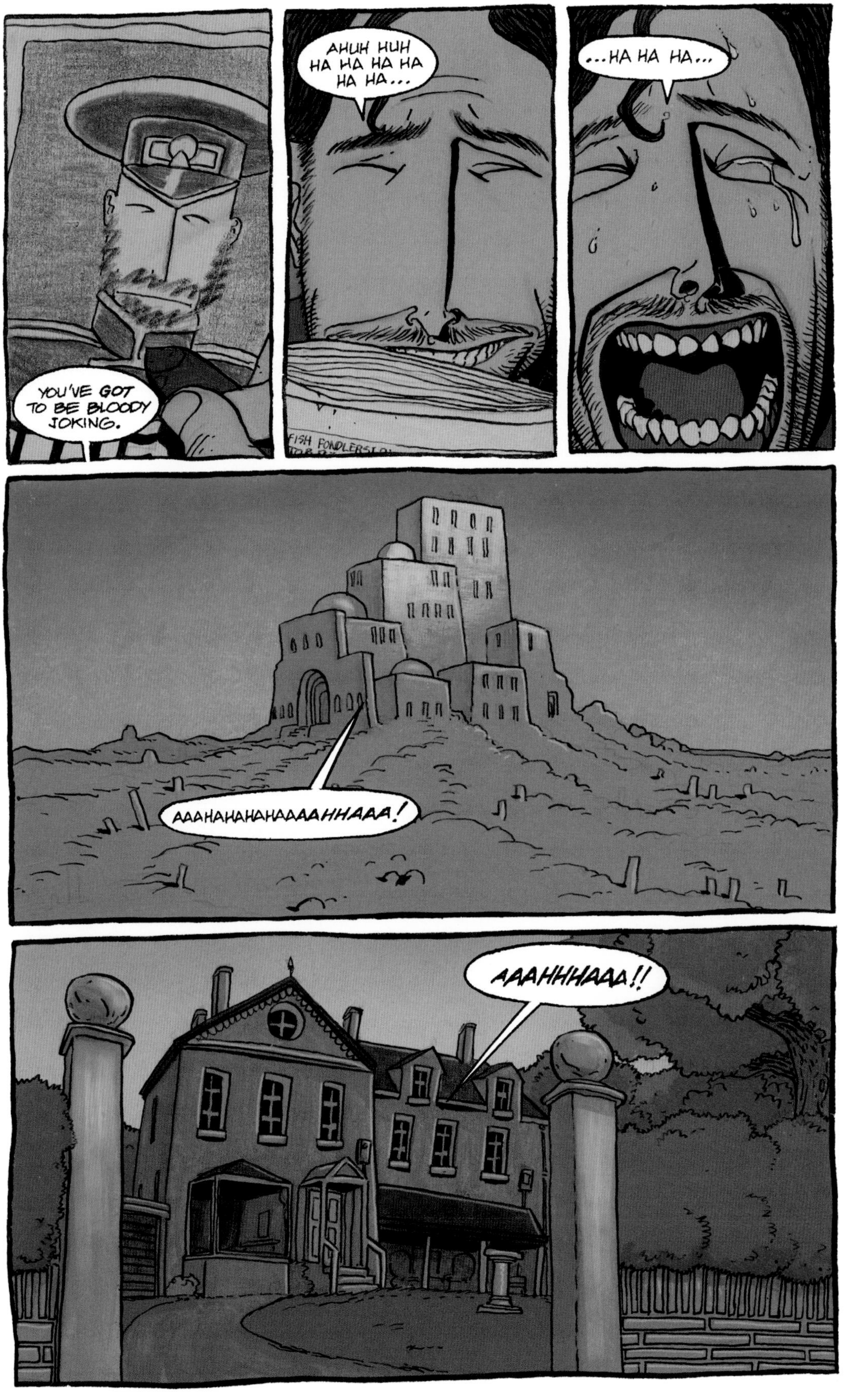
YOU'VE GOT TO BE BLOODY JOKING.
FISH FONDLERS
AHUH HUH HA HA HA HA HA HA...
...HA HA HA...
AAAHAHAHAHAAAAHHAAA!
AAAHHHAAA!!

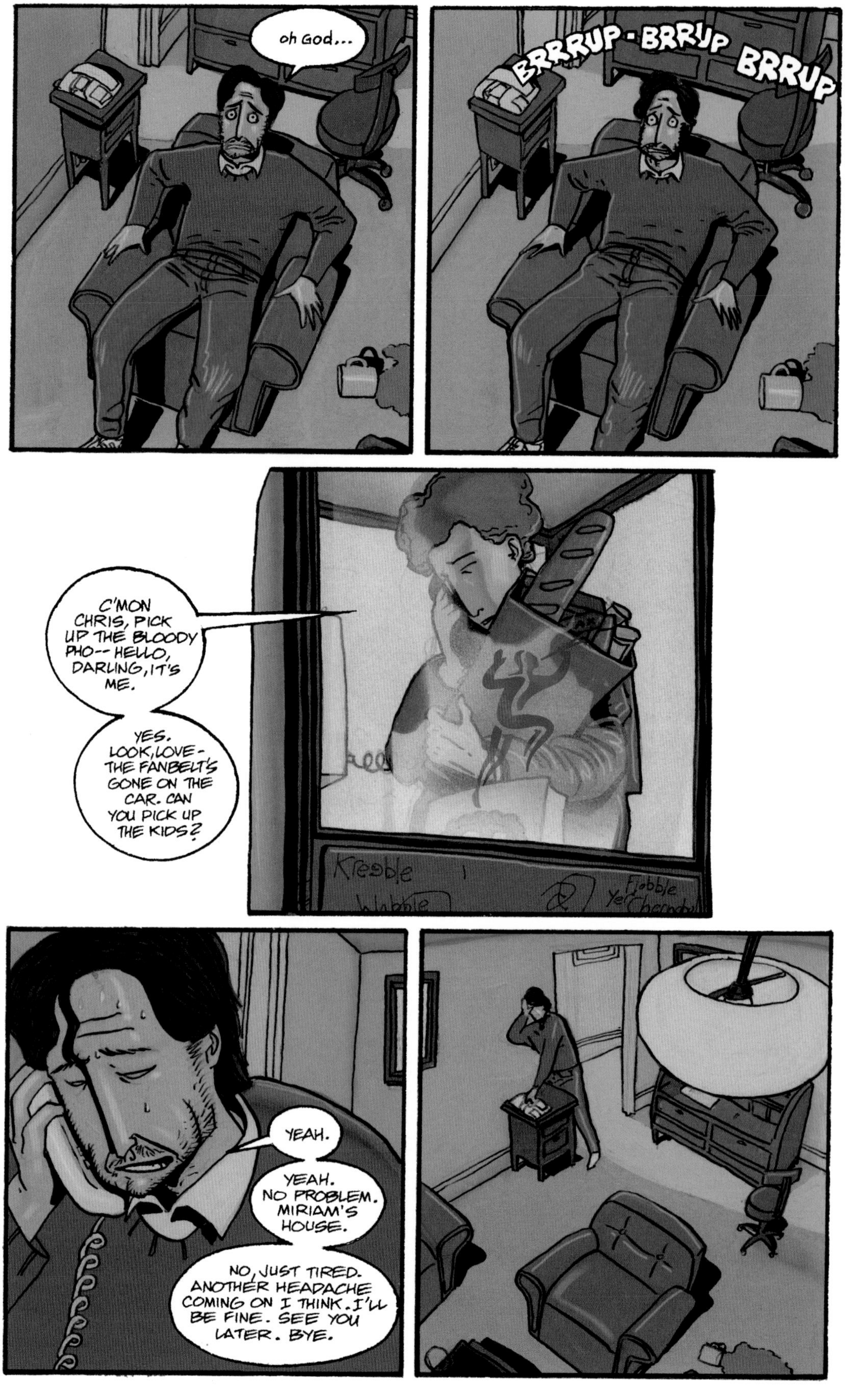
oh God...
BRRRUP - BRRUP BRRUP
C'MON CHRIS, PICK UP THE BLOODY PHO-- HELLO, DARLING, IT'S ME.
YES. LOOK, LOVE - THE FANBELT'S GONE ON THE CAR. CAN YOU PICK UP THE KIDS?
Kreeble
Flobble
YEAH.
YEAH. NO PROBLEM. MIRIAM'S HOUSE.
NO, JUST TIRED. ANOTHER HEADACHE COMING ON I THINK. I'LL BE FINE. SEE YOU LATER. BYE.

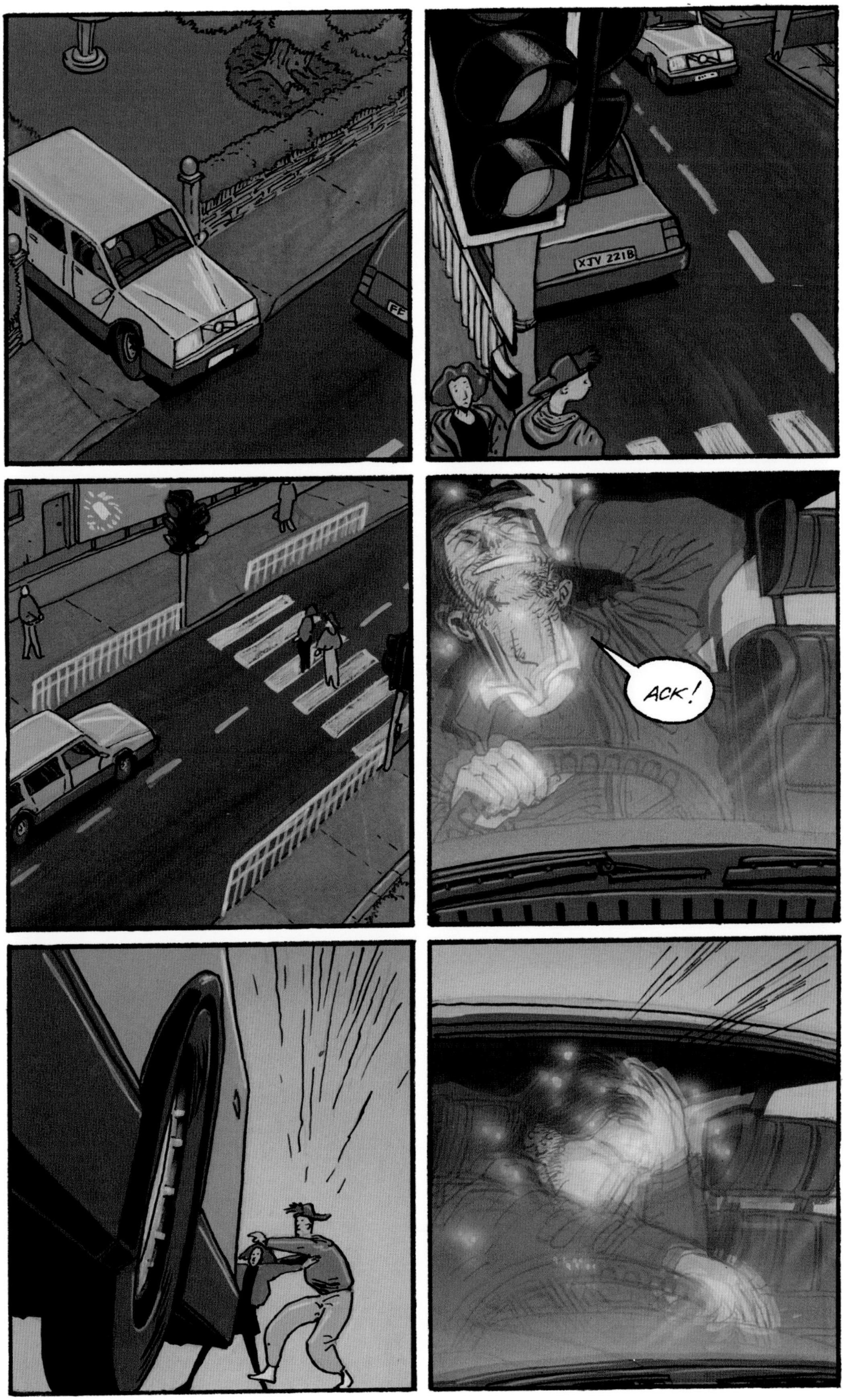
XJV 221B
ACK!

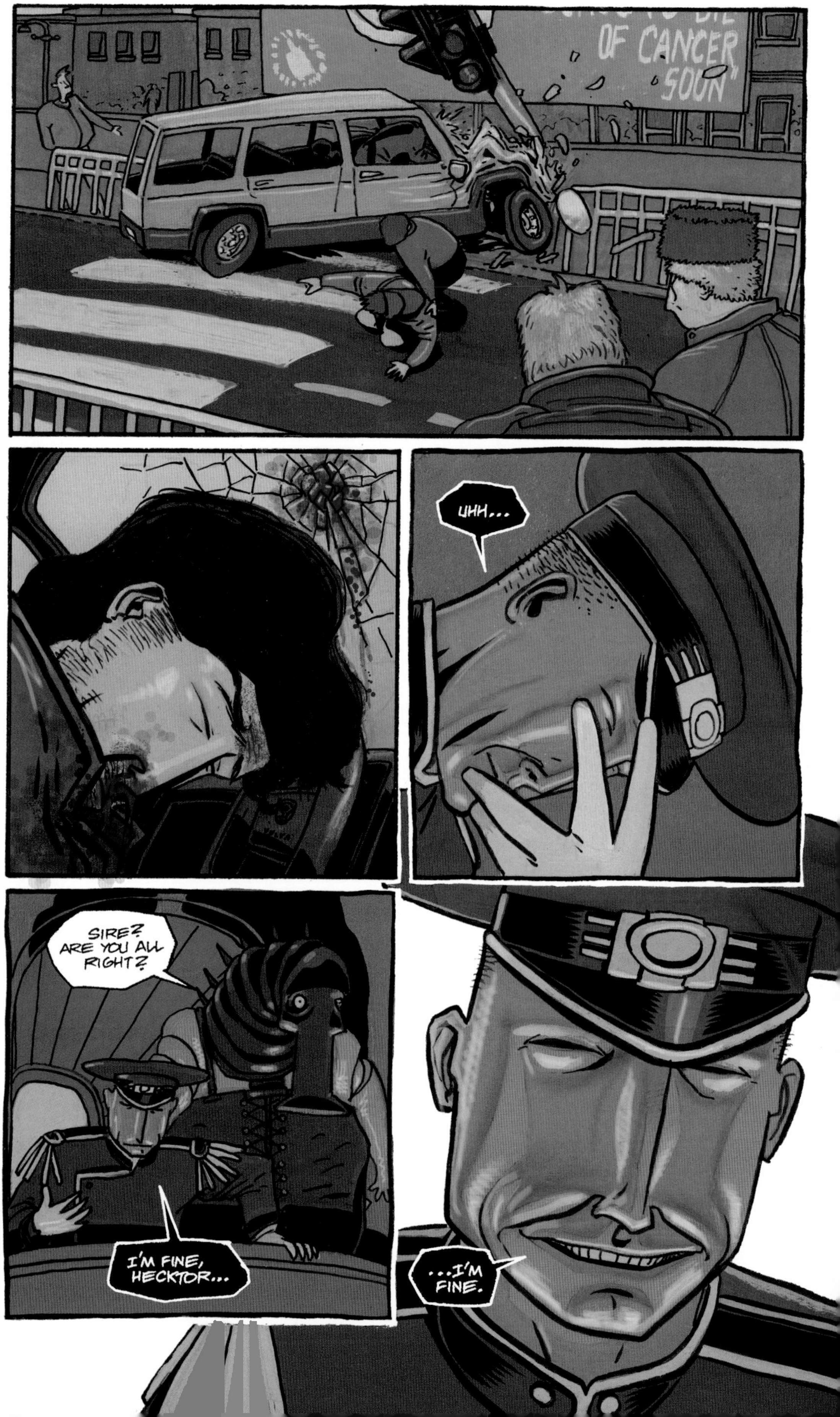
OF CANCER
SOON
UHH...
SIRE? ARE YOU ALL RIGHT?
I'M FINE, HECKTOR...
...I'M FINE.

Chapter
Three

◆◆◆

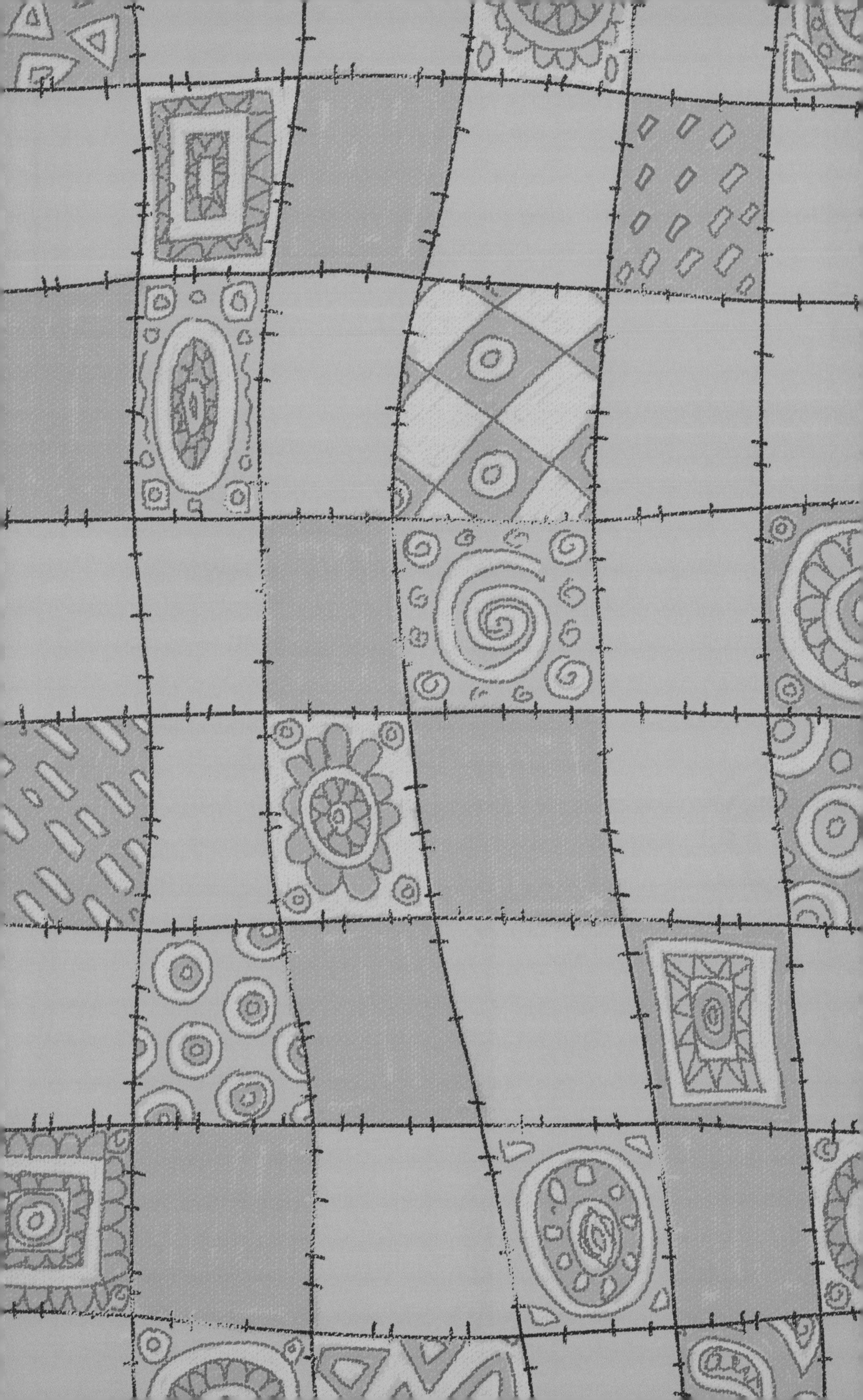

I KNOW A PLACE WHERE DARKNESS LIVES.

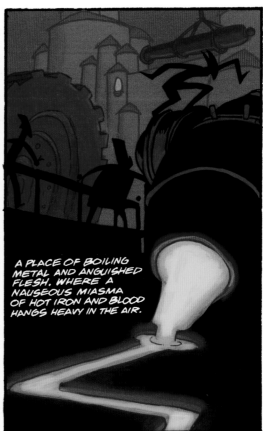

A PLACE OF BOILING METAL AND ANGUISHED FLESH, WHERE A NAUSEOUS MIASMA OF HOT IRON AND BLOOD HANGS HEAVY IN THE AIR.

THIS IS WHERE THE WILD THINGS ARE... WHERE BAD DREAMS FERMENT

THIS IS HELL... THIS IS MY HOME...

...AND I'M EXPECTING COMPANY.

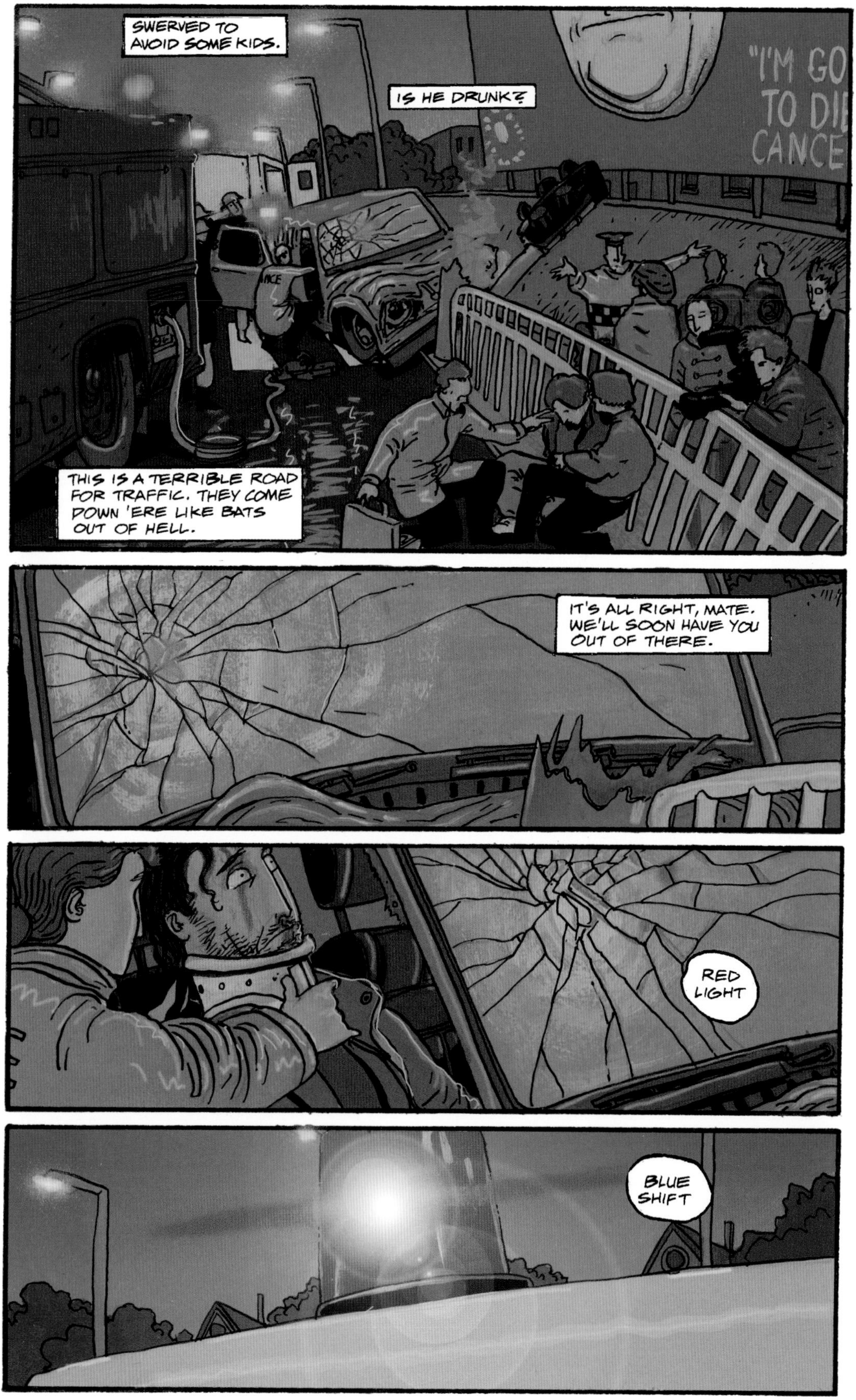
SWERVED TO AVOID SOME KIDS.
IS HE DRUNK?
THIS IS A TERRIBLE ROAD FOR TRAFFIC. THEY COME DOWN 'ERE LIKE BATS OUT OF HELL.
IT'S ALL RIGHT, MATE. WE'LL SOON HAVE YOU OUT OF THERE.
RED LIGHT
BLUE SHIFT

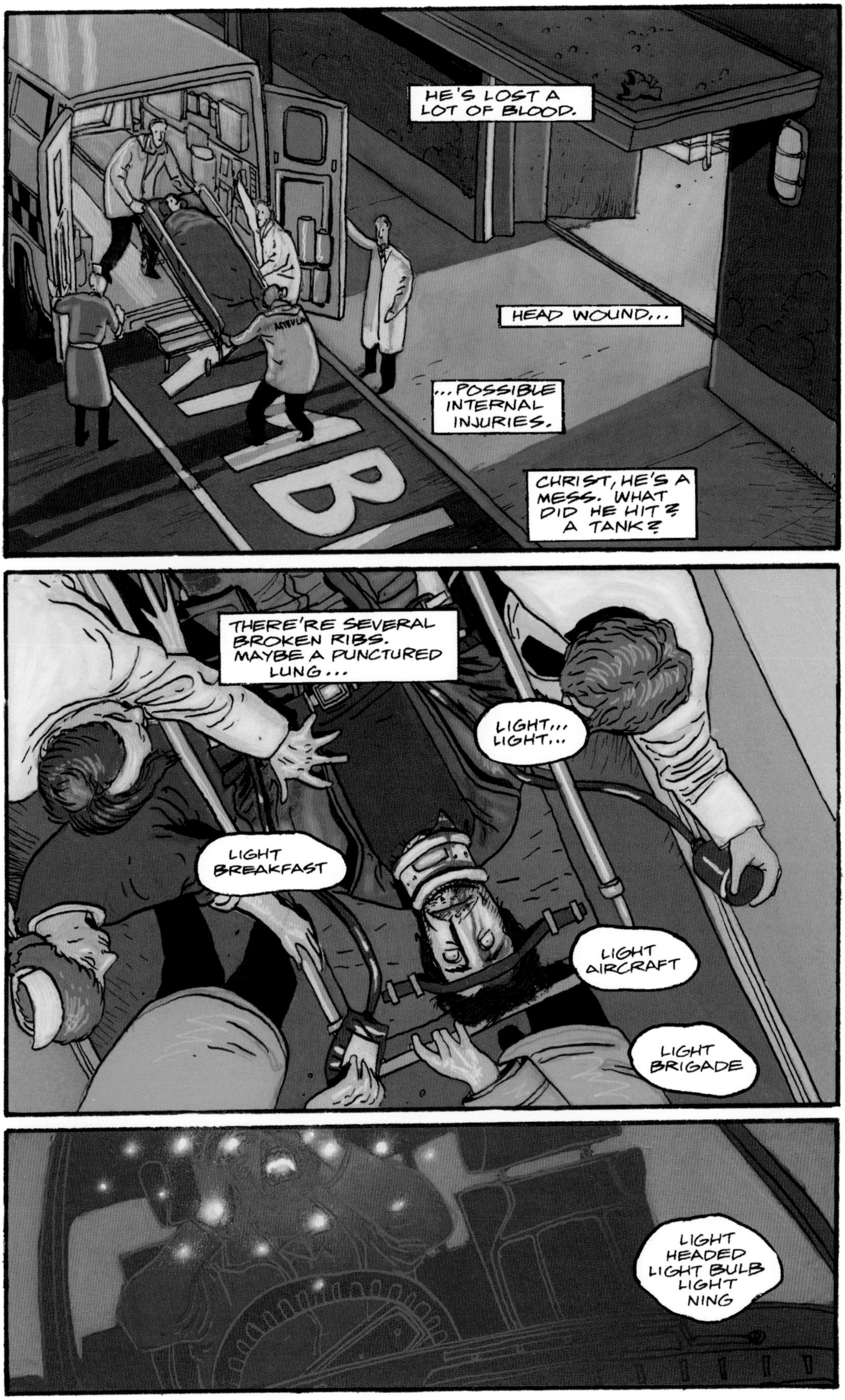
HE'S LOST A LOT OF BLOOD.
HEAD WOUND...
...POSSIBLE INTERNAL INJURIES.
CHRIST, HE'S A MESS. WHAT DID HE HIT? A TANK?
THERE'RE SEVERAL BROKEN RIBS. MAYBE A PUNCTURED LUNG...
LIGHT... LIGHT...
LIGHT BREAKFAST
LIGHT AIRCRAFT
LIGHT BRIGADE
LIGHT HEADED LIGHT BULB LIGHT NING

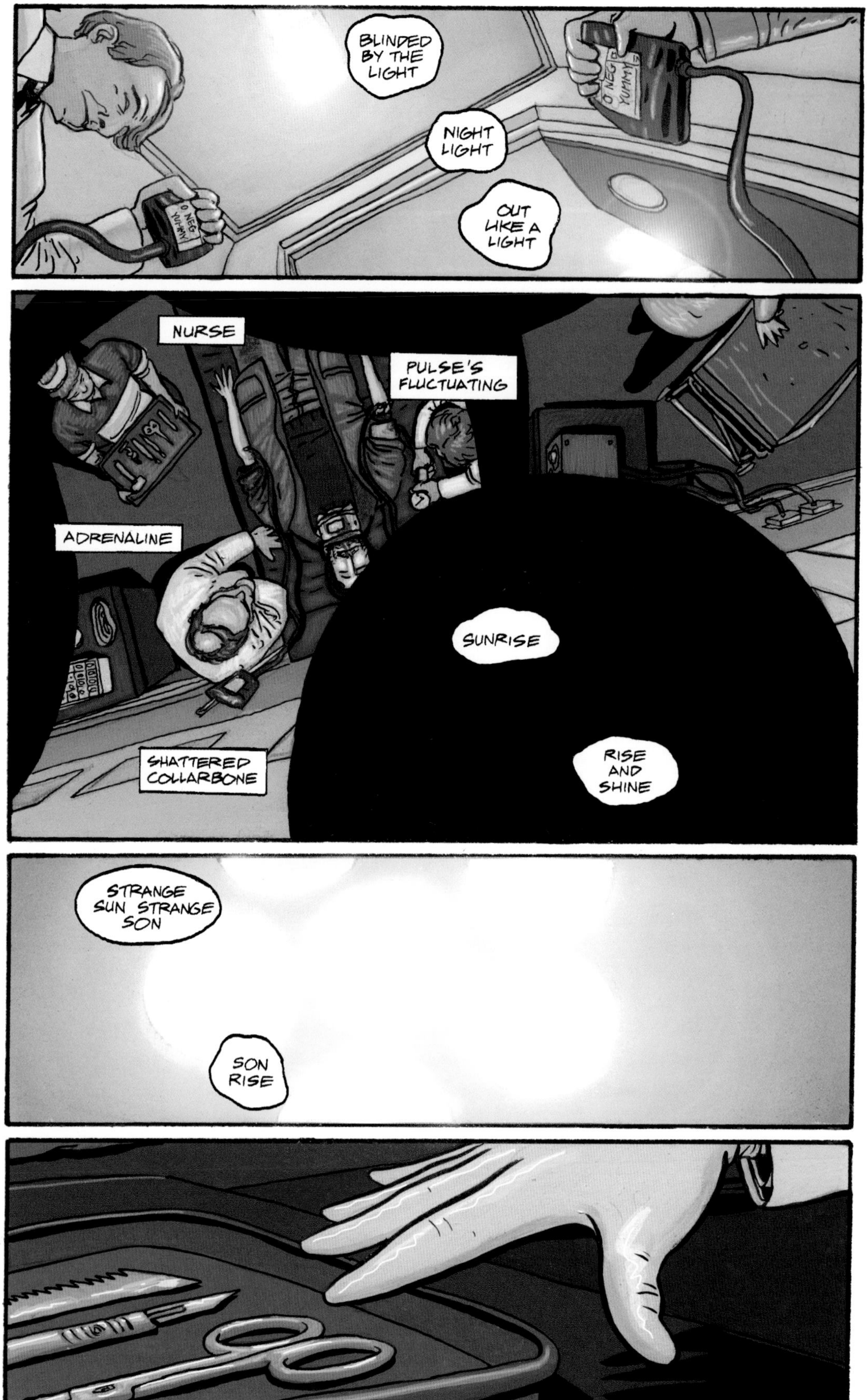
BLINDED BY THE LIGHT
NIGHT LIGHT
OUT LIKE A LIGHT
NURSE
PULSE'S FLUCTUATING
ADRENALINE
SHATTERED COLLARBONE
SUNRISE
RISE AND SHINE
STRANGE SUN STRANGE SON
SON RISE

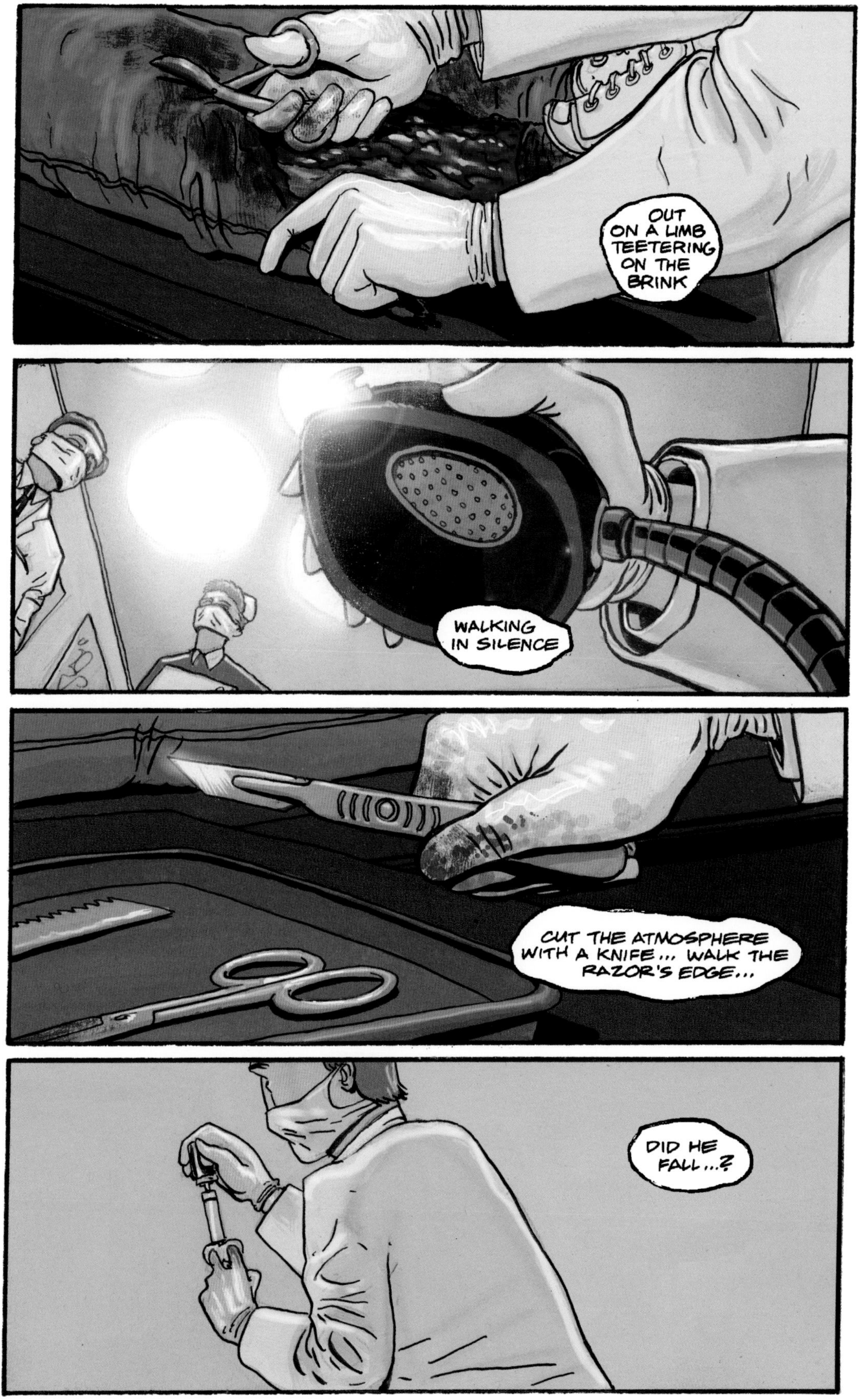
OUT ON A LIMB TEETERING ON THE BRINK
WALKING IN SILENCE
CUT THE ATMOSPHERE WITH A KNIFE... WALK THE RAZOR'S EDGE...
DID HE FALL...?

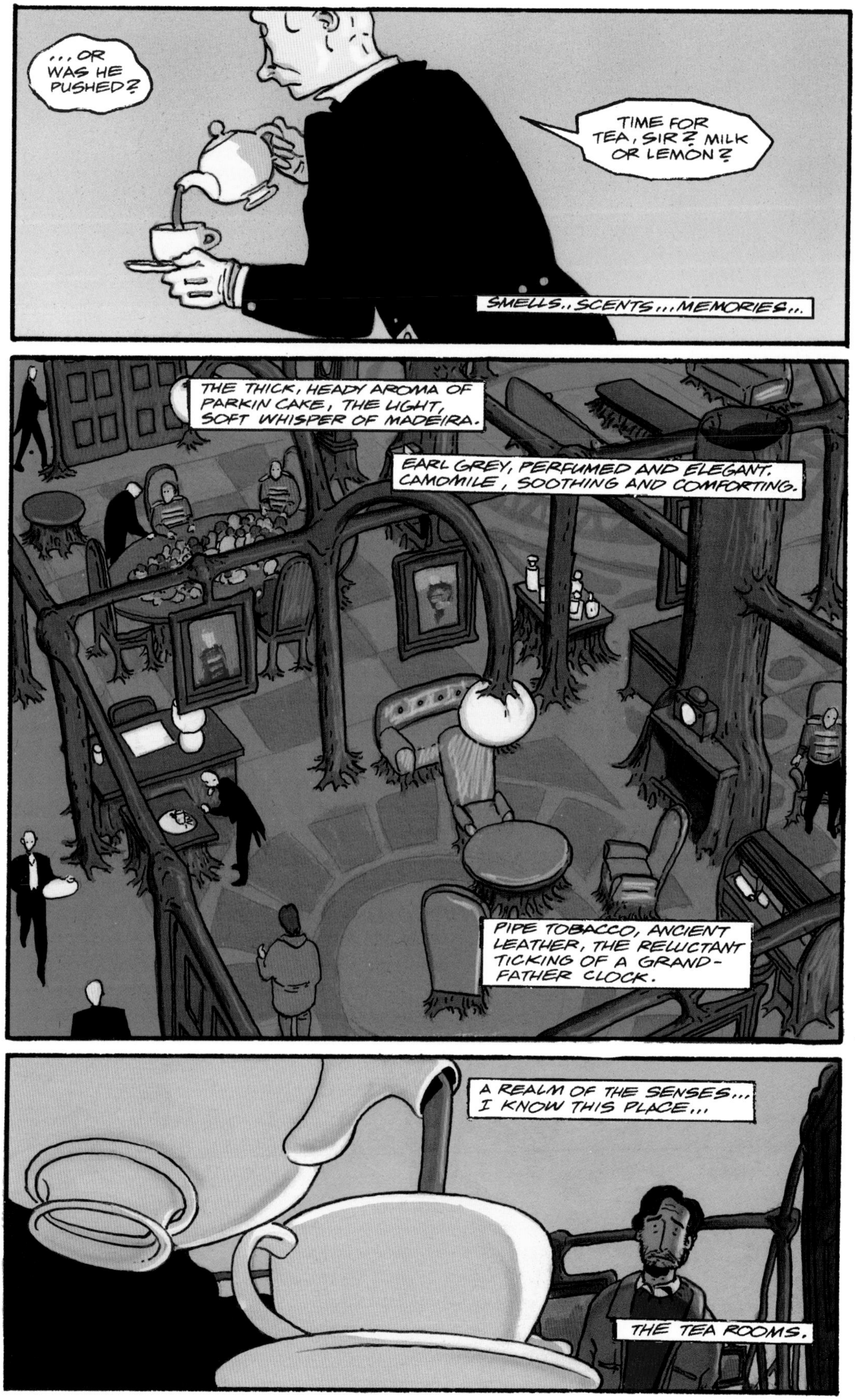
...OR WAS HE PUSHED?
TIME FOR TEA, SIR? MILK OR LEMON?
SMELLS.. SCENTS... MEMORIES...
THE THICK, HEADY AROMA OF PARKIN CAKE, THE LIGHT, SOFT WHISPER OF MADEIRA.
EARL GREY, PERFUMED AND ELEGANT. CAMOMILE, SOOTHING AND COMFORTING.
PIPE TOBACCO, ANCIENT LEATHER, THE RELUCTANT TICKING OF A GRAND-FATHER CLOCK.
A REALM OF THE SENSES... I KNOW THIS PLACE...
THE TEA ROOMS.

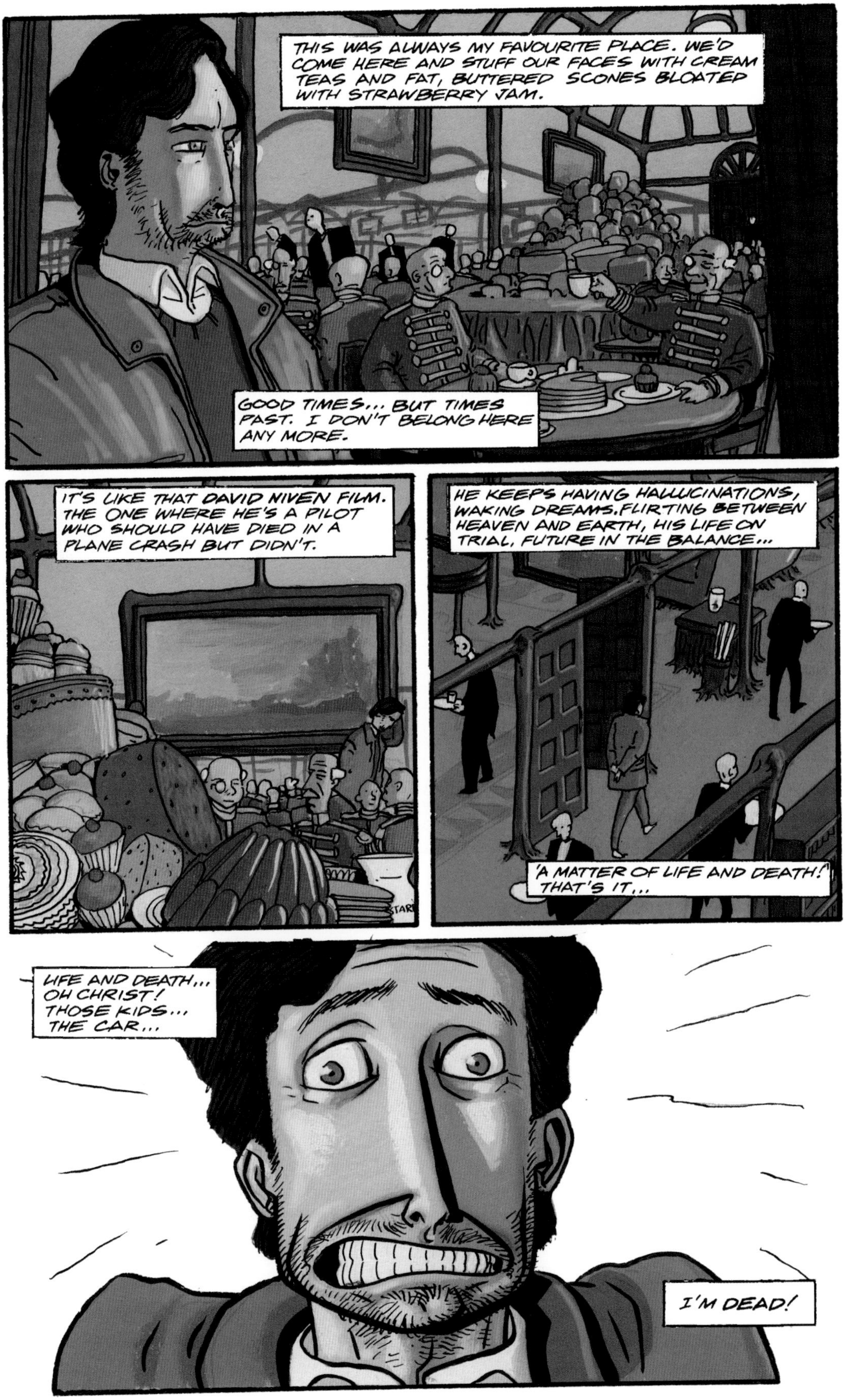
THIS WAS ALWAYS MY FAVOURITE PLACE. WE'D COME HERE AND STUFF OUR FACES WITH CREAM TEAS AND FAT, BUTTERED SCONES BLOATED WITH STRAWBERRY JAM.
GOOD TIMES... BUT TIMES PAST. I DON'T BELONG HERE ANY MORE.
IT'S LIKE THAT DAVID NIVEN FILM. THE ONE WHERE HE'S A PILOT WHO SHOULD HAVE DIED IN A PLANE CRASH BUT DIDN'T.
HE KEEPS HAVING HALLUCINATIONS, WAKING DREAMS. FLIRTING BETWEEN HEAVEN AND EARTH, HIS LIFE ON TRIAL, FUTURE IN THE BALANCE...
'A MATTER OF LIFE AND DEATH!' THAT'S IT...
LIFE AND DEATH... OH CHRIST! THOSE KIDS... THE CAR...
I'M DEAD!

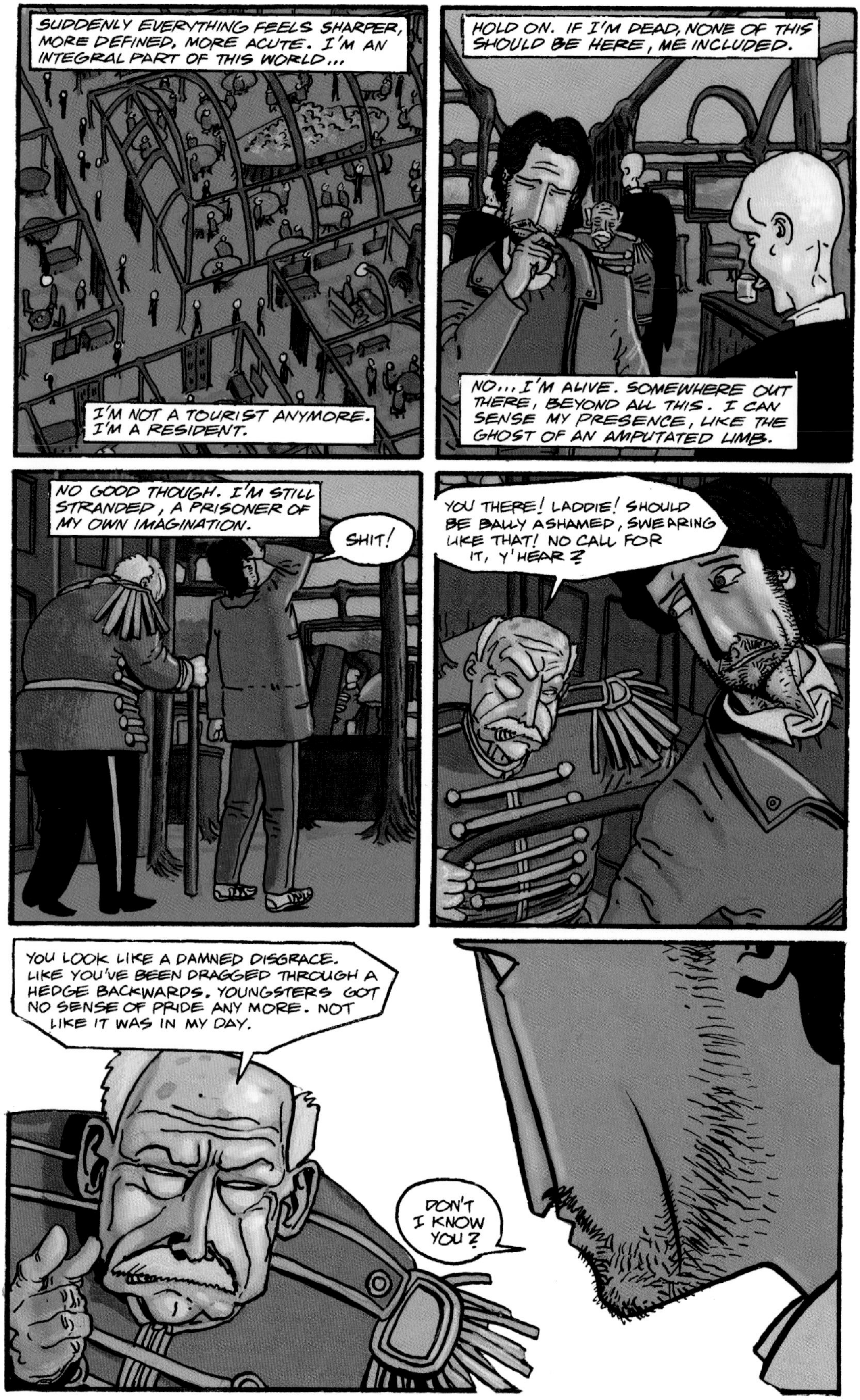
SUDDENLY EVERYTHING FEELS SHARPER, MORE DEFINED, MORE ACUTE. I'M AN INTEGRAL PART OF THIS WORLD...
I'M NOT A TOURIST ANYMORE. I'M A RESIDENT.
HOLD ON. IF I'M DEAD, NONE OF THIS SHOULD BE HERE, ME INCLUDED.
NO... I'M ALIVE. SOMEWHERE OUT THERE, BEYOND ALL THIS. I CAN SENSE MY PRESENCE, LIKE THE GHOST OF AN AMPUTATED LIMB.
NO GOOD THOUGH. I'M STILL STRANDED, A PRISONER OF MY OWN IMAGINATION.
SHIT!
YOU THERE! LADDIE! SHOULD BE BALLY ASHAMED, SWEARING LIKE THAT! NO CALL FOR IT, Y'HEAR?
YOU LOOK LIKE A DAMNED DISGRACE. LIKE YOU'VE BEEN DRAGGED THROUGH A HEDGE BACKWARDS. YOUNGSTERS GOT NO SENSE OF PRIDE ANY MORE. NOT LIKE IT WAS IN MY DAY.
DON'T I KNOW YOU?

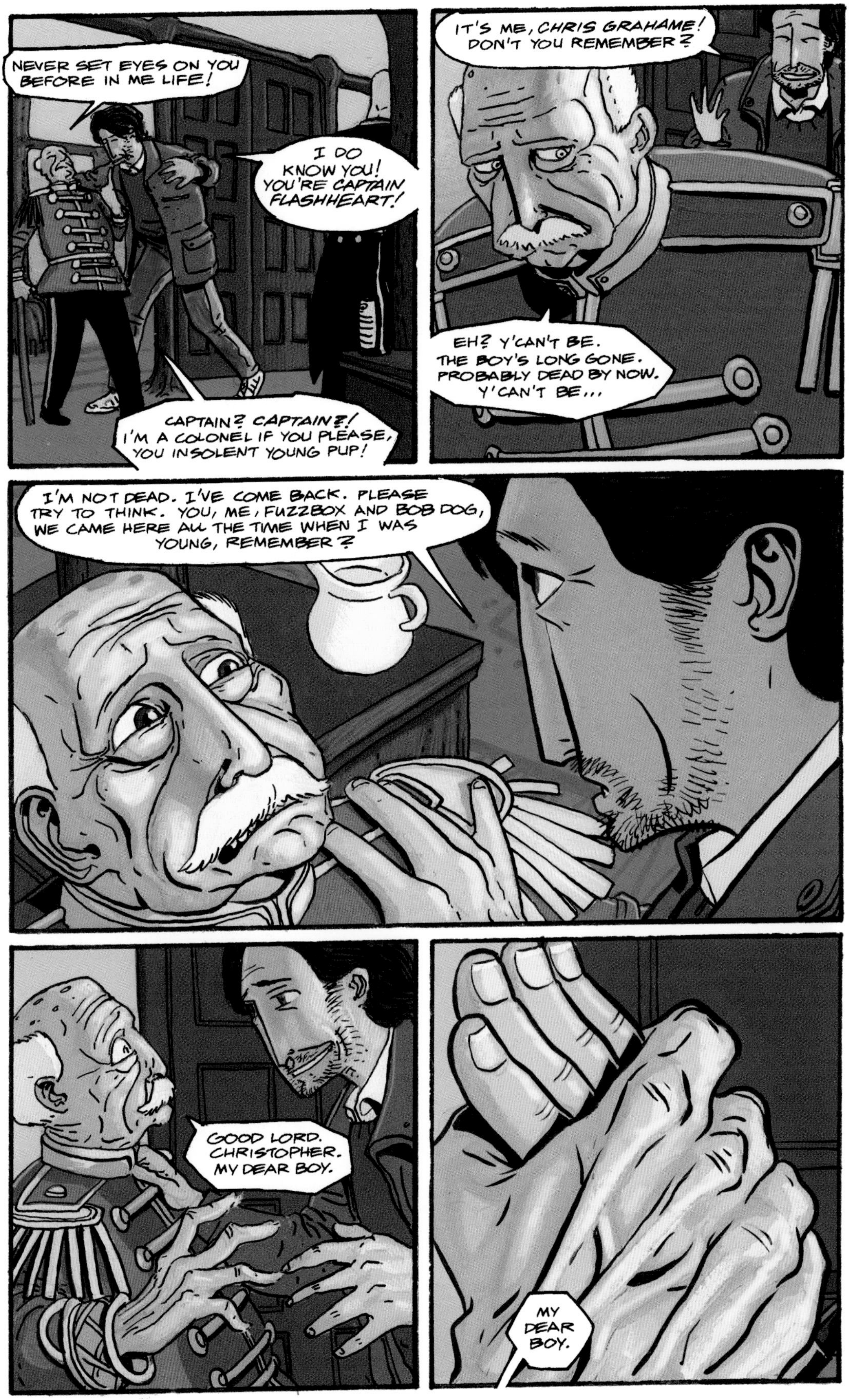
NEVER SET EYES ON YOU BEFORE IN ME LIFE!
I DO KNOW YOU! YOU'RE CAPTAIN FLASHHEART!
CAPTAIN? CAPTAIN?! I'M A COLONEL IF YOU PLEASE, YOU INSOLENT YOUNG PUP!
IT'S ME, CHRIS GRAHAME! DON'T YOU REMEMBER?
EH? Y'CAN'T BE. THE BOY'S LONG GONE. PROBABLY DEAD BY NOW. Y'CAN'T BE...
I'M NOT DEAD. I'VE COME BACK. PLEASE TRY TO THINK. YOU, ME, FUZZBOX AND BOB DOG, WE CAME HERE ALL THE TIME WHEN I WAS YOUNG, REMEMBER?
GOOD LORD. CHRISTOPHER. MY DEAR BOY.
MY DEAR BOY.

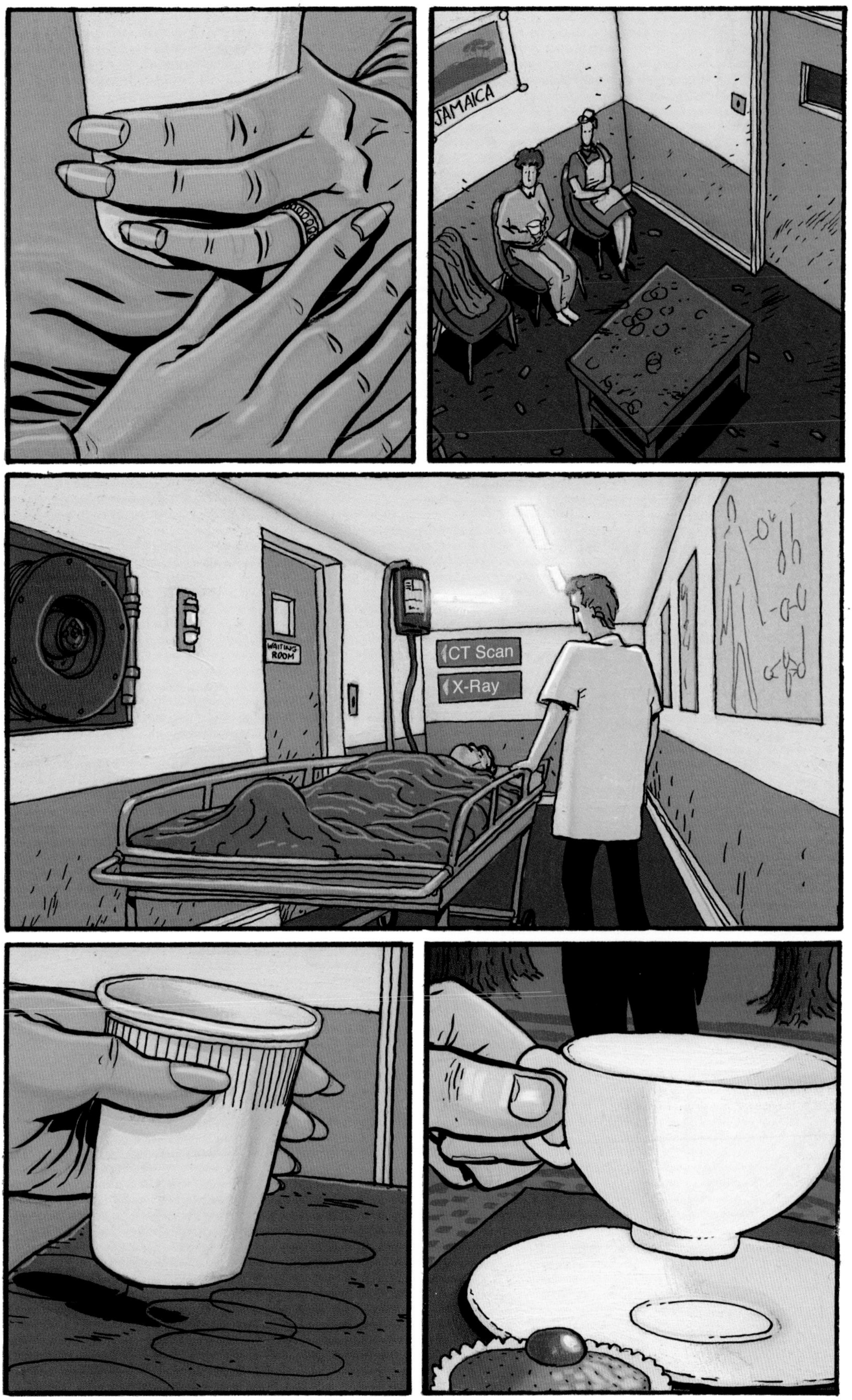
JAMAICA
WAITING ROOM
CT Scan
X-Ray

I SIT, LIKE A SEVEN YEAR OLD, LISTENING, RAPT, TO TALES TOLD AT HIS GRANDFATHER'S KNEE.

OF BATTLE CRIES AND CAVALRY CHARGES, SWORD PLAY AND CANNON FIRE, UNCOMMON VALOUR AND NOBLE HEROICS...

WAR STORIES.

HIS HANDS, ARTHRITIC ROOTS OF OAK AND WALNUT, WIELD PHANTOM SABRES, REIN GHOSTLY HORSES.

COUNT THE WHORLS, READ THE AGE. OLD SOLDIERS NEVER DIE...

...ONLY THE YOUNG ONES.

THOSE FALLEN IN

J. ASHFORTH

3RD SILVER CITY HUSSARS

H. CARTER
I. EDGINTON
D. ELLIOTT
W. ELLIS
S. WHITE
L. WILKES
F. WYNNE

4TH SILVER CITY HUSSARS

S. WHITAKER
P. SCHREEDER
N. ABADZIS
R. BALL

1ST ROYAL FUSILLIERS

M. BUCKINGHAM
A. ELLIOTT

S.L. OAKLEY
A. JOXALL

2ND ROYAL FUSILLIERS

L. ELLERY
D. KING
V. MORGAN
A. ROBERTS
J. SCOTT
R. TIMER
N. VINCE
S. WESTON

3RD ROYAL FUSILLIERS

E. DEVILLE
E. HALES
A. HARRIES
J. McCREA
W. PHOENIX
E. TIMMINS
TIMOLO

IT WAS CARNAGE. MEN AND HORSES AGAINST THOSE INFERNAL DEVICES OF HIS. WE NEVER STOOD A CHANCE BUT BY GOD WE TRIED, WE TRIED.

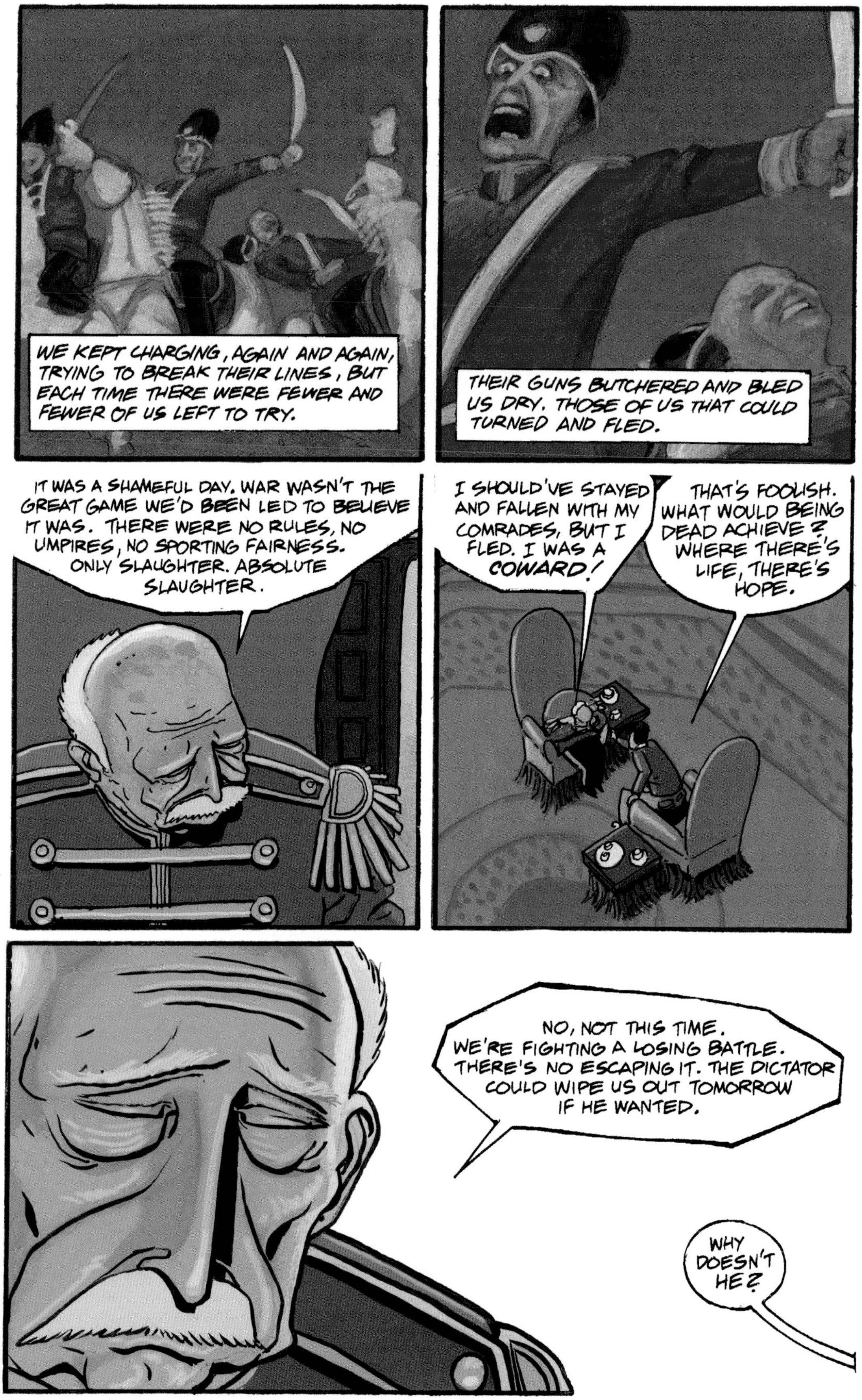
WE KEPT CHARGING, AGAIN AND AGAIN, TRYING TO BREAK THEIR LINES, BUT EACH TIME THERE WERE FEWER AND FEWER OF US LEFT TO TRY.
THEIR GUNS BUTCHERED AND BLED US DRY. THOSE OF US THAT COULD TURNED AND FLED.
IT WAS A SHAMEFUL DAY. WAR WASN'T THE GREAT GAME WE'D BEEN LED TO BELIEVE IT WAS. THERE WERE NO RULES, NO UMPIRES, NO SPORTING FAIRNESS. ONLY SLAUGHTER. ABSOLUTE SLAUGHTER.
I SHOULD'VE STAYED AND FALLEN WITH MY COMRADES, BUT I FLED. I WAS A COWARD!
THAT'S FOOLISH. WHAT WOULD BEING DEAD ACHIEVE? WHERE THERE'S LIFE, THERE'S HOPE.
NO, NOT THIS TIME. WE'RE FIGHTING A LOSING BATTLE. THERE'S NO ESCAPING IT. THE DICTATOR COULD WIPE US OUT TOMORROW IF HE WANTED.
WHY DOESN'T HE?

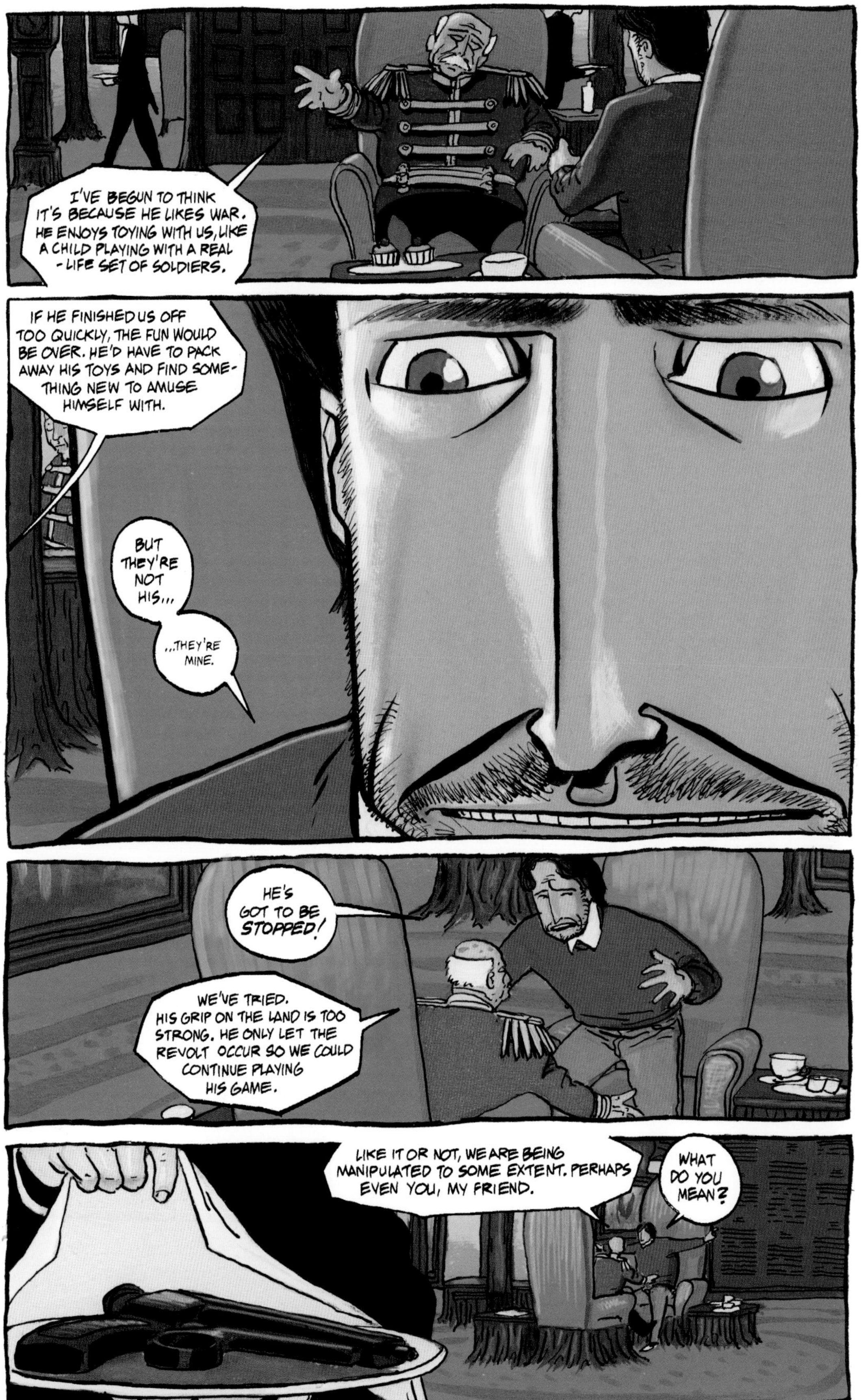
I'VE BEGUN TO THINK IT'S BECAUSE HE LIKES WAR. HE ENJOYS TOYING WITH US, LIKE A CHILD PLAYING WITH A REAL -LIFE SET OF SOLDIERS.
IF HE FINISHED US OFF TOO QUICKLY, THE FUN WOULD BE OVER. HE'D HAVE TO PACK AWAY HIS TOYS AND FIND SOME-THING NEW TO AMUSE HIMSELF WITH.
BUT THEY'RE NOT HIS...
...THEY'RE MINE.
HE'S GOT TO BE STOPPED!
WE'VE TRIED. HIS GRIP ON THE LAND IS TOO STRONG. HE ONLY LET THE REVOLT OCCUR SO WE COULD CONTINUE PLAYING HIS GAME.
LIKE IT OR NOT, WE ARE BEING MANIPULATED TO SOME EXTENT. PERHAPS EVEN YOU, MY FRIEND.
WHAT DO YOU MEAN?

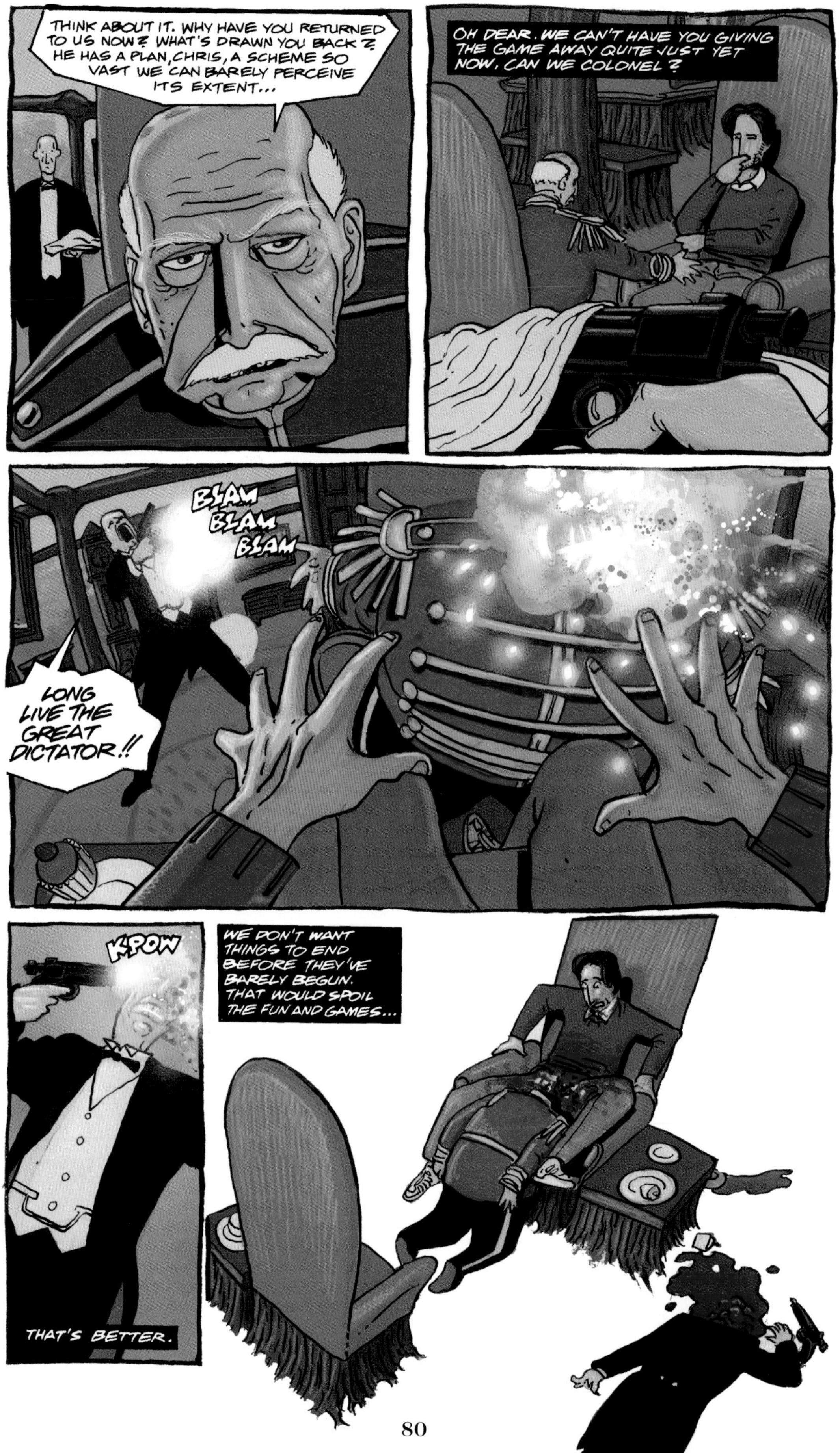
THINK ABOUT IT. WHY HAVE YOU RETURNED TO US NOW? WHAT'S DRAWN YOU BACK? HE HAS A PLAN, CHRIS, A SCHEME SO VAST WE CAN BARELY PERCEIVE ITS EXTENT...
OH DEAR. WE CAN'T HAVE YOU GIVING THE GAME AWAY QUITE JUST YET NOW, CAN WE COLONEL?
BLAM
BLAM
BLAM
LONG LIVE THE GREAT DICTATOR!!
KPOW
THAT'S BETTER.
WE DON'T WANT THINGS TO END BEFORE THEY'VE BARELY BEGUN. THAT WOULD SPOIL THE FUN AND GAMES...

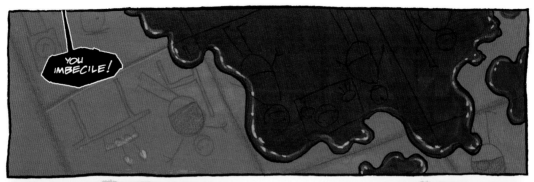

YOU IMBECILE!

IT...IT WAS AN ACCIDENT, HIGHNESS. I'LL FETCH ANOTHER BOTTLE.

THERE ISN'T ANOTHER BOTTLE, YOU MORON! THAT WAS IT! I EVEN BURNED DOWN THE VINEYARD TO MAKE IT AN EXCLUSIVE VINTAGE!

I...I'M SORRY, HIGHNESS.

WELL THAT'S NOT GOOD ENOUGH.

KER·BLAM!

HEKTOR, CLEAR A PATH BETWEEN HERE AND THE TEA ROOMS. I'M ANTICIPATING THE ARRIVAL OF A VERY SPECIAL GUEST AND I WANT HIM TO PASS UNMOLESTED.

81

IF ANY LITTLE 'ACCIDENT' SHOULD OCCUR, I WILL PERSONALLY FLAY YOUR LIVING HIDE FOR A NEW PAIR OF BOOTS. IS THAT CLEAR?

YES SIRE.

OH AND GET SOMEONE TO CLEAN THAT UP OTHERWISE THE STAINS WILL NEVER COME OUT.

THIS IS IT. FINALLY, AFTER INTERMINABLE DECADES OF WAITING, THE WHEEL TURNS. MY TIME HAS COME!

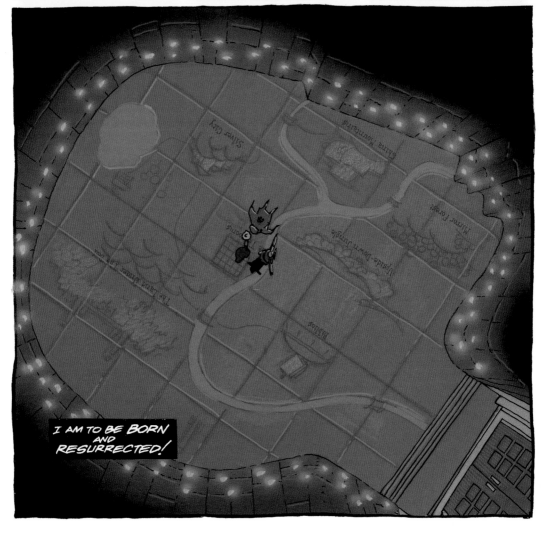

I AM TO BE BORN AND RESURRECTED!

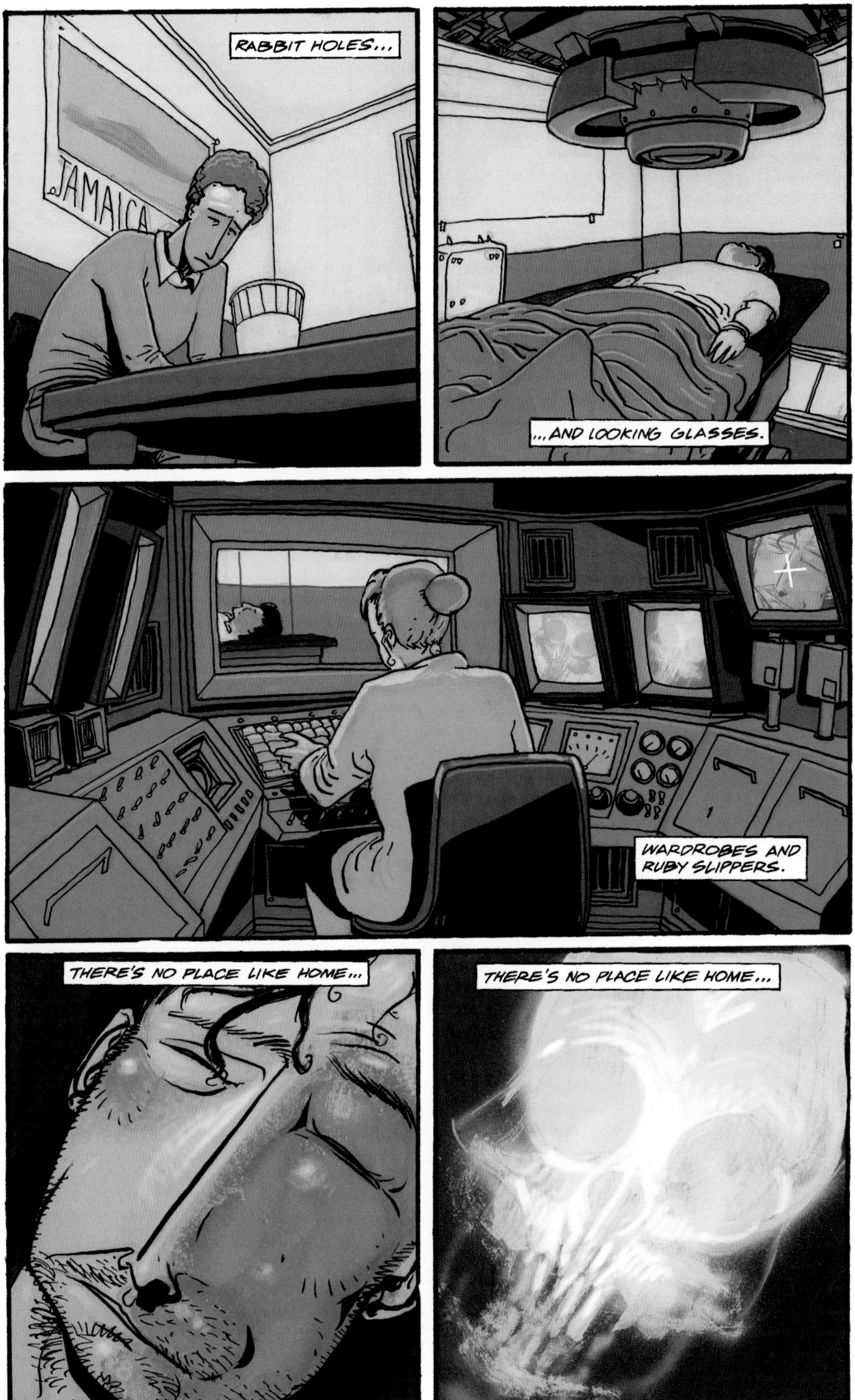
RABBIT HOLES...
...AND LOOKING GLASSES.
WARDROBES AND RUBY SLIPPERS.
THERE'S NO PLACE LIKE HOME...
THERE'S NO PLACE LIKE HOME...

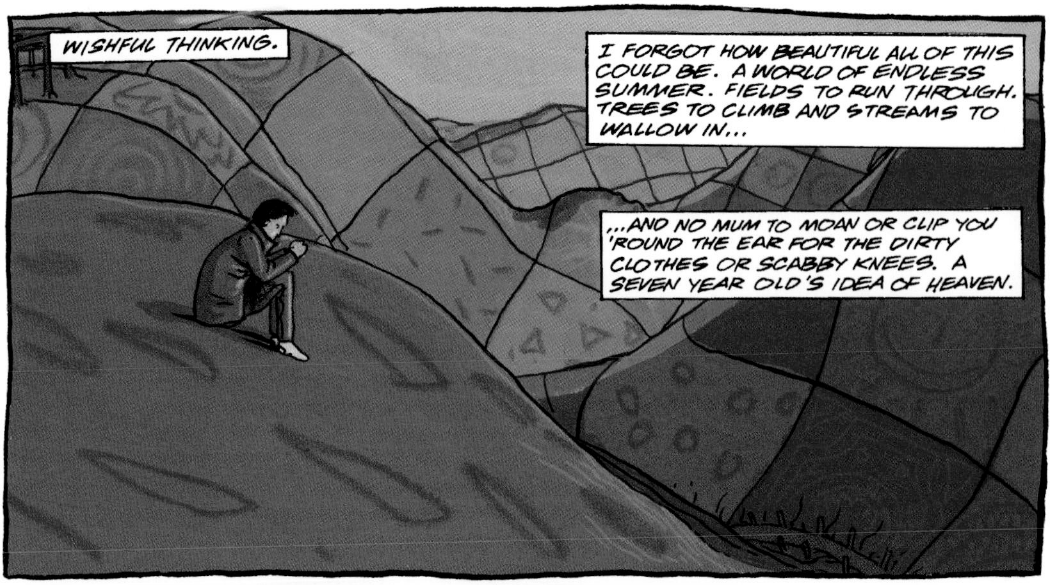
WISHFUL THINKING.
I FORGOT HOW BEAUTIFUL ALL OF THIS COULD BE. A WORLD OF ENDLESS SUMMER. FIELDS TO RUN THROUGH. TREES TO CLIMB AND STREAMS TO WALLOW IN...
...AND NO MUM TO MOAN OR CLIP YOU 'ROUND THE EAR FOR THE DIRTY CLOTHES OR SCABBY KNEES. A SEVEN YEAR OLD'S IDEA OF HEAVEN.

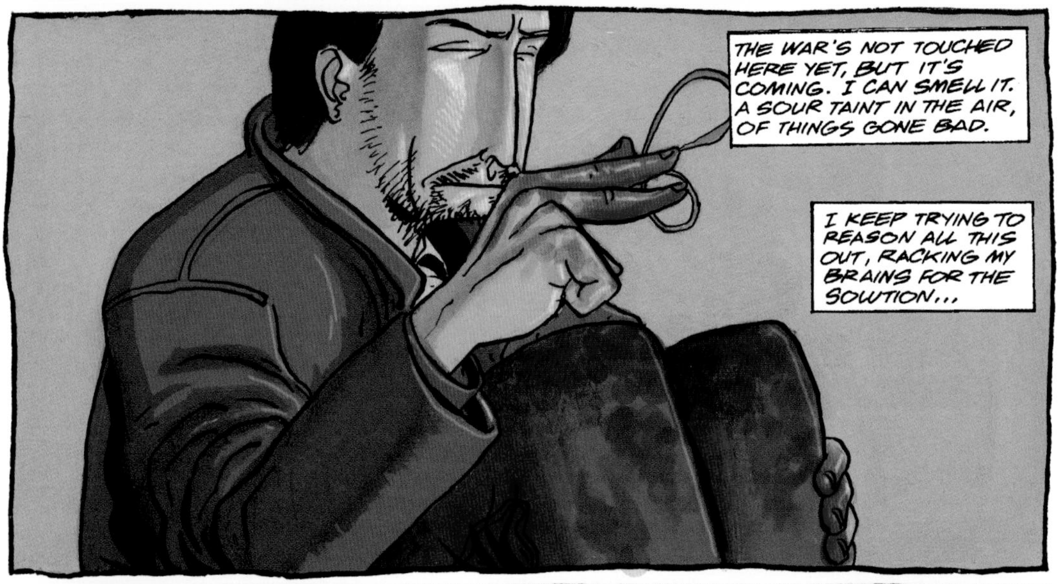
THE WAR'S NOT TOUCHED HERE YET, BUT IT'S COMING. I CAN SMELL IT. A SOUR TAINT IN THE AIR, OF THINGS GONE BAD.
I KEEP TRYING TO REASON ALL THIS OUT, RACKING MY BRAINS FOR THE SOLUTION...

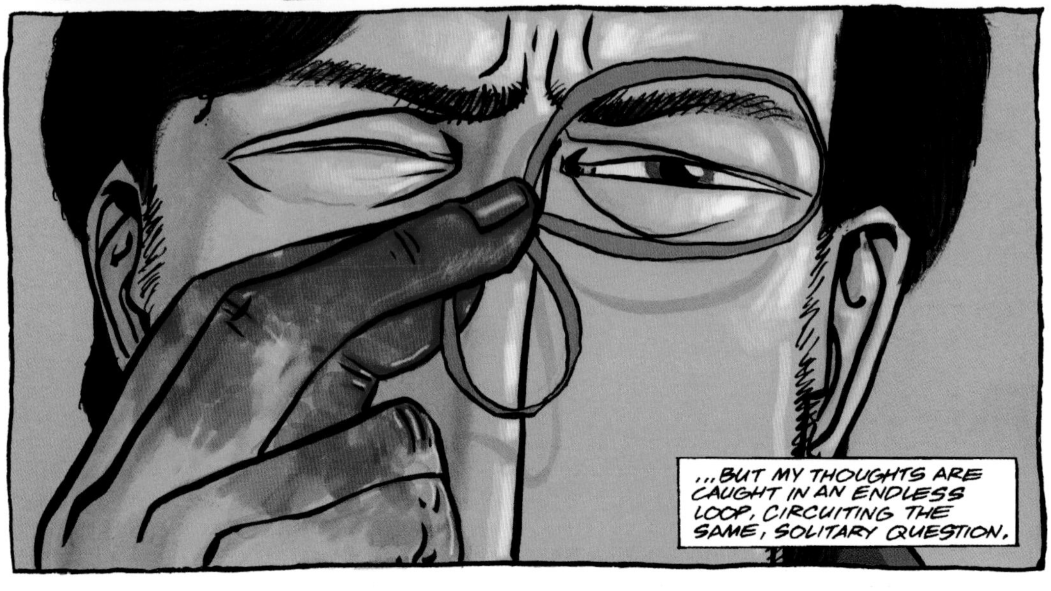
...BUT MY THOUGHTS ARE CAUGHT IN AN ENDLESS LOOP, CIRCUITING THE SAME, SOLITARY QUESTION.

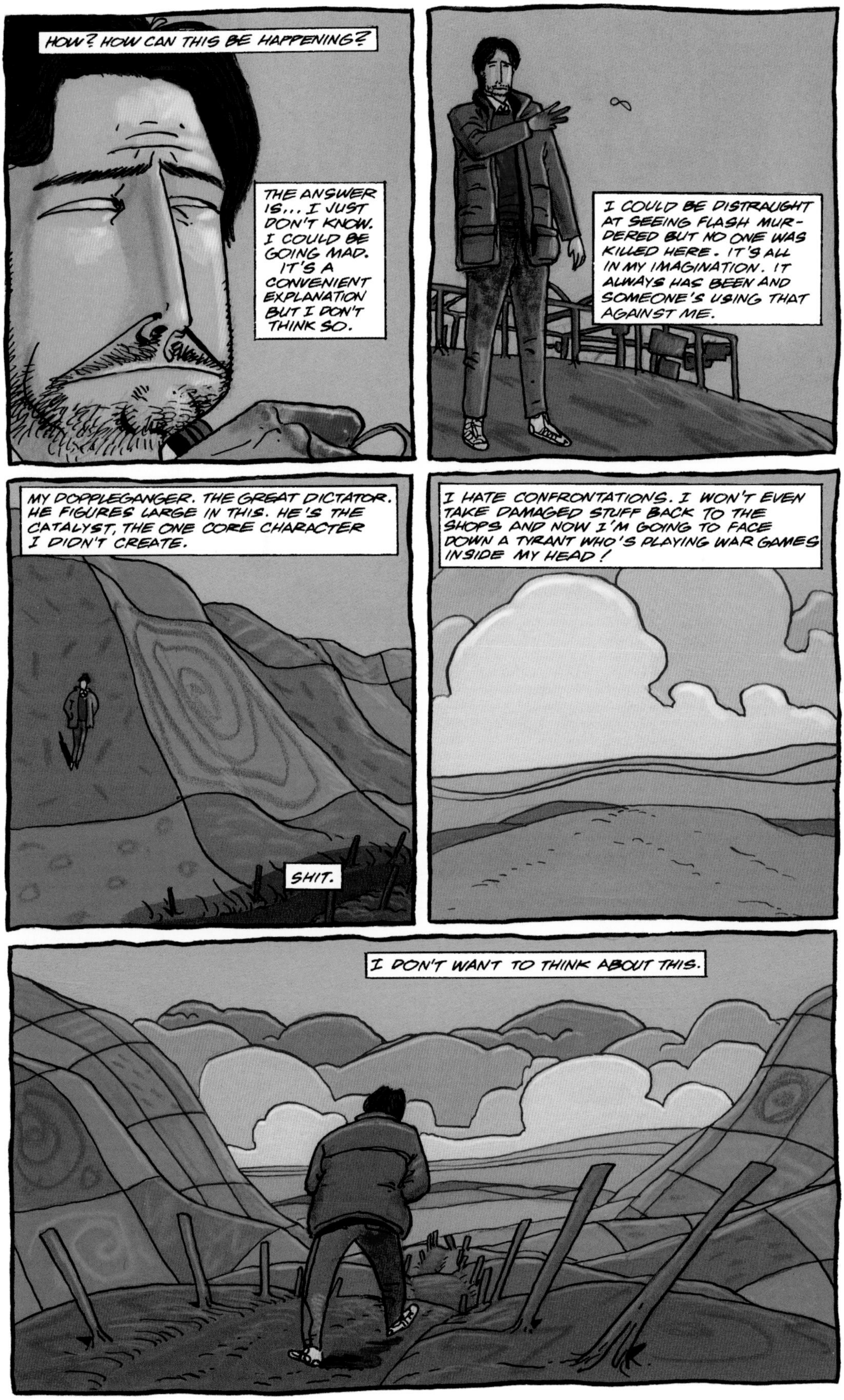
HOW? HOW CAN THIS BE HAPPENING?
THE ANSWER IS... I JUST DON'T KNOW. I COULD BE GOING MAD. IT'S A CONVENIENT EXPLANATION BUT I DON'T THINK SO.
I COULD BE DISTRAUGHT AT SEEING FLASH MURDERED BUT NO ONE WAS KILLED HERE. IT'S ALL IN MY IMAGINATION. IT ALWAYS HAS BEEN AND SOMEONE'S USING THAT AGAINST ME.
MY DOPPLEGANGER. THE GREAT DICTATOR. HE FIGURES LARGE IN THIS. HE'S THE CATALYST, THE ONE CORE CHARACTER I DIDN'T CREATE.
SHIT.
I HATE CONFRONTATIONS. I WON'T EVEN TAKE DAMAGED STUFF BACK TO THE SHOPS AND NOW I'M GOING TO FACE DOWN A TYRANT WHO'S PLAYING WAR GAMES INSIDE MY HEAD!
I DON'T WANT TO THINK ABOUT THIS.

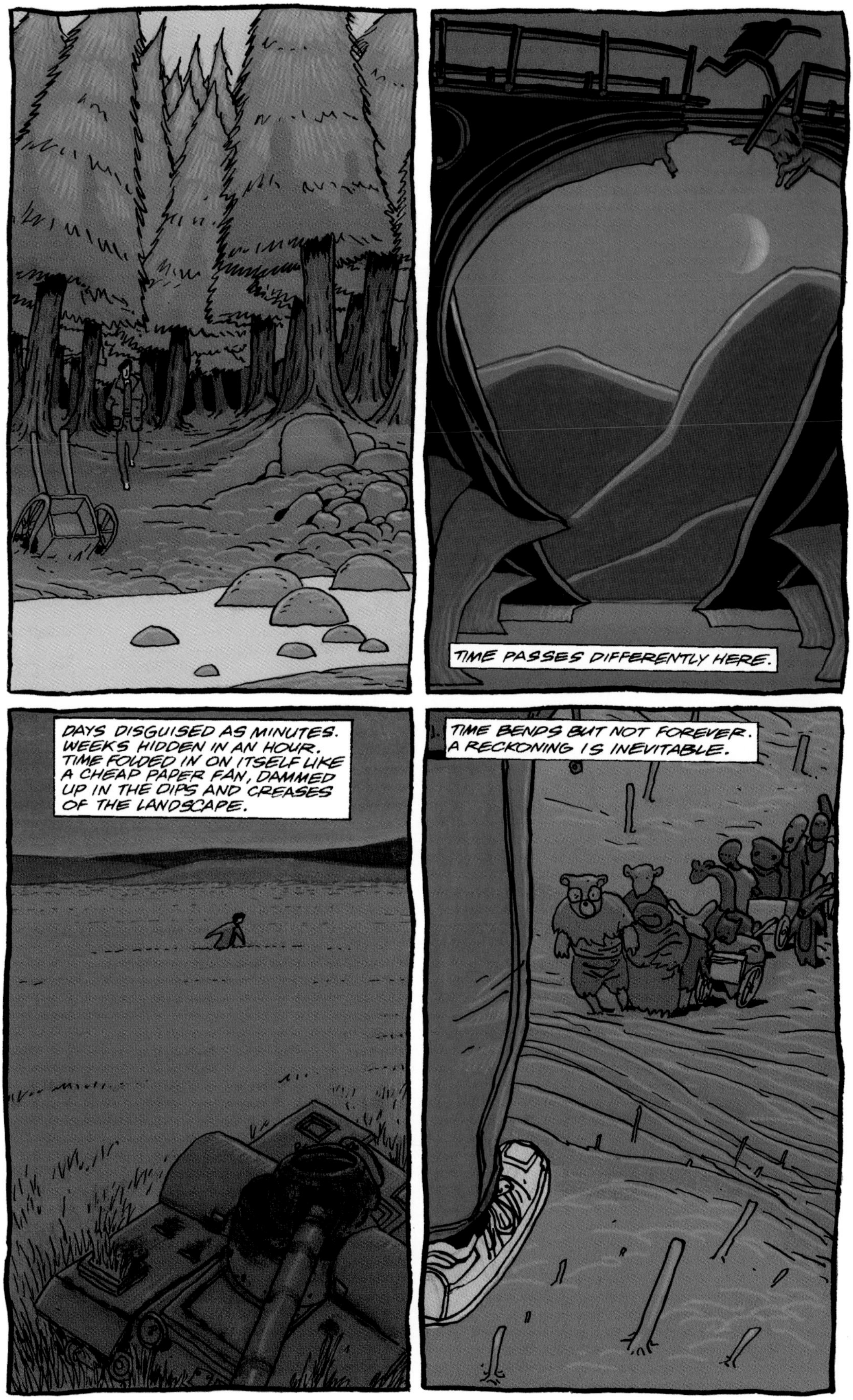
TIME PASSES DIFFERENTLY HERE.
DAYS DISGUISED AS MINUTES. WEEKS HIDDEN IN AN HOUR. TIME FOLDED IN ON ITSELF LIKE A CHEAP PAPER FAN, DAMMED UP IN THE DIPS AND CREASES OF THE LANDSCAPE.
TIME BENDS BUT NOT FOREVER. A RECKONING IS INEVITABLE.

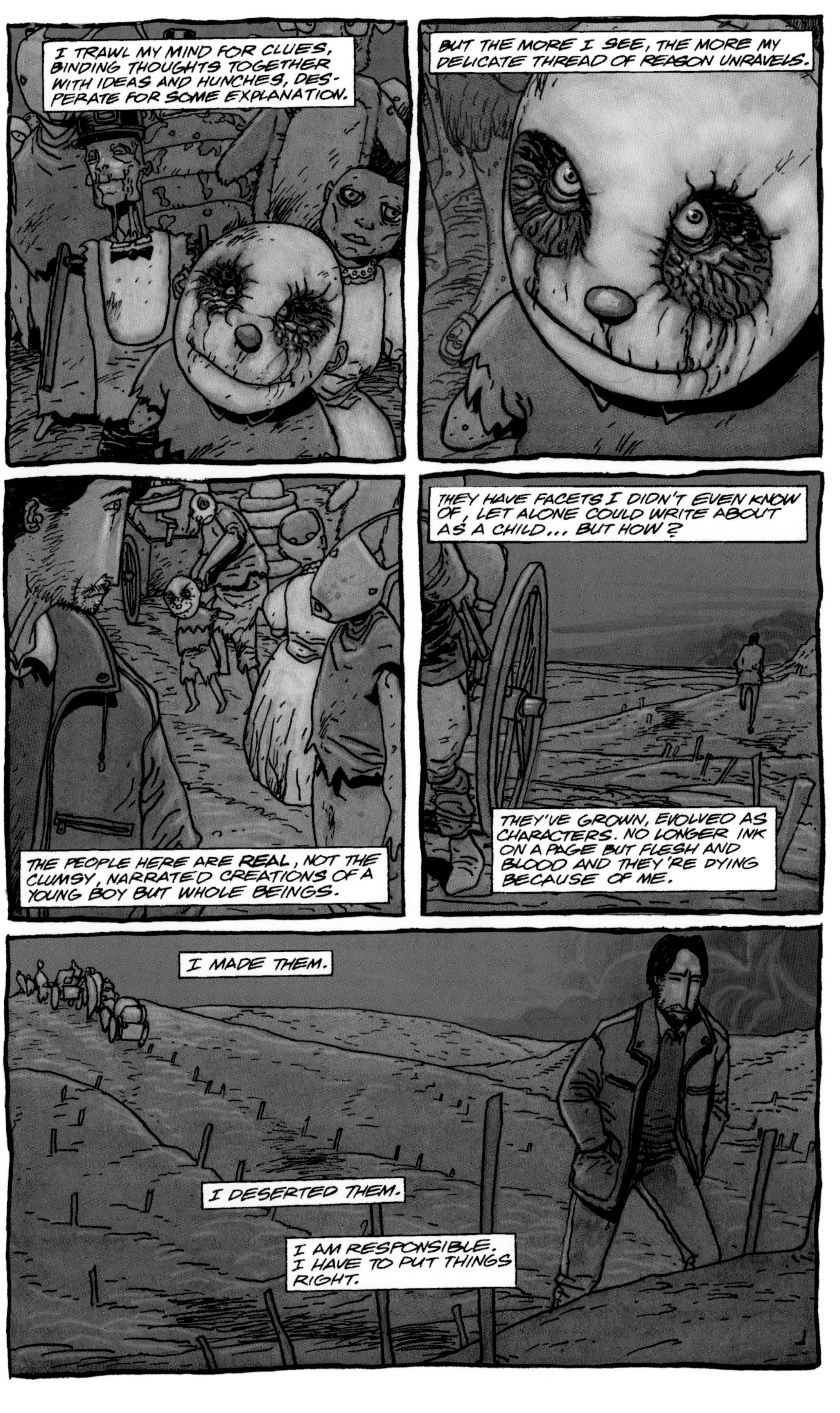
I TRAWL MY MIND FOR CLUES, BINDING THOUGHTS TOGETHER WITH IDEAS AND HUNCHES, DESPERATE FOR SOME EXPLANATION.
BUT THE MORE I SEE, THE MORE MY DELICATE THREAD OF REASON UNRAVELS.
THE PEOPLE HERE ARE REAL, NOT THE CLUMSY, NARRATED CREATIONS OF A YOUNG BOY BUT WHOLE BEINGS.
THEY HAVE FACETS I DIDN'T EVEN KNOW OF, LET ALONE COULD WRITE ABOUT AS A CHILD... BUT HOW?
THEY'VE GROWN, EVOLVED AS CHARACTERS. NO LONGER INK ON A PAGE BUT FLESH AND BLOOD AND THEY'RE DYING BECAUSE OF ME.
I MADE THEM.
I DESERTED THEM.
I AM RESPONSIBLE. I HAVE TO PUT THINGS RIGHT.

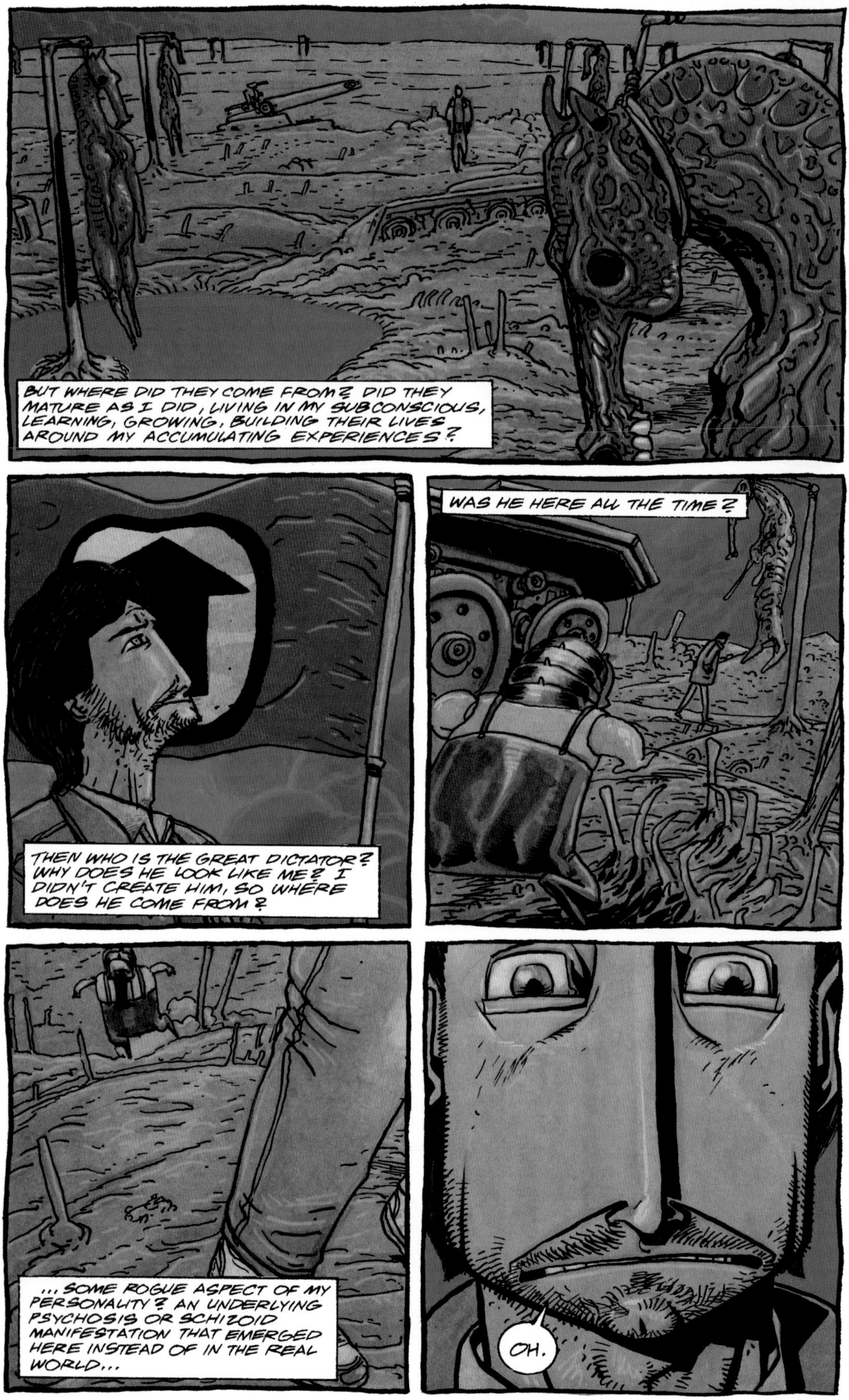
BUT WHERE DID THEY COME FROM? DID THEY MATURE AS I DID, LIVING IN MY SUBCONSCIOUS, LEARNING, GROWING, BUILDING THEIR LIVES AROUND MY ACCUMULATING EXPERIENCES?
THEN WHO IS THE GREAT DICTATOR? WHY DOES HE LOOK LIKE ME? I DIDN'T CREATE HIM, SO WHERE DOES HE COME FROM?
WAS HE HERE ALL THE TIME?
...SOME ROGUE ASPECT OF MY PERSONALITY? AN UNDERLYING PSYCHOSIS OR SCHIZOID MANIFESTATION THAT EMERGED HERE INSTEAD OF IN THE REAL WORLD...
OH.

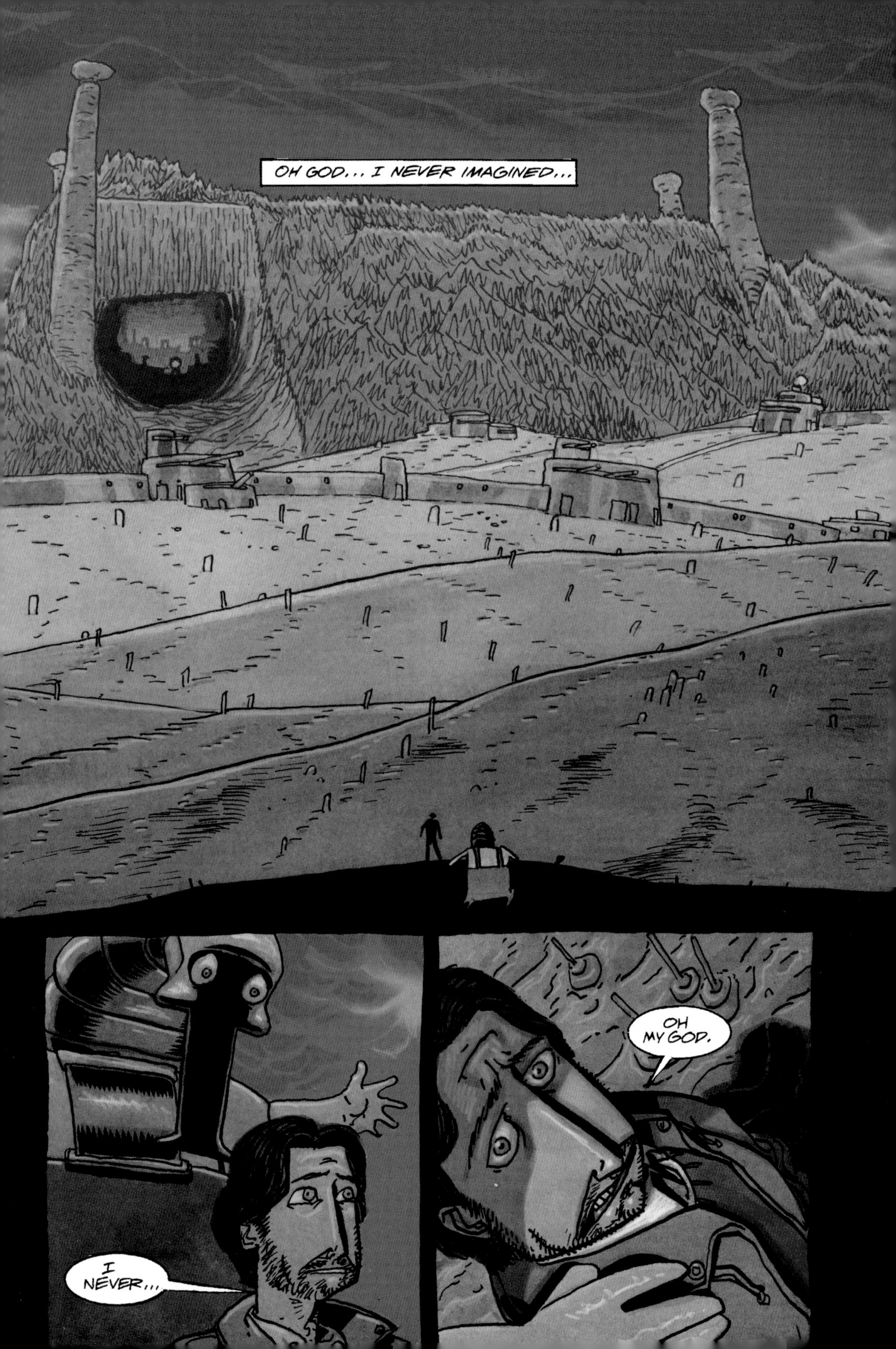
OH GOD... I NEVER IMAGINED...
I NEVER...
OH MY GOD.

THIS IS INCREDIBLE.

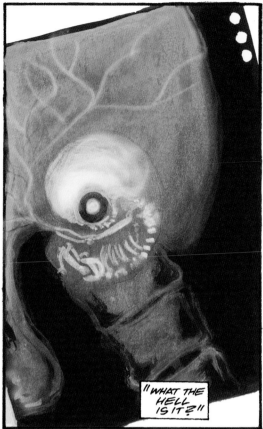

"WHAT THE HELL IS IT?"

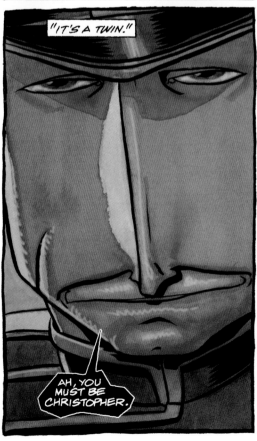

"IT'S A TWIN."

AH, YOU MUST BE CHRISTOPHER.

HOW DO YOU DO? I'M THE GREAT DICTATOR. I'VE BEEN SO LOOKING FORWARD TO MEETING YOU. I'M SURE WE'RE GOING TO GET ALONG *FAMOUSLY*.

Chapter
Four

◆◆◆

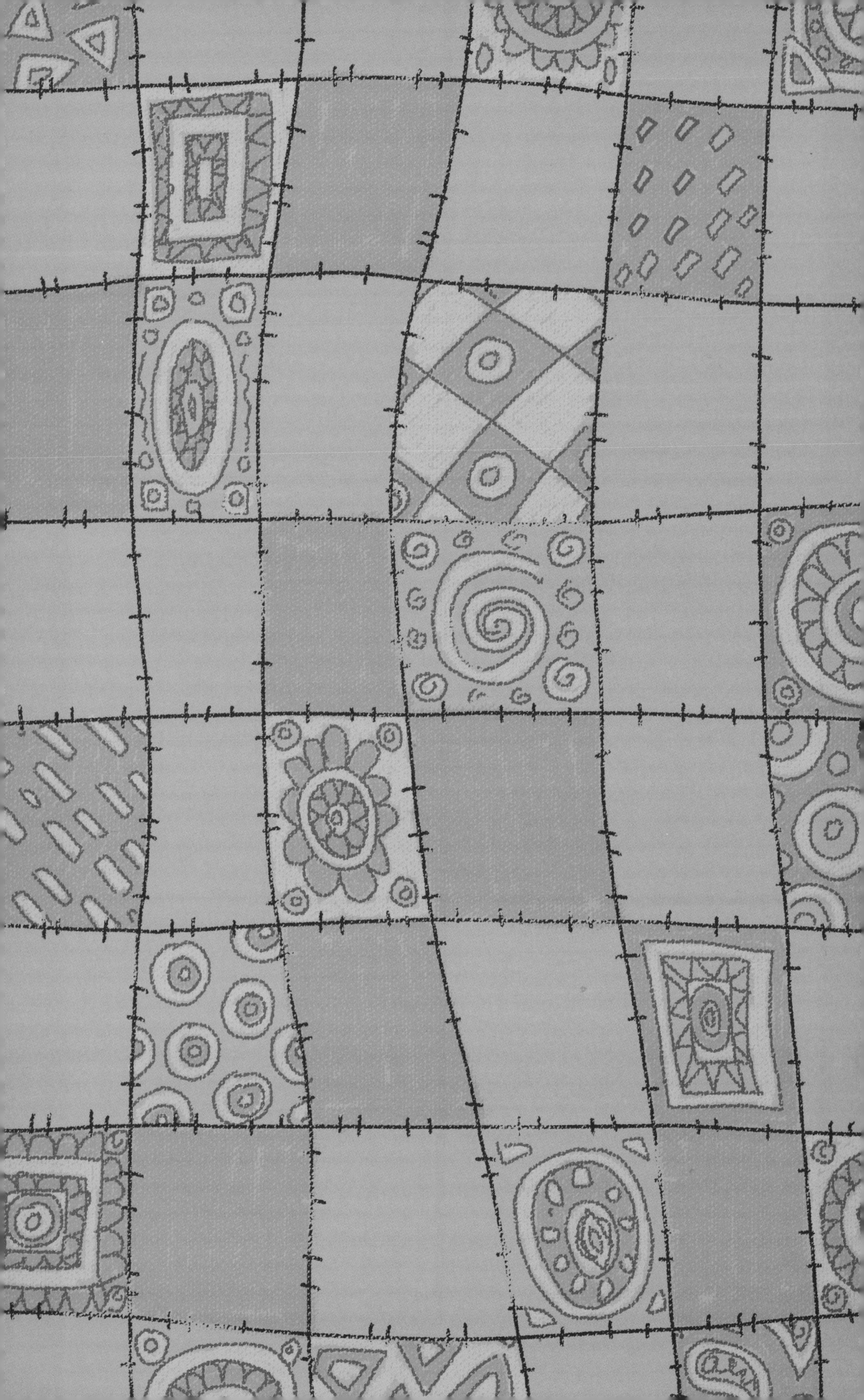

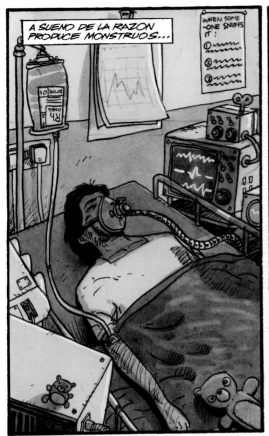

A SUENO DE LA RAZON PRODUCE MONSTRUOS...
WHEN SOME-ONE SNUFFS IT :
...THE SLEEP OF REASON BRINGS FORTH MONSTERS.
PARTS OF THE BODY
HAIR (LOTS)
EYE
HEAD
MOUTH
EAR
ARM
FINGERS (LOTS)
AN INTERNAL
THIS IS A NIGHTMARE. EVEN WITH THE DAMN THING IN FRONT OF ME, I STILL FIND IT HARD TO BELIEVE.
BUT THE CAMERA NEVER LIES. ALL THE MIRACLES OF NATURE ARE LAID BARE BEFORE THE LENS...

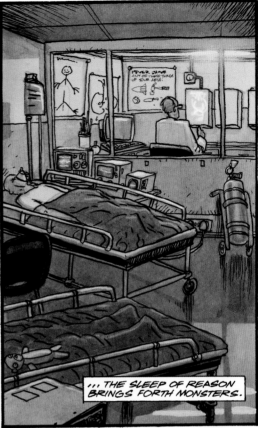

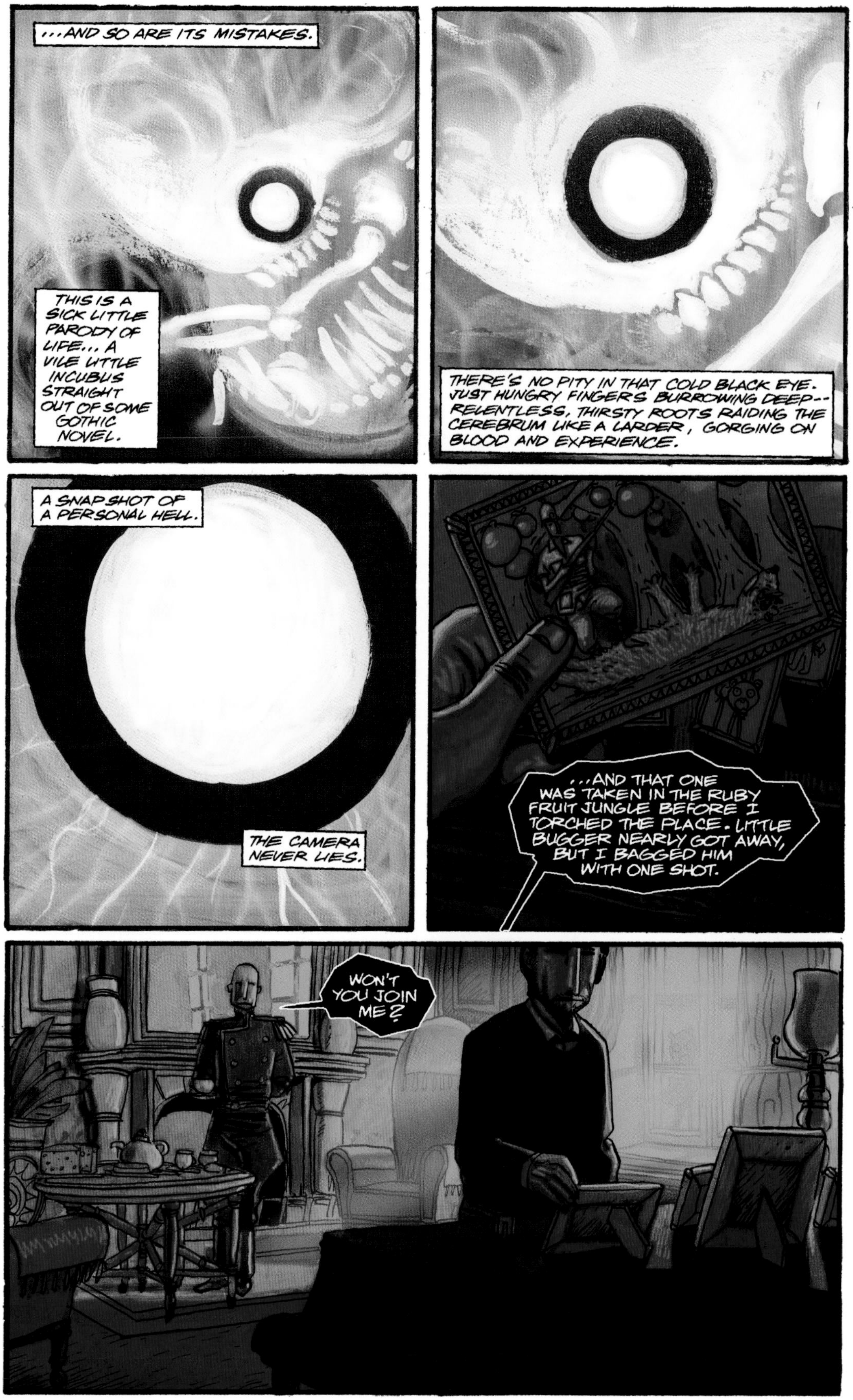
...AND SO ARE ITS MISTAKES.
THIS IS A SICK LITTLE PARODY OF LIFE... A VILE LITTLE INCUBUS STRAIGHT OUT OF SOME GOTHIC NOVEL.
THERE'S NO PITY IN THAT COLD BLACK EYE. JUST HUNGRY FINGERS BURROWING DEEP-- RELENTLESS, THIRSTY ROOTS RAIDING THE CEREBRUM LIKE A LARDER, GORGING ON BLOOD AND EXPERIENCE.
A SNAPSHOT OF A PERSONAL HELL.
THE CAMERA NEVER LIES.
...AND THAT ONE WAS TAKEN IN THE RUBY FRUIT JUNGLE BEFORE I TORCHED THE PLACE. LITTLE BUGGER NEARLY GOT AWAY, BUT I BAGGED HIM WITH ONE SHOT.
WON'T YOU JOIN ME?

YOU SIMPLY CAN'T IMAGINE HOW LONG I'VE BEEN LOOKING FORWARD TO OUR MEETING. I'VE SPENT A LIFETIME PLANNING FOR THIS DAY.

I WISH I COULD SAY THE SAME.

COME NOW, DON'T BE SURLY. CAN'T WE BE FRIENDS? I'M SURE THERE ARE DOZENS OF QUESTIONS YOU WANT TO ASK ME.

COCONUT MACAROON?

THE AIR SMELLS SICKLY SWEET, OF BISCUITS AND VOMIT...

I CAN'T STOMACH ANYMORE OF THIS!

A BUTTERED SCONE THEN?

I DON'T WANT ANY OF YOUR BLOODY SCONES!

ARE YOU INSANE? YOU'VE TURNED THIS PLACE INTO A NIGHTMARE AND YOU CALMLY STAND THERE OFFERING ME TEA AND CAKES! DON'T YOU KNOW WHAT YOU'VE DONE?!

IS THIS SOME KIND OF SICK JOKE?

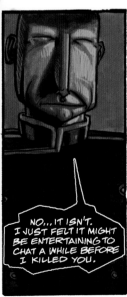

NO...IT ISN'T. I JUST FELT IT MIGHT BE ENTERTAINING TO CHAT A WHILE BEFORE I KILLED YOU.

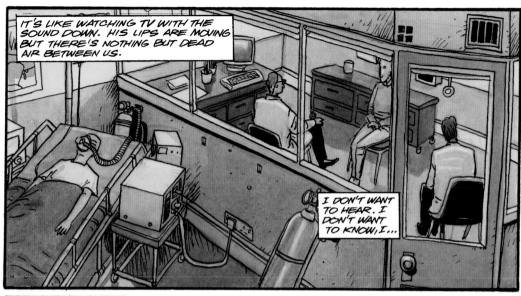

IT'S LIKE WATCHING TV WITH THE SOUND DOWN. HIS LIPS ARE MOVING BUT THERE'S NOTHING BUT DEAD AIR BETWEEN US.

I DON'T WANT TO HEAR. I DON'T WANT TO KNOW, I...

THIS THING IN HIS HEAD, YOU'RE SAYING IF IT'S NOT REMOVED, IT COULD KILL HIM?

IT'S A POSSIBILITY.

WHAT'S IT DOING?

WELL, IT'S A COMPLEX PROCESS, I'M NOT SURE YOU'D --

DOCTOR, I'M NOT A MORON SO PLEASE DON'T TREAT ME LIKE ONE. MY HUSBAND MAY BE DYING AND I WANT TO KNOW WHY! I HAVE A RIGHT TO KNOW, SO DON'T PATRONISE ME, OKAY?!

YES, OF COURSE. I'M SORRY.

THIS PARASITE HAS EMBEDDED ITSELF IN YOUR HUSBAND'S BRAIN, PARTICULARLY THE TEMPORAL AND OCCIPITAL LOBES.

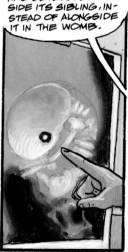

IT APPEARS TO BE A VESTIGIAL TWIN THAT HAS DEVELOPED IN-SIDE ITS SIBLING, IN-STEAD OF ALONGSIDE IT IN THE WOMB.

HAS IT BEEN THERE ALL HIS LIFE?

OH YES.

IT'S RARE BUT NOT UNUSUAL. THERE'S A FAMOUS CASE OF A BRAZILIAN WOMAN THAT GAVE BIRTH TO A BABY GIRL THAT WAS ACTUALLY BORN PREGNANT, AN EMBRYONIC TWIN BROTHER INSIDE HER...

...SADLY, NEITHER SURVIVED.

THEN THE HEADACHES... ALL THIS TIME. MY POOR CHRIS...

A CUP OF TEA, MAYBE?

NO, PLEASE CARRY ON.

THE PARASITE IS SUSTAINING ITSELF BY DRAWING UPON THE RESOURCES OF HIS BODY. GIVEN YOUR HUSBAND'S PRESENT CONDITION, THIS MAY PROVE FATAL.

UNFORTUNATELY, YOUR HUSBAND AND THE PARASITE ARE VERY CLOSELY INTEGRATED...

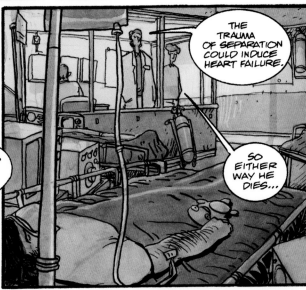

THE TRAUMA OF SEPARATION COULD INDUCE HEART FAILURE.

SO EITHER WAY HE DIES...

NOT NECESSARILY... THERE IS A SLIM CHANCE, BUT WE'VE NO GUARANTEES ...AS HIS NEXT OF KIN, WE'D NEED YOUR CONSENT...

DO IT.

CUT THAT THING OUT OF HIS HEAD.

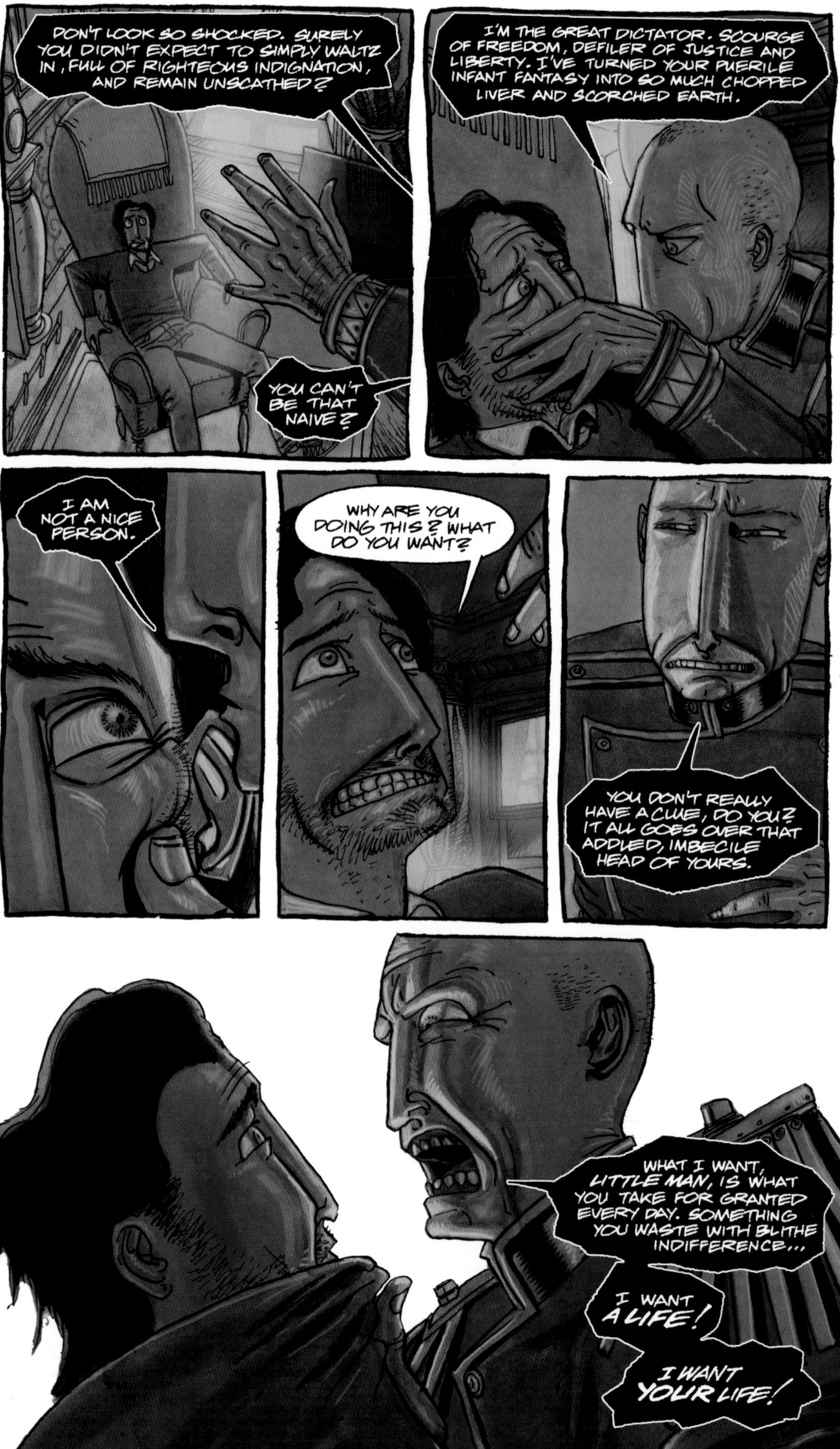
DON'T LOOK SO SHOCKED. SURELY YOU DIDN'T EXPECT TO SIMPLY WALTZ IN, FULL OF RIGHTEOUS INDIGNATION, AND REMAIN UNSCATHED?
YOU CAN'T BE THAT NAIVE?
I'M THE GREAT DICTATOR. SCOURGE OF FREEDOM, DEFILER OF JUSTICE AND LIBERTY. I'VE TURNED YOUR PUERILE INFANT FANTASY INTO SO MUCH CHOPPED LIVER AND SCORCHED EARTH.
I AM NOT A NICE PERSON.
WHY ARE YOU DOING THIS? WHAT DO YOU WANT?
YOU DON'T REALLY HAVE A CLUE, DO YOU? IT ALL GOES OVER THAT ADDLED, IMBECILE HEAD OF YOURS.
WHAT I WANT, LITTLE MAN, IS WHAT YOU TAKE FOR GRANTED EVERY DAY. SOMETHING YOU WASTE WITH BLITHE INDIFFERENCE...
I WANT A LIFE!
I WANT YOUR LIFE!

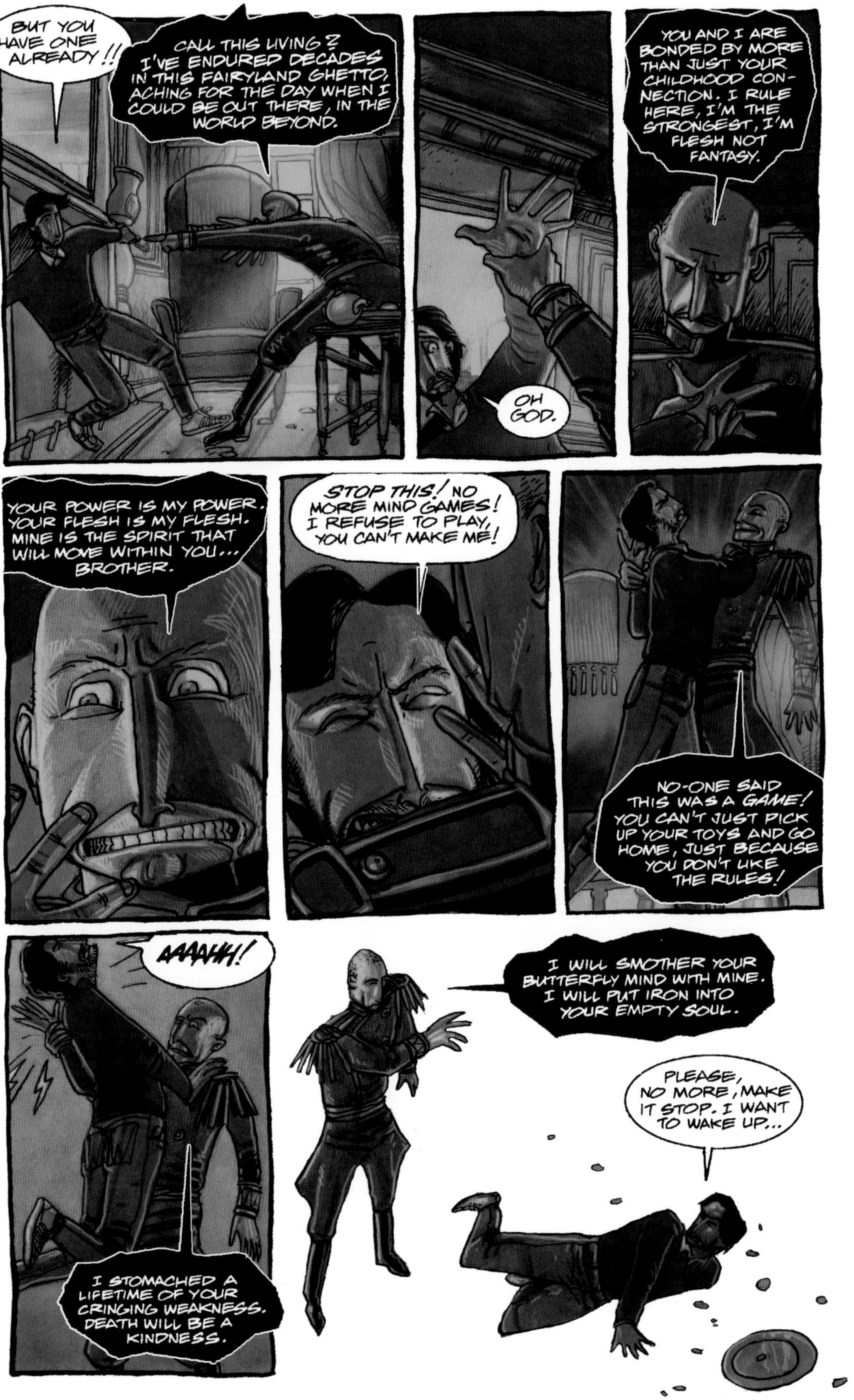
BUT YOU HAVE ONE ALREADY!!
CALL THIS LIVING? I'VE ENDURED DECADES IN THIS FAIRYLAND GHETTO, ACHING FOR THE DAY WHEN I COULD BE OUT THERE, IN THE WORLD BEYOND.
OH GOD.
YOU AND I ARE BONDED BY MORE THAN JUST YOUR CHILDHOOD CON-NECTION. I RULE HERE, I'M THE STRONGEST, I'M FLESH NOT FANTASY.
YOUR POWER IS MY POWER. YOUR FLESH IS MY FLESH. MINE IS THE SPIRIT THAT WILL MOVE WITHIN YOU... BROTHER.
STOP THIS! NO MORE MIND GAMES! I REFUSE TO PLAY, YOU CAN'T MAKE ME!
NO-ONE SAID THIS WAS A GAME! YOU CAN'T JUST PICK UP YOUR TOYS AND GO HOME, JUST BECAUSE YOU DON'T LIKE THE RULES!
AAAAHH!
I STOMACHED A LIFETIME OF YOUR CRINGING WEAKNESS. DEATH WILL BE A KINDNESS.
I WILL SMOTHER YOUR BUTTERFLY MIND WITH MINE. I WILL PUT IRON INTO YOUR EMPTY SOUL.
PLEASE, NO MORE, MAKE IT STOP. I WANT TO WAKE UP...

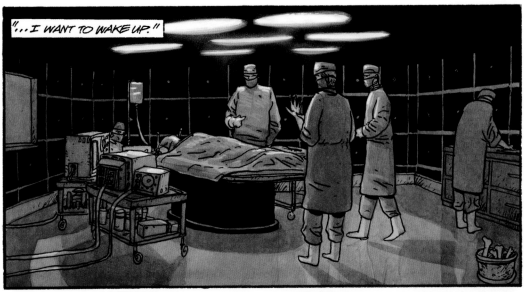

"...I WANT TO WAKE UP."

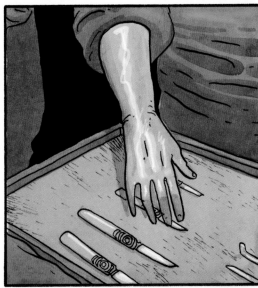

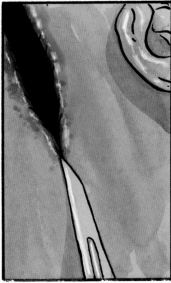

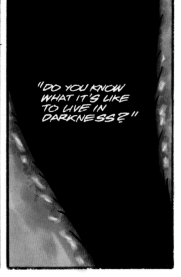

"DO YOU KNOW WHAT IT'S LIKE TO LIVE IN DARKNESS?"

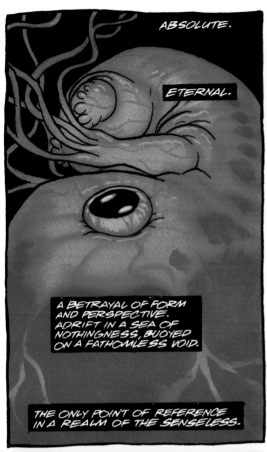

ABSOLUTE.

ETERNAL.

A BETRAYAL OF FORM AND PERSPECTIVE. ADRIFT IN A SEA OF NOTHINGNESS, BUOYED ON A FATHOMLESS VOID.

THE ONLY POINT OF REFERENCE IN A REALM OF THE SENSELESS.

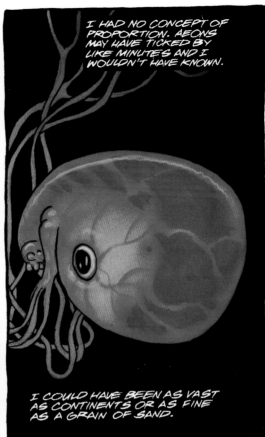

I HAD NO CONCEPT OF PROPORTION. AEONS MAY HAVE TICKED BY LIKE MINUTES AND I WOULDN'T HAVE KNOWN.

I COULD HAVE BEEN AS VAST AS CONTINENTS OR AS FINE AS A GRAIN OF SAND.

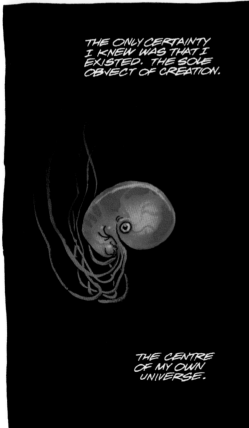

THE ONLY CERTAINTY I KNEW WAS THAT I EXISTED. THE SOLE OBJECT OF CREATION.

THE CENTRE OF MY OWN UNIVERSE.

BUT, OF COURSE, I WAS WRONG.

101

IT WAS SOMETHING OF A REVELATION TO DISCOVER YOU WERE THE STAR OF THE SHOW WHILE I WAS MERELY AN IMPOTENT BACK-SEAT DRIVER.

I WAS NOT HAPPY.

IWANTTO WAKEUPIWANT TOWAKEUPI WANTTOWAKE UP

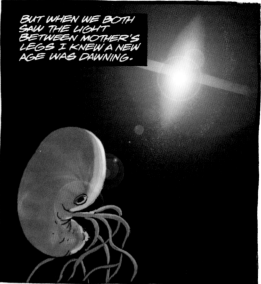

BUT WHEN WE BOTH SAW THE LIGHT BETWEEN MOTHER'S LEGS I KNEW A NEW AGE WAS DAWNING.

I LIVED, EXILED, BEHIND YOUR EYES, ALL SEEING, ALL HEARING... PARALYSED LIKE SOME DUMB QUADRIPLEGIC TRAPPED IN A CINEMA WATCHING ENDLESS RUNS OF BERGMAN FILMS.

GOD, YOU WERE A DULL CHILD.

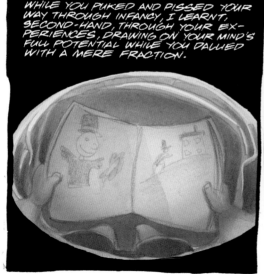

WHILE YOU PUKED AND PISSED YOUR WAY THROUGH INFANCY, I LEARNT, SECOND-HAND, THROUGH YOUR EX-PERIENCES, DRAWING ON YOUR MIND'S FULL POTENTIAL WHILE YOU DALLIED WITH A MERE FRACTION.

I WAS AMUSED TO FIND I COULD READ YOUR THOUGHTS, BUT 'EAT', 'SLEEP', 'SHIT' ONLY HOLD THE ATTENTION FOR SO LONG.

YOU'VE NEVER BEEN MUCH OF A DEEP THINKER, HAVE YOU?

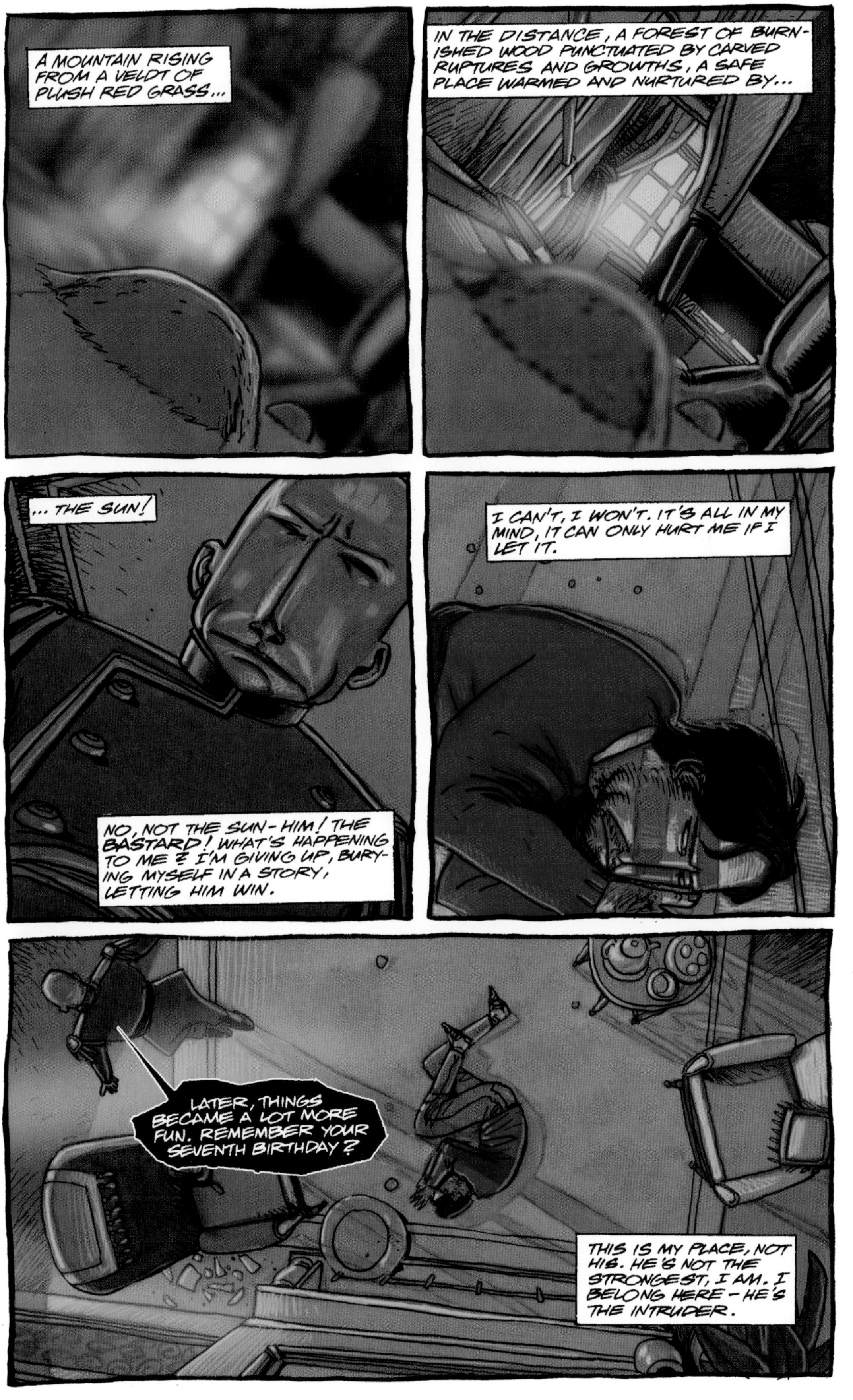
A MOUNTAIN RISING FROM A VELDT OF PLUSH RED GRASS...
IN THE DISTANCE, A FOREST OF BURNISHED WOOD PUNCTUATED BY CARVED RUPTURES AND GROWTHS, A SAFE PLACE WARMED AND NURTURED BY...
...THE SUN!
NO, NOT THE SUN- HIM! THE BASTARD! WHAT'S HAPPENING TO ME? I'M GIVING UP, BURYING MYSELF IN A STORY, LETTING HIM WIN.
I CAN'T, I WON'T. IT'S ALL IN MY MIND, IT CAN ONLY HURT ME IF I LET IT.
LATER, THINGS BECAME A LOT MORE FUN. REMEMBER YOUR SEVENTH BIRTHDAY?
THIS IS MY PLACE, NOT HIS. HE'S NOT THE STRONGEST, I AM. I BELONG HERE - HE'S THE INTRUDER.

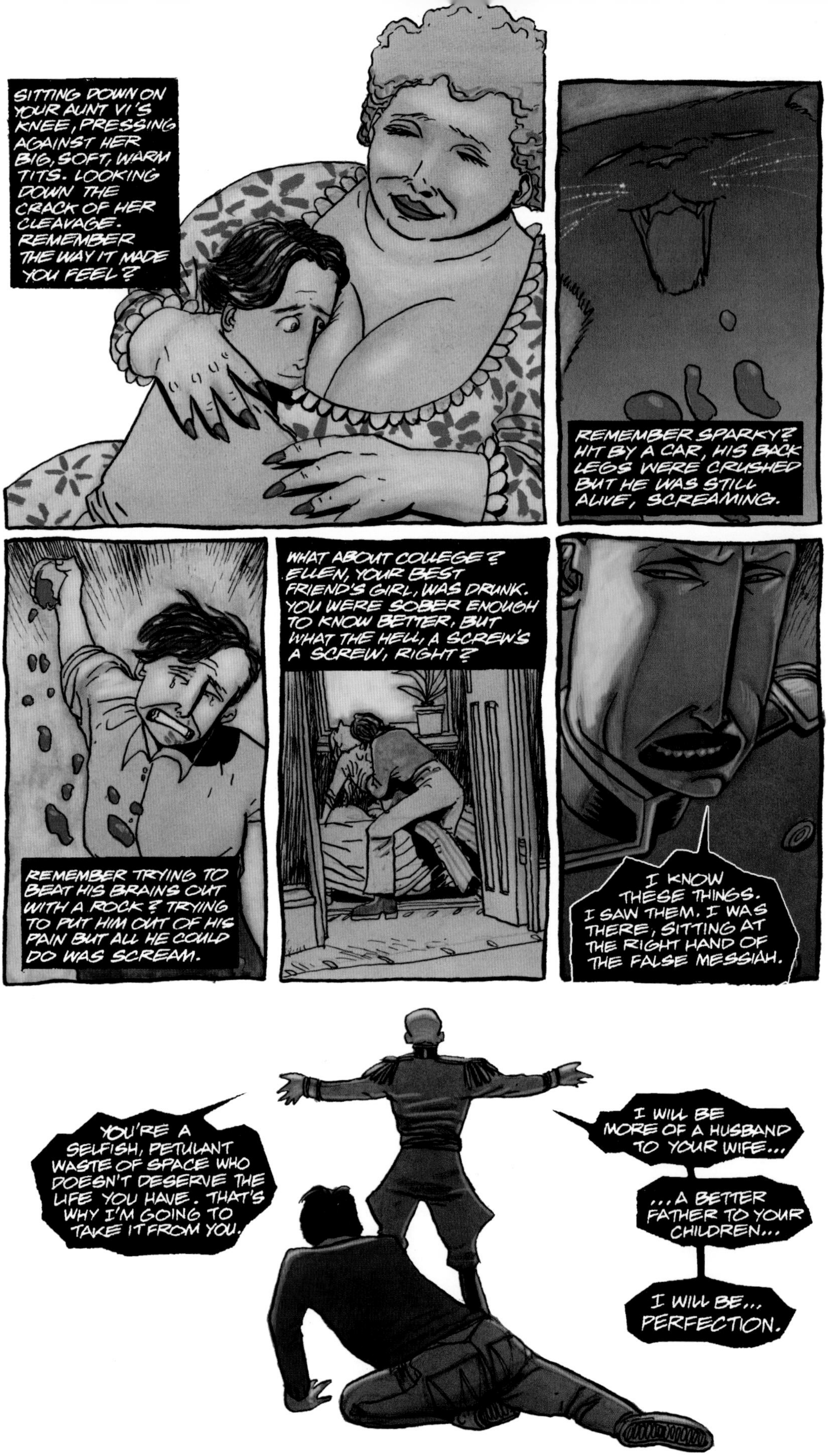
SITTING DOWN ON YOUR AUNT VI'S KNEE, PRESSING AGAINST HER BIG, SOFT, WARM TITS. LOOKING DOWN THE CRACK OF HER CLEAVAGE. REMEMBER THE WAY IT MADE YOU FEEL?
REMEMBER SPARKY? HIT BY A CAR, HIS BACK LEGS WERE CRUSHED BUT HE WAS STILL ALIVE, SCREAMING.
REMEMBER TRYING TO BEAT HIS BRAINS OUT WITH A ROCK? TRYING TO PUT HIM OUT OF HIS PAIN BUT ALL HE COULD DO WAS SCREAM.
WHAT ABOUT COLLEGE? ELLEN, YOUR BEST FRIEND'S GIRL, WAS DRUNK. YOU WERE SOBER ENOUGH TO KNOW BETTER, BUT WHAT THE HELL, A SCREW'S A SCREW, RIGHT?
I KNOW THESE THINGS. I SAW THEM. I WAS THERE, SITTING AT THE RIGHT HAND OF THE FALSE MESSIAH.
YOU'RE A SELFISH, PETULANT WASTE OF SPACE WHO DOESN'T DESERVE THE LIFE YOU HAVE. THAT'S WHY I'M GOING TO TAKE IT FROM YOU.
I WILL BE MORE OF A HUSBAND TO YOUR WIFE...
...A BETTER FATHER TO YOUR CHILDREN...
I WILL BE... PERFECTION.

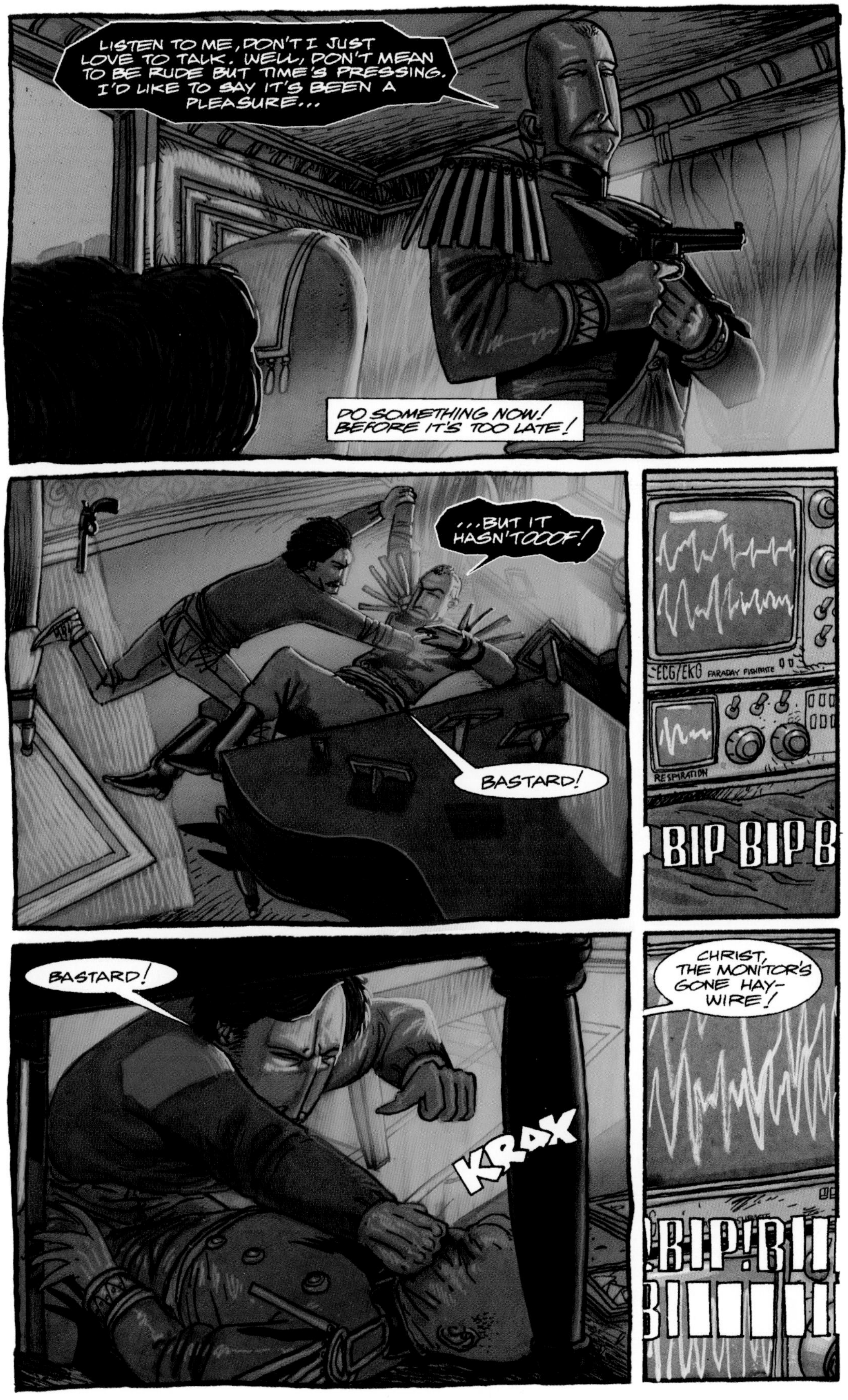
LISTEN TO ME, DON'T I JUST LOVE TO TALK. WELL, DON'T MEAN TO BE RUDE BUT TIME'S PRESSING. I'D LIKE TO SAY IT'S BEEN A PLEASURE...
DO SOMETHING NOW! BEFORE IT'S TOO LATE!
...BUT IT HASN'T OOOF!
BASTARD!
ECG/EKG FARADAY FISHPASTE
RESPIRATION
BIP BIP B
BASTARD!
KRAX
CHRIST, THE MONITOR'S GONE HAY-WIRE!
BIP!BI

BASTARD!

CUAK

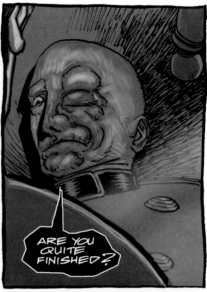

ARE YOU QUITE FINISHED?

NO.

YOU ARE NOW.

GUUUH!

AH, THERE YOU ARE.

YOU'RE TENACIOUS, I MUST SAY. BUT I'VE SPENT A LIFETIME FIGHTING WARS. I DON'T THINK A CHILDREN'S AUTHOR WILL POSE MUCH OF A PROBLEM. DO YOU?

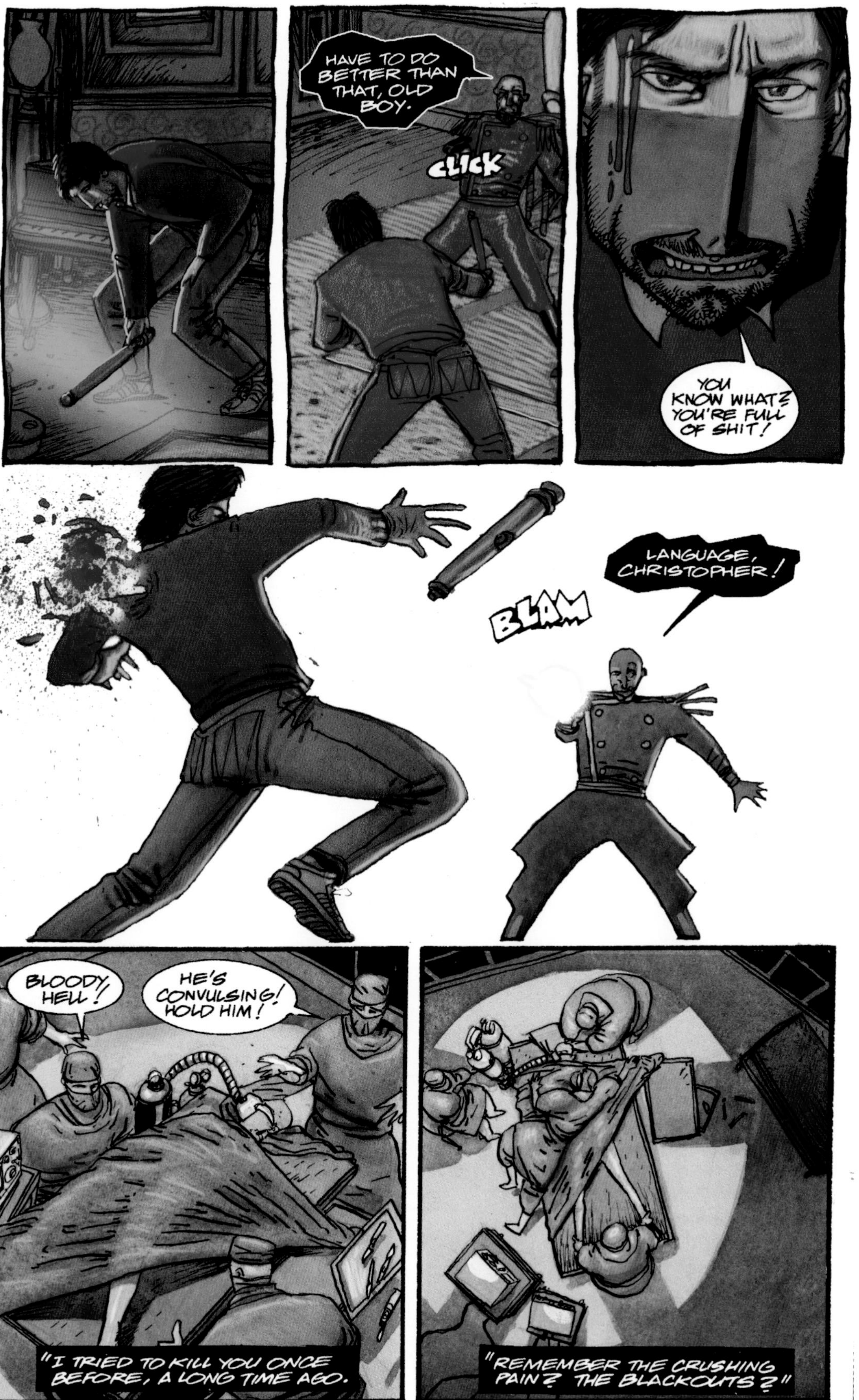
HAVE TO DO BETTER THAN THAT, OLD BOY.
CLICK
YOU KNOW WHAT? YOU'RE FULL OF SHIT!
LANGUAGE, CHRISTOPHER!
BLAM
BLOODY HELL!
HE'S CONVULSING! HOLD HIM!
"I TRIED TO KILL YOU ONCE BEFORE, A LONG TIME AGO.
"REMEMBER THE CRUSHING PAIN? THE BLACKOUTS?"

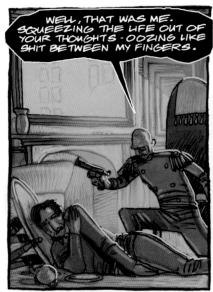

WELL, THAT WAS ME. SQUEEZING THE LIFE OUT OF YOUR THOUGHTS - OOZING LIKE SHIT BETWEEN MY FINGERS.

NEARLY KILLED US BOTH, SO I RECALL.

WHEN I RETIRED TO RETHINK A SUBTLER STRATEGY, I DISCOVERED SOMETHING QUITE UNIQUE HAD TAKEN PLACE IN MY ABSENCE.

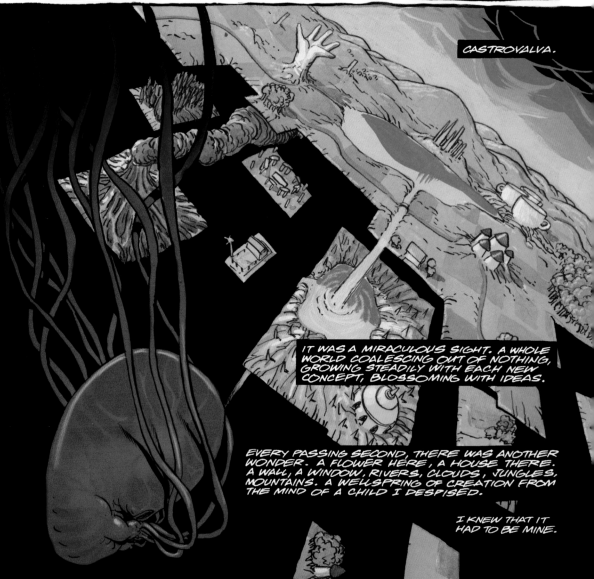

CASTROVALVA.

IT WAS A MIRACULOUS SIGHT. A WHOLE WORLD COALESCING OUT OF NOTHING, GROWING STEADILY WITH EACH NEW CONCEPT, BLOSSOMING WITH IDEAS.

EVERY PASSING SECOND, THERE WAS ANOTHER WONDER. A FLOWER HERE, A HOUSE THERE. A WALL, A WINDOW, RIVERS, CLOUDS, JUNGLES, MOUNTAINS. A WELLSPRING OF CREATION FROM THE MIND OF A CHILD I DESPISED.

I KNEW THAT IT HAD TO BE MINE.

I COULD HAVE TAKEN IT THEN, BUT I CHOSE NOT TO.

I WANTED TO PLAY...

...GAMES LIKE YOU WOULDN'T BELIEVE. BUT IT WASN'T ENOUGH.

I SOON TIRED OF BREAKING YOUR TOYS. THERE WAS BETTER FUN TO BE HAD, BUT FIRST, I NEEDED YOUR CO-OPERATION.

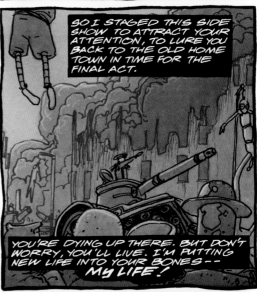

SO I STAGED THIS SIDE SHOW TO ATTRACT YOUR ATTENTION, TO LURE YOU BACK TO THE OLD HOME TOWN IN TIME FOR THE FINAL ACT.

YOU'RE DYING UP THERE. BUT DON'T WORRY, YOU'LL LIVE. I'M PUTTING NEW LIFE INTO YOUR BONES-- MY LIFE!

WHEN THEY CUT OUT MY OWN TWISTED FORM, I WON'T CARE. I'M MOVING INTO NEW PREMISES AND, WHETHER YOU LIKE IT OR NOT, YOU'RE ABOUT TO BE EVICTED.

BLAM

CHEERIO, OLD SON. DON'T FORGET TO WRITE.

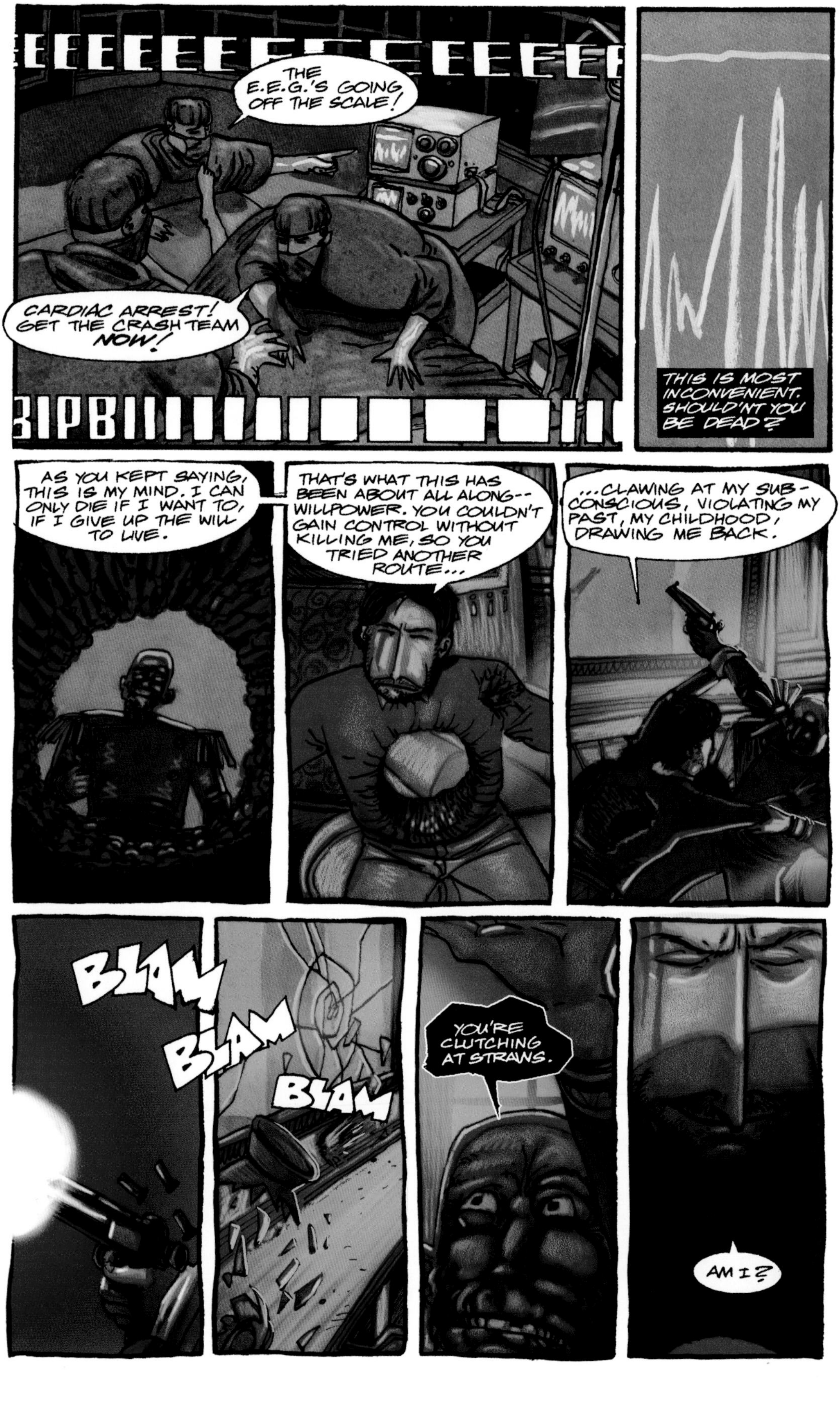
EEEEEEEEEEEEEEEEEE
THE E.E.G.'S GOING OFF THE SCALE!
CARDIAC ARREST! GET THE CRASH TEAM NOW!
BIPBIIIIIIIIIII
THIS IS MOST INCONVENIENT. SHOULD'NT YOU BE DEAD?
AS YOU KEPT SAYING, THIS IS MY MIND. I CAN ONLY DIE IF I WANT TO, IF I GIVE UP THE WILL TO LIVE.
THAT'S WHAT THIS HAS BEEN ABOUT ALL ALONG-- WILLPOWER. YOU COULDN'T GAIN CONTROL WITHOUT KILLING ME, SO YOU TRIED ANOTHER ROUTE...
...CLAWING AT MY SUB-CONSCIOUS, VIOLATING MY PAST, MY CHILDHOOD, DRAWING ME BACK.
BLAM
BLAM
BLAM
YOU'RE CLUTCHING AT STRAWS.
AM I?

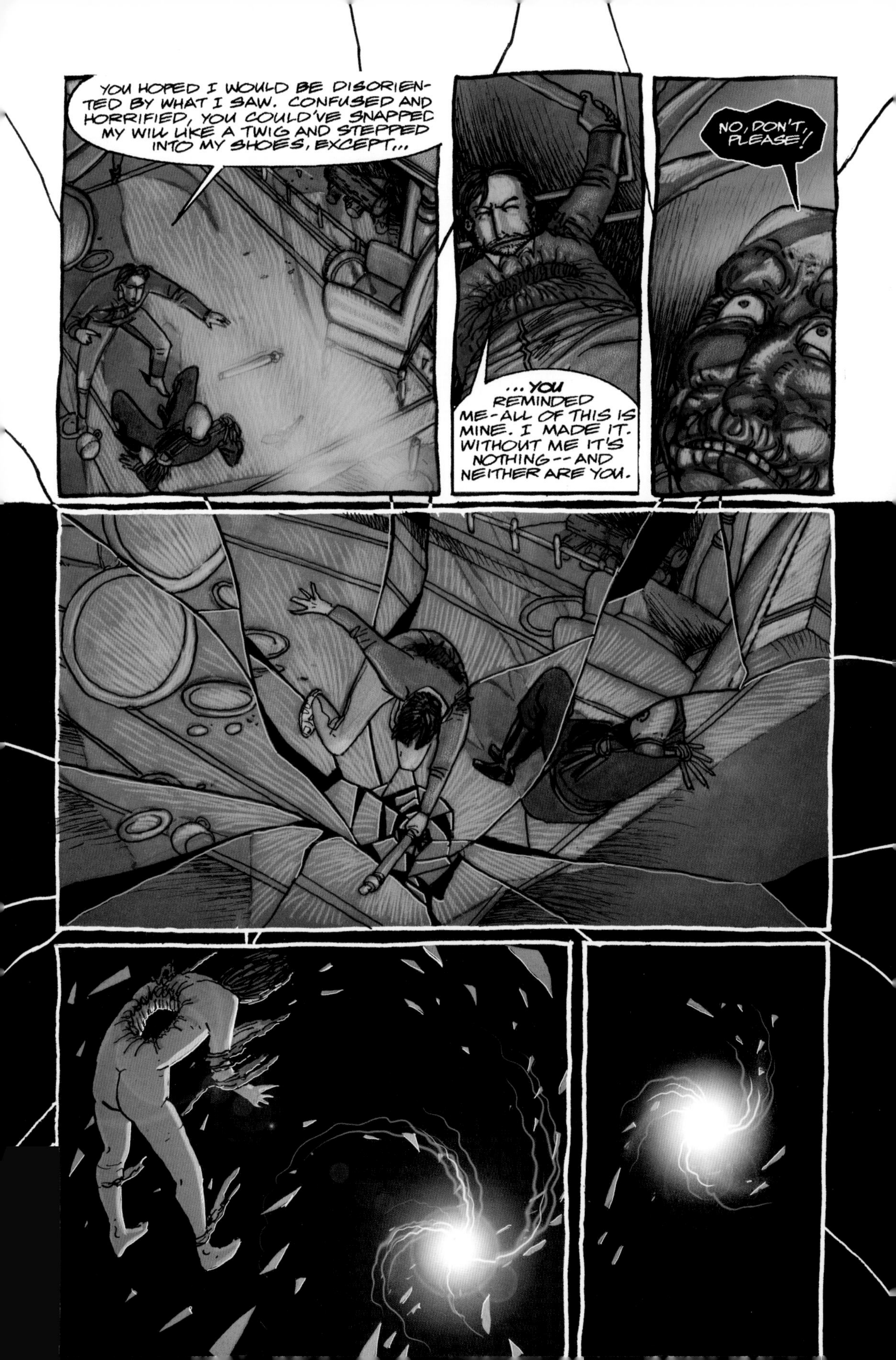
YOU HOPED I WOULD BE DISORIENTED BY WHAT I SAW. CONFUSED AND HORRIFIED, YOU COULD'VE SNAPPED MY WILL LIKE A TWIG AND STEPPED INTO MY SHOES, EXCEPT...
...YOU REMINDED ME - ALL OF THIS IS MINE. I MADE IT. WITHOUT ME IT'S NOTHING -- AND NEITHER ARE YOU.
NO, DON'T, PLEASE!

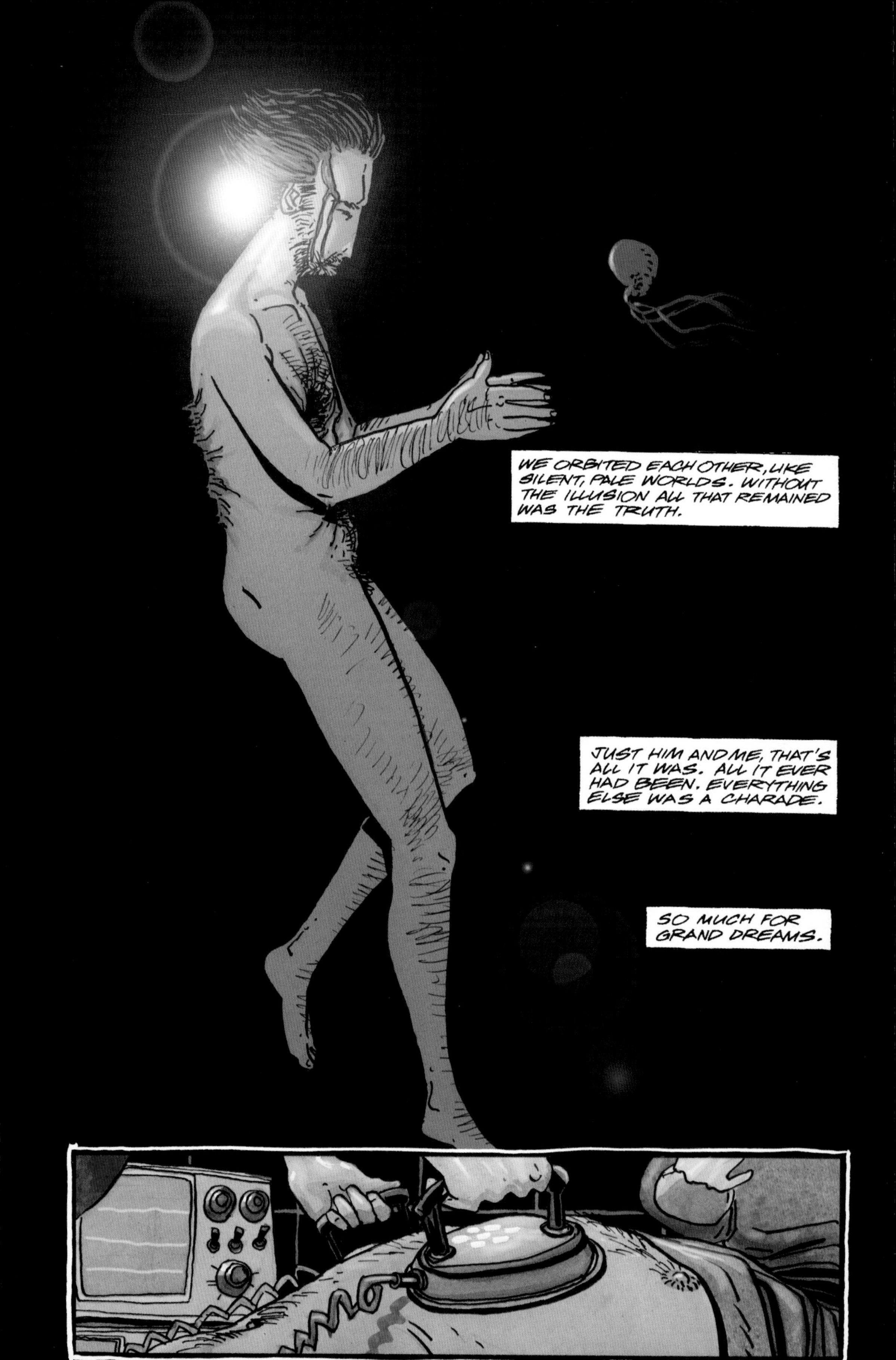
WE ORBITED EACH OTHER, LIKE SILENT, PALE WORLDS. WITHOUT THE ILLUSION ALL THAT REMAINED WAS THE TRUTH.
JUST HIM AND ME, THAT'S ALL IT WAS. ALL IT EVER HAD BEEN. EVERYTHING ELSE WAS A CHARADE.
SO MUCH FOR GRAND DREAMS.

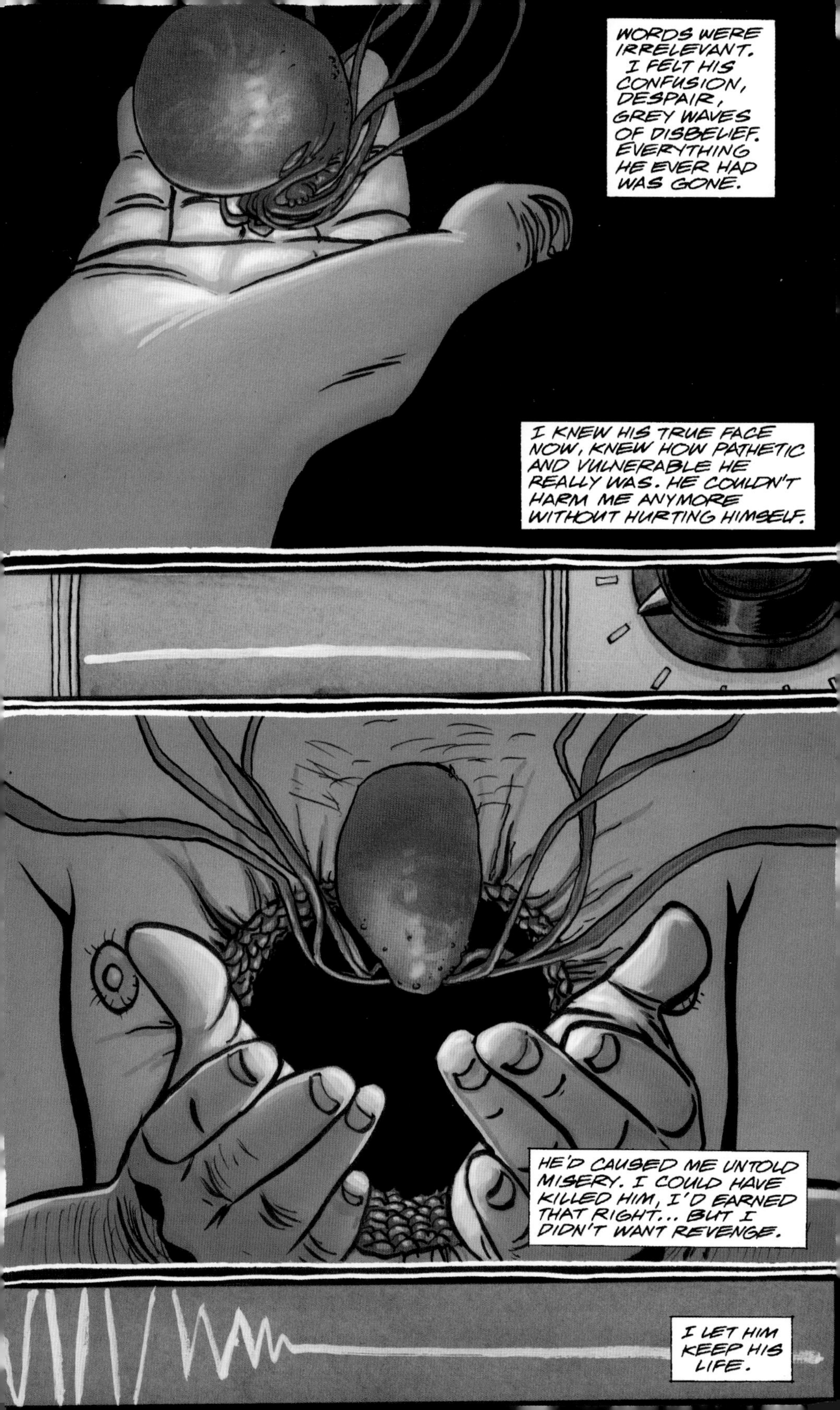
WORDS WERE IRRELEVANT. I FELT HIS CONFUSION, DESPAIR, GREY WAVES OF DISBELIEF. EVERYTHING HE EVER HAD WAS GONE.
I KNEW HIS TRUE FACE NOW, KNEW HOW PATHETIC AND VULNERABLE HE REALLY WAS. HE COULDN'T HARM ME ANYMORE WITHOUT HURTING HIMSELF.
HE'D CAUSED ME UNTOLD MISERY. I COULD HAVE KILLED HIM, I'D EARNED THAT RIGHT... BUT I DIDN'T WANT REVENGE.
I LET HIM KEEP HIS LIFE.

HE DIED ANYWAY. I DON'T KNOW WHY.

THE DEFEAT? HUMILIATION? THE LOSS OF HIS IDEAL? WITH NOTHING LEFT TO LIVE FOR HE SIMPLY GAVE UP LIVING; A SOFT, DEAD PEBBLE IN MY HAND.

I HAD ONE LAST TASK TO PERFORM...

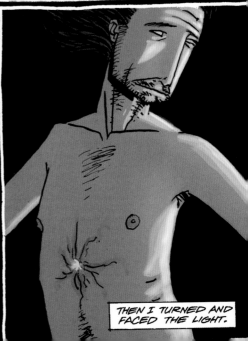

THEN I TURNED AND FACED THE LIGHT.

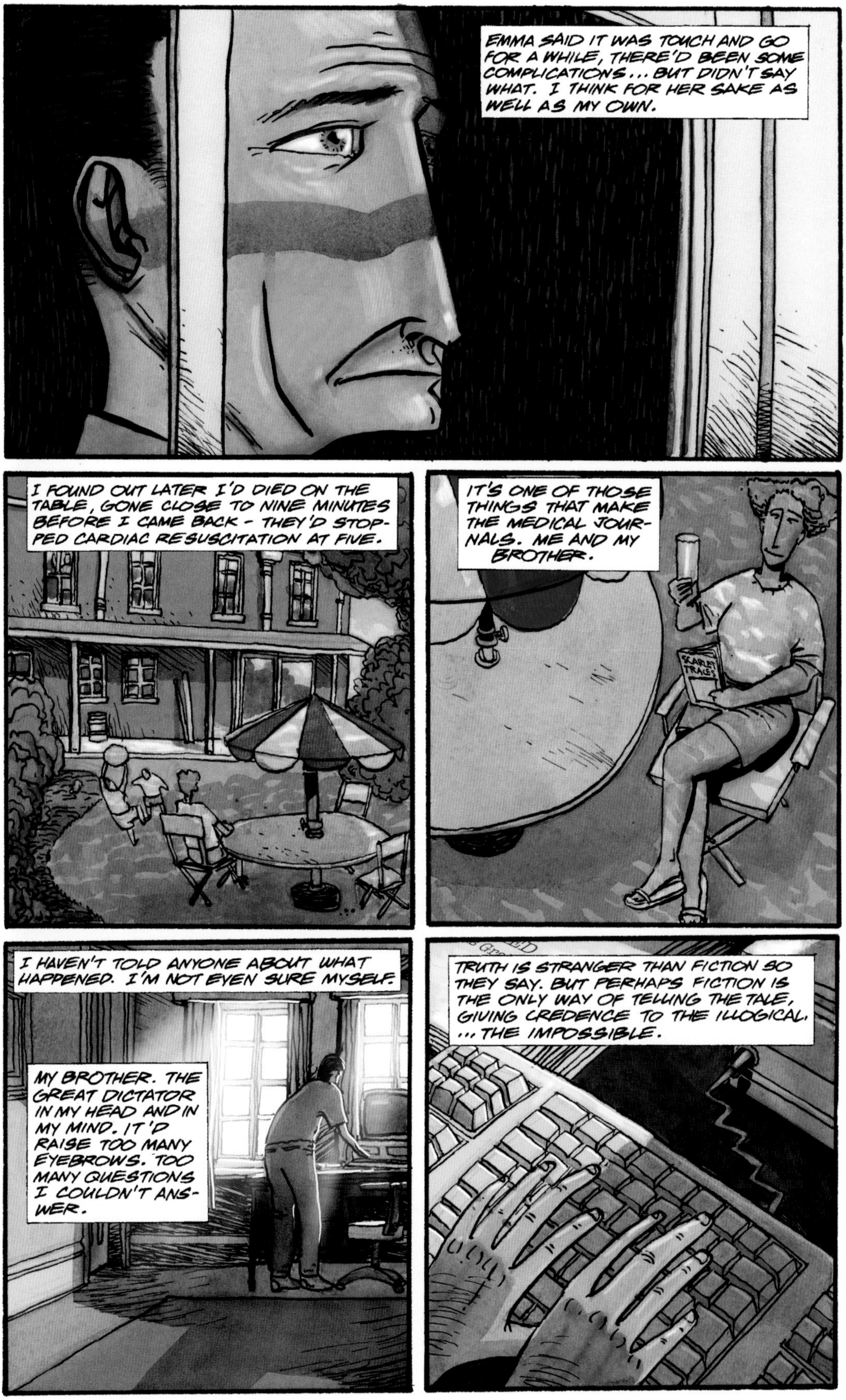
EMMA SAID IT WAS TOUCH AND GO FOR A WHILE, THERE'D BEEN SOME COMPLICATIONS... BUT DIDN'T SAY WHAT. I THINK FOR HER SAKE AS WELL AS MY OWN.
I FOUND OUT LATER I'D DIED ON THE TABLE, GONE CLOSE TO NINE MINUTES BEFORE I CAME BACK - THEY'D STOPPED CARDIAC RESUSCITATION AT FIVE.
IT'S ONE OF THOSE THINGS THAT MAKE THE MEDICAL JOURNALS. ME AND MY BROTHER.
SCARLET TRACES
I HAVEN'T TOLD ANYONE ABOUT WHAT HAPPENED. I'M NOT EVEN SURE MYSELF.
MY BROTHER. THE GREAT DICTATOR IN MY HEAD AND IN MY MIND. IT'D RAISE TOO MANY EYEBROWS. TOO MANY QUESTIONS I COULDN'T ANSWER.
TRUTH IS STRANGER THAN FICTION SO THEY SAY. BUT PERHAPS FICTION IS THE ONLY WAY OF TELLING THE TALE, GIVING CREDENCE TO THE ILLOGICAL, ...THE IMPOSSIBLE.

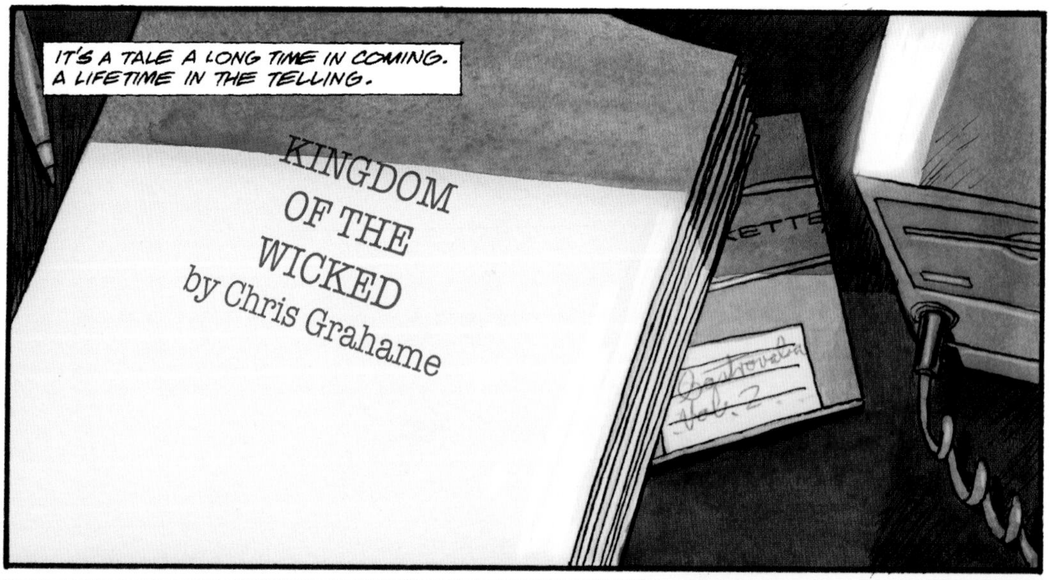
IT'S A TALE A LONG TIME IN COMING. A LIFETIME IN THE TELLING.
KINGDOM OF THE WICKED
by Chris Grahame

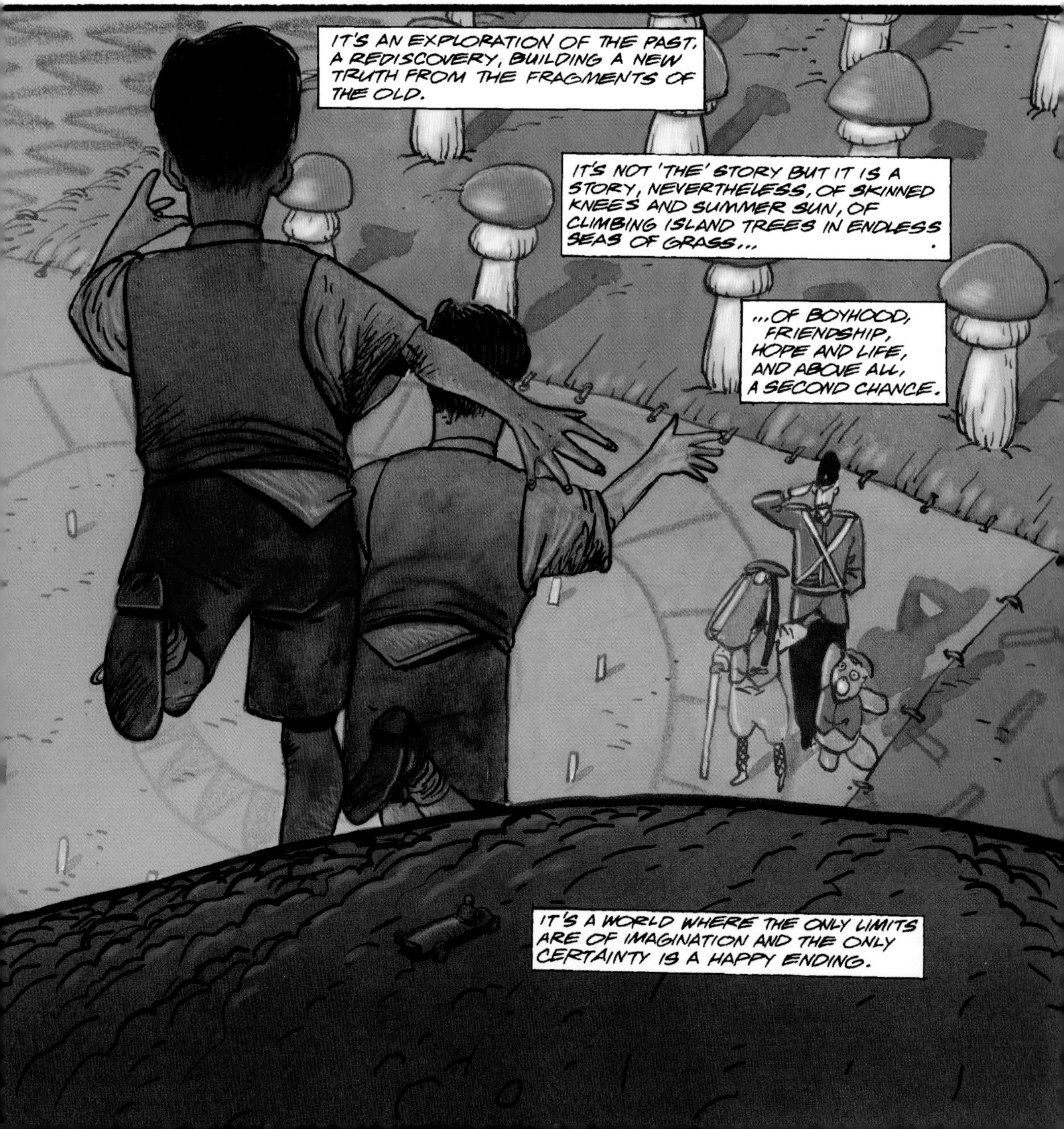
IT'S AN EXPLORATION OF THE PAST, A REDISCOVERY, BUILDING A NEW TRUTH FROM THE FRAGMENTS OF THE OLD.
IT'S NOT 'THE' STORY BUT IT IS A STORY, NEVERTHELESS, OF SKINNED KNEES AND SUMMER SUN, OF CLIMBING ISLAND TREES IN ENDLESS SEAS OF GRASS...
...OF BOYHOOD, FRIENDSHIP, HOPE AND LIFE, AND ABOVE ALL, A SECOND CHANCE.
IT'S A WORLD WHERE THE ONLY LIMITS ARE OF IMAGINATION AND THE ONLY CERTAINTY IS A HAPPY ENDING.

A completist curio, this was my second ever piece of comics work and the beginning of a long-standing collaboration with Matt. A silent movie morality tale about life, death, spacemen, God, and baked beans. As soon as I saw he'd put the Almighty in a flat cap and a comfy cardigan I knew I'd found someone with a wonderfully skewed mind set. What else would you expect from an Esperanto-speaking ballroom dancer?!

—Ian Edginton

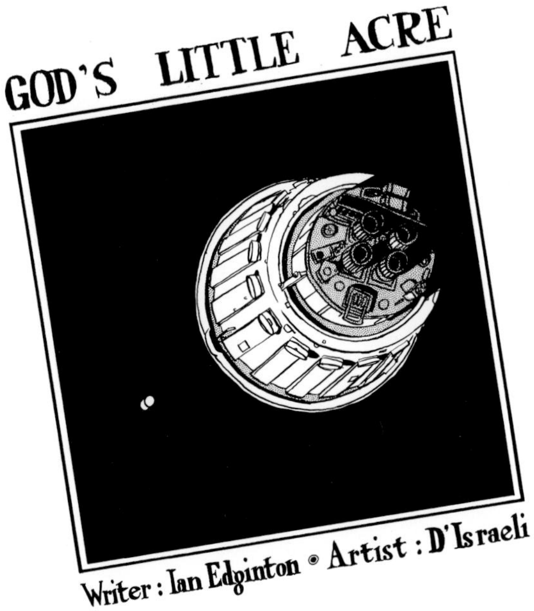
GOD'S LITTLE ACRE
Writer : Ian Edginton • Artist : D'Israeli

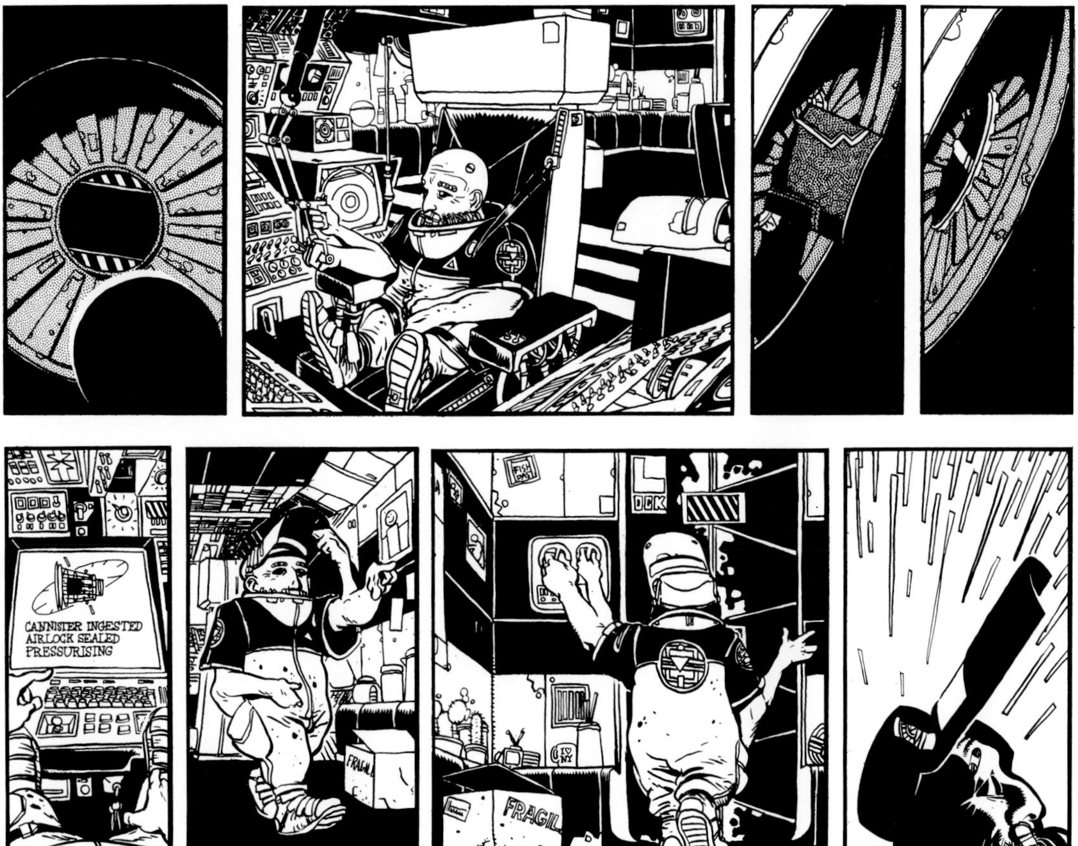
CANNISTER INGESTED
AIRLOCK SEALED
PRESSURISING
FRAGIL
DCK
FRAGIL

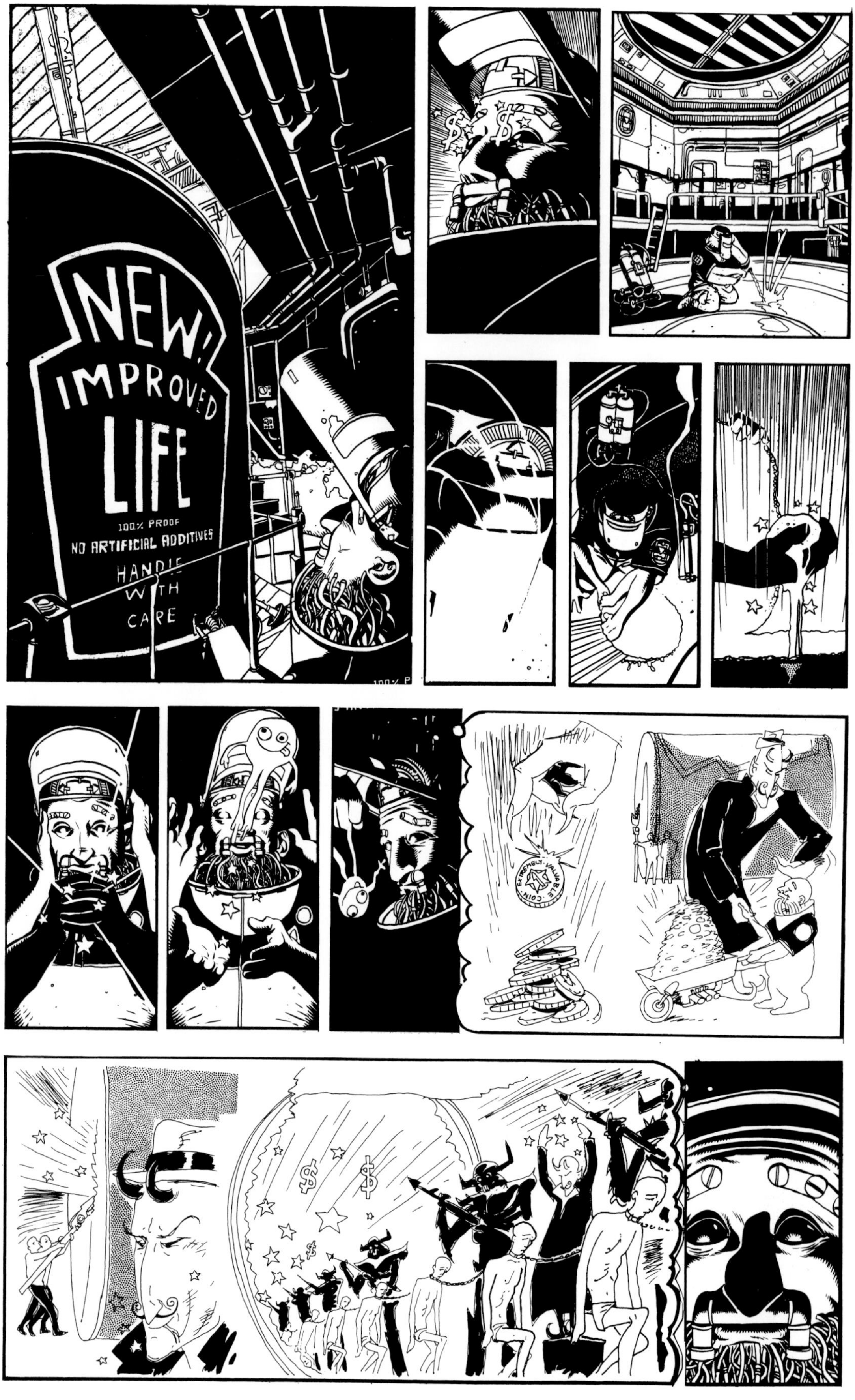
NEW!
IMPROVED
LIFE
100% PROOF
NO ARTIFICIAL ADDITIVES
HANDLE
WITH
CARE
EXTREMELY · VALUABLE · COIN

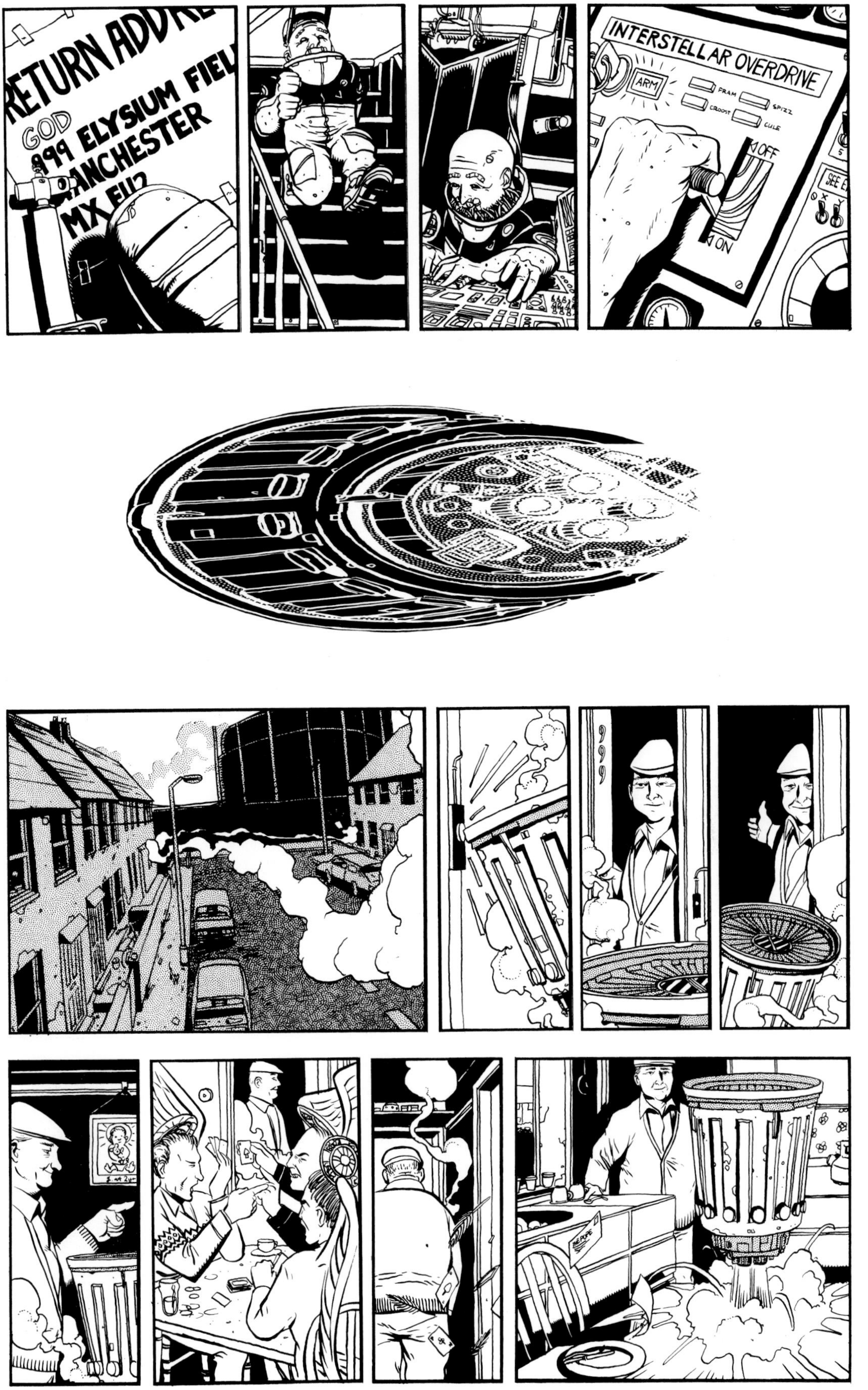
RETURN ADDRE
GOD
999 ELYSIUM FIEL
ANCHESTER
MX EU2
INTERSTELLAR OVERDRIVE
ARM
FRAM
SPIZZ
CROOST
CULE
OFF
ON
999
THE POPE

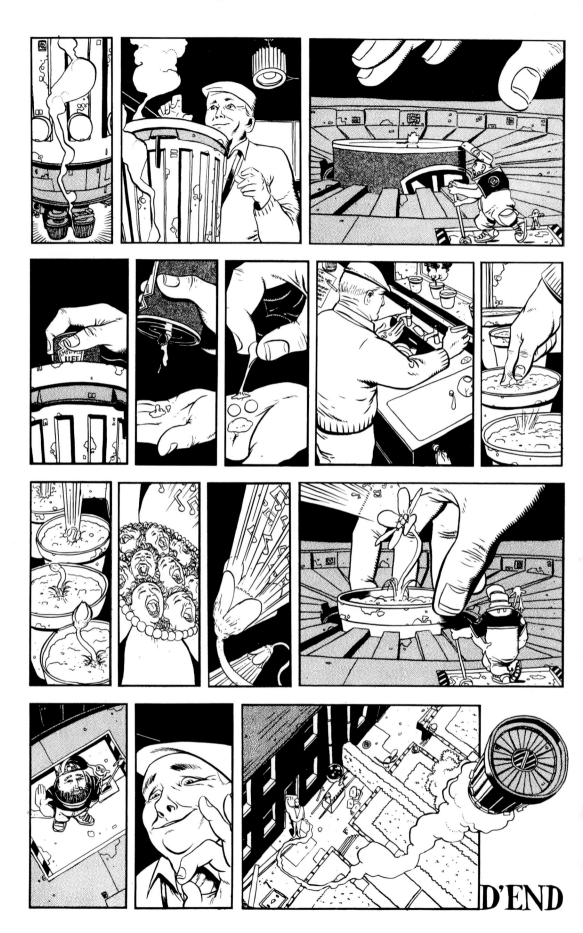

D'END

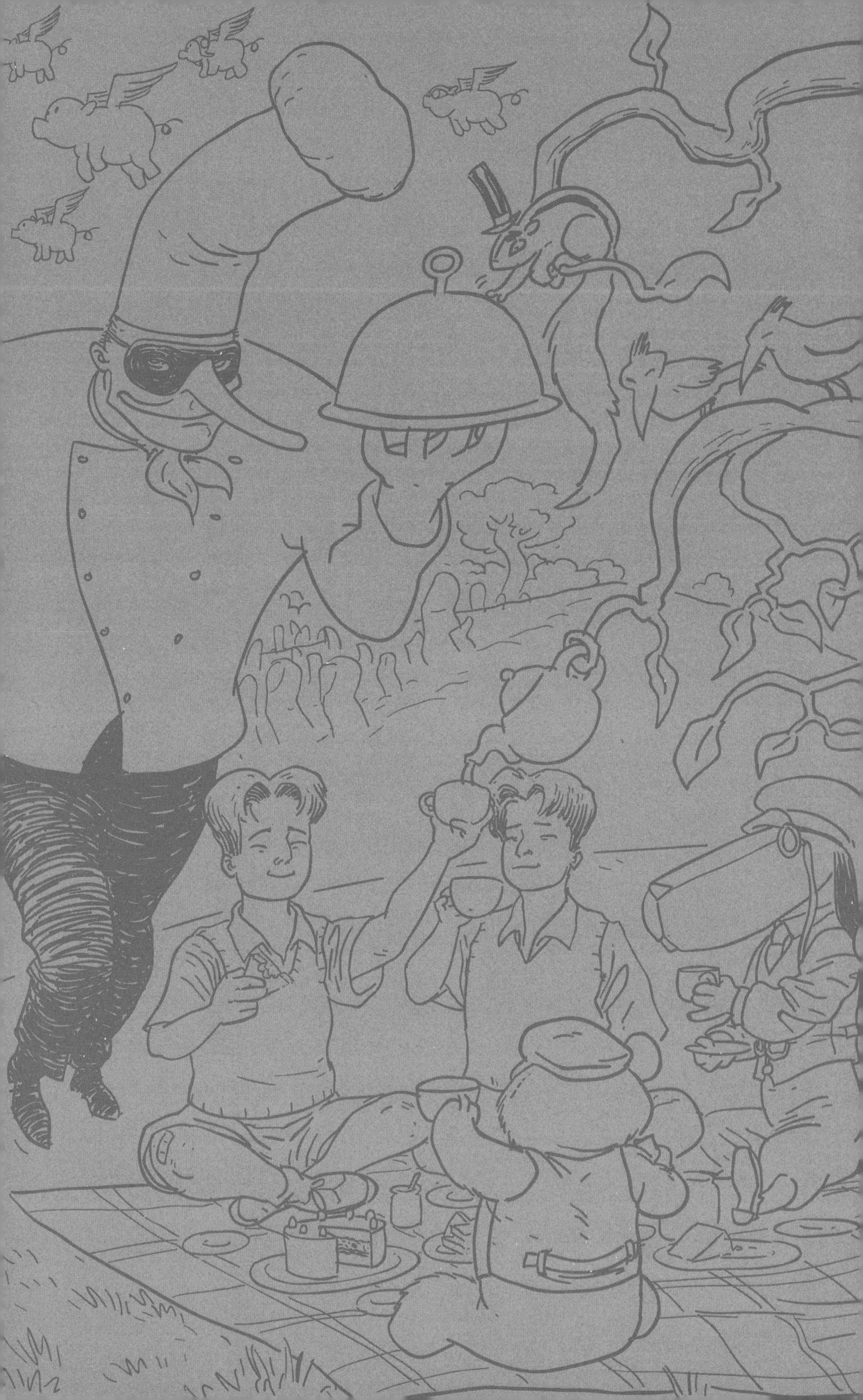